*A*dventure Guide to
2nd Edition
Barbados

Harry S. Pariser

HUNTER
PUBLISHING

Hunter Publishing, Inc.
300 Raritan Center Parkway
Edison NJ 08818
Tel (908) 225 1900
Fax (908) 417 0482

ISBN 1-55650-707-0

Cover photo: Tony Arruza Photography
All other photos by author, except where indicated

Other books by Harry S. Pariser from Hunter Publishing:

Jamaica: A Visitor's Guide, 3rd Ed 1-55650-703-8 $14.95
Adventure Guide to Costa Rica, 2nd Ed 1-55650-598-1 $15.95
Adventure Guide to Belize, 3rd Ed 1-55650-647-3 $14.95
Adventure Guide to the Dominican Republic, 2nd Ed 1-55650-629-5 $14.95
Adventure Guide to Puerto Rico, 2nd Ed 1-55650-628-7 $14.95
Adventure Guide to the Virgin Islands, 3rd Ed 1-55650-597-3 $14.95

We Love to Get Mail

In today's world, things change so rapidly that it's impossible to keep up with everything that's happening in any one place. Travel books are like automobiles: they require fine tuning and frequent overhauls if they are to stay in top condition. We need input from readers so that we can continue to provide the best, most current information available. Please write to let us know about any inaccuracies, new information, or misleading suggestions. Although we try to make our maps as accurate as possible, errors can occur. If you have suggestions for improvement or places that should be included, please let us know.

We especially appreciate letters from female travelers, local residents, hikers, and other outdoor enthusiasts. We also like learning from experts in the field as well as from local hotel owners and individuals wishing to accommodate visitors from abroad. Send your comments to Harry S. Pariser, c/o Hunter Publishing, 300 Raritan Center Parkway, Edison NJ 08818. Fax (908) 417 0482.

Reader's Response Form

Adventure Guide To Barbados, 2nd Edition

I found your book:

Your book could be improved by:

The best places I stayed in were (explain why):

I found the best food at:

Some good and bad experiences were:

Will you return to Barbados?

If so, where do you plan to go? If not, why not?

I purchased this book at:

Please include any other comments on a separate sheet and mail completed form to Harry. S. Pariser, c/o Hunter Publishing, 300 Raritan Center Parkway, Edison NJ 08818, USA. Or e-mail to salsa@slip.net.

Acknowledgements

I would like to thank my publisher, Michael Hunter, and his staff as well as my mapmakers, Joyce Huber and Kim André. For their invaluable comments, I would like to thank Francis Roman and Dr. John Gilmore as well as Betty-Carillo-Shannon. Others to thank include Calvin A. Howell, Haxel E. Gaskin, George Forte, Penelope Hynam Roach, Leroy Foster, Matthew Roberts, Samuel Farley, Bill Sutherland, Paul Howard, Anthony Johnson, Ron Lippert, Glyne Murray, Lionel Sandiford, Jacqueline Rogers, Sally Adamson Taylor, Dr. Carrington, and Norbert Bailey. A special thanks to my mother who always worries about me.

About the Author

Harry S. Pariser was born in Pittsburgh and grew up in a small town in southwestern Pennsylvania. After graduating from Boston University with a B.S. in Public Communications in 1975, Harry hitched and camped his way through Europe, traveled down the Nile by steamer, and by train through Sudan. After visiting Uganda, Rwanda and Tanzania, he traveled by passenger ship from Mombasa to Bombay, and then on through Asia before settling down in Kyoto, Japan, where he studied Japanese and ceramics. While there, he supported himself by teaching English to everyone from tiny tots to Buddhist priests. Using Japan as a base, he trekked to the vicinity of Mount Everest in Nepal, taking tramp steamers to remote Indonesian islands like Adorana, Timor, Sulawesi and Ternate, and visiting rural parts of China. He returned to the US in 1984, via the Caribbean, where he researched two travel guides: *Guide to Jamaica* and *Guide to Puerto Rico and the Virgin Islands*. The first editions of these were published in 1986. Returning to Japan in 1986, lived in the city of Kagoshima at the southern end of Kyushu, which lies across the bay from an active volcano. During that year and part of the next, he taught English and wrote for *The Japan Times*. He currently lives in San Francisco. Besides traveling and writing, his other pursuits include printmaking, painting, cooking, backpacking, and listening to music – especially jazz, salsa, and African pop.

"Your *Adventure Guide to Barbados* proved to be a delightful introduction to the Barbados I have come to know as a visitor among the local agricultural community."
Sally Adamson Taylor, Barbados.

Abbreviations

B$ - Barbados Dollars
C. - Century
CP - Continental Plan
d - Double
E - East
EP - European Plan
FAP - Full American Plan
m - Meter
MAP - Modified American Plan
N - North
OW - One Way
pn - Per Night
pp - Per Person
RT - Round Trip
s - Single
S - South
t - Triple
W - West

Note: Prices are listed in Barbados dollars (B$) and are subject to fluctuation. Be sure to ask about taxes and service charges before booking a hotel. Listing a hotel or restaurant does not constitute a recommendation.

Contents

Maps

Charts

Introduction

Barbados: the very name conjures up an aura of mystery. There's almost a rhythmic beat to it. In fact, its name is Portuguese – allegedly after the island's bearded fig trees which indelibly impressed the first explorers. A hybrid blend of Africa and England set in the tropics, this "singular isle" combines British institutions, architecture, and style with open, African-style hospitality. Nowhere in the world have African and British cultures combined in such a remarkable synthesis.

It has been nicknamed "Bimshire" or "Little England" because its land, reforested with green and yellow slopes of sugarcane fields, came to resemble the motherland. The island's shape has been compared to that of a ham, a leg of mutton, a pear-shaped emerald, or a lopsided pear with the stem end pointing north. Barbados, 21 miles long by a "smile" wide, is an island of dramatic contrasts and offers many picture-postcard terrains. Its gentle W coast, graced with pink and white beaches, contrasts vividly with the rough and ragged eastern-facing Atlantic coast. In addition to a smorgasbord of beaches, there are fantastic panoramas, densely-foliated tropical gullies, and breathtaking stretches of craggy coastline.

For such a small island, there's an enormous amount to take in. The island's geological history has transformed it into a living laboratory for studying the workings of the earth, from the nature-rendered ecological effects of erosion in the Scotland District to the manmade transformation of a heavily forested island into a vast plain of sugarcane. In addition, the intelligent and perceptive visitor gains a great deal just by traveling around and interacting. In few places throughout the world are the people as receptive to strangers. Finally, the island's greathouses, old churches, and forts bring history to life for all who travel here.

The Land

THE BIG PICTURE: The islands of the Caribbean are laid out in a 2,800-mile (4,500-km) arc from the western tip of Cuba to the small Dutch island of Aruba. The region is sometimes extended to include the Central and S. American countries of Belize (the former

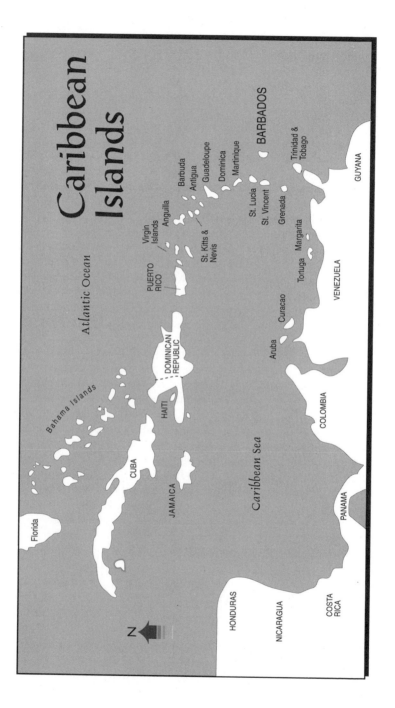

Caribbean Islands

Atlantic Ocean

Bahama Islands

Florida

CUBA

HAITI

DOMINICAN
REPUBLIC

PUERTO
RICO

Virgin
Islands

Anguilla

St. Kitts &
Nevis

Barbuda

Antigua

Guadeloupe

Dominica

Martinique

St. Lucia

St. Vincent

Grenada

BARBADOS

Trinidad &
Tobago

JAMAICA

Caribbean Sea

Aruba

Curacao

Tortuga

Margarita

VENEZUELA

COLOMBIA

PANAMA

COSTA
RICA

NICARAGUA

HONDURAS

GUYANA

N

colony of British Honduras), the Yucatán, Surinam, Guiana, and Guyana. The islands of Jamaica, Hispaniola, Puerto Rico, the US and British Virgin Islands, along with Cuba, the Caymans, and Turks and Caicos islands form the Greater Antilles. This name derives from the early geographers who gave the name "Antilia" to hypothetical islands thought to lie beyond the no less imaginary "Antilades." In general, the land is steep and volcanic in origin. To the S are the Lesser Antilles, whose islands include the Windwards and Leewards, Barbados, Trinidad, Tobago, and Grenada.

GEOGRAPHY: Lying as far E as Nova Scotia and as far S as Senegal, Barbados is the most easterly of the Caribbean islands, situated 200 miles (322 km) NNE of Trinidad and 100 miles (161 km) ESE of St. Lucia. Farther afield to the N are Miami, 1,611 miles (2,592 km); New York City, 2,000 miles (3,220 km); and Toronto, 2,429 miles (3,908 km). On the other side of the ocean to the E lie London, 4,195 miles (6,750 km) and Luxembourg, 4,500 miles (7,240 km). With an area of 166 sq. miles (430 sq. km) extending 21 miles (34 km) N to S and 14 miles (23 km) E to W, it is one of the Americas' most miniscule nations. Viewed from the S and W, the island appears flat with ridges extending up to about 1,000 feet (300 m) and then falling steeply off to the sea. Barbados has literally pulled itself up by its own bootstraps, unlike the Windward Islands 100 miles W. Its base originated with the compression, folding, and uplifting of the sea floor. During the course of subsequent uplift-ings and sea level fluctuations, billions of coral polyps willed their skeletal structures so that the island might secure a limestone cap – over 300 feet (90 m) thick in some locations – atop its sedimentary base. Later movements formed the island's terraced landscape which rises toward the Atlantic side.

Geologically speaking, the island is young: somewhere be-tween 750,000 and a million years old (parts of Western Australia are more than three billion years old). In places like Hackleton's Cliff and at Cherry Tree Hill in the Scotland District, the land falls away abruptly, having eroded swiftly without the protection of the spongelike coral cap which soaks up the rain. In turn, it's the only area with stable streams. In other locations streams only arise during flash floods in coral gullies, most of which are believed to have been formed by a cracking in the coral cap or by collapsed underground stream channels that once interconnected caverns. The most famous gully is Welchman Hall, which is administered by the National Trust. Others contain dense vegetation and pro-vide sanctuary for animals. The lack of rivers is compensated for somewhat by the deliciousness of the drinking water. And there's a good reason why it tastes so delectable. Because seawater has a higher specific gravity than fresh, it serves as a seal to lock in the enormous reservoirs of freshwater it surrounds. The largest of these stores lies under St. George's Valley, but the best known is Cole's Cave.

The highest point is Mt. Hillaby at 1,105 feet (336 m) near the island's center. The land descends steeply heading S to the broad St. George Valley. Christ Church Ridge rises 400 feet between the valley and the sea. It is estimated to be a comparatively youthful 350,000 years old. Coral reefs encircle the coast.

Climate

The island has a delightful climate. Located within the belt of the steady NE tradewinds, its mild, subtropical weather varies little. Winter temperatures average from 70-85°; summers (76-87°) are humid. The island's lowest recorded temperature is 59°. Few days are entirely without sunshine. The E and SE coasts cool down delightfully at night during the winter. Rain (usually short showers) is most frequent between July through the end of Nov.; the driest months are Feb. and March. The average annual rainfall is 60 inches, although totals actually vary from 40 inches (101.60 cm) on the coasts to 90 inches (228.60 cm) along the central ridge region. Winds prevail from the N during the winter and early spring months, but turn around to come in from the SE during the rest of the year.

HURRICANES: There's aways something to spoil a utopia, and the Caribbean is by no means immune. The region as a whole ranks third worldwide in the number of hurricanes per year. These low-pressure zones are serious business and should not be taken lightly. The majority of structures here are poorly constructed and property damage from a hurricane may run into hundreds of millions of dollars.

A hurricane begins as a relatively small tropical storm, known as a cyclone when its winds reach a velocity of 39 mph (62 kph). At 74 mph (118 kph) it is upgraded to hurricane status, with winds of up to 200 mph (320 kph) and ranging in size from 60-1,000 miles (100-1,600 km) in diameter. A small hurricane releases energy equivalent to the explosions of six atomic bombs per second. Hurricanes draw on the moist air and water of the tropics carried by eastern tradewinds which intensify as they move across warm ocean waters. As it heads N, the cooler, drier air infiltrates it and the hurricane begins to die, cut off from the life-sustaining ocean currents that have nourished it from infancy. Routes and patterns are unpredictable. As for their frequency:

> "June – too soon; July – stand by; August – it must;
> September – remember."

So goes the old rhyme. Unfortunately, hurricanes are not confined to July and Aug. Hurricanes forming in Aug. and Sept. typically last for two weeks, while those that form in June, July, Oct., and Nov. (many of which originate in the Caribbean and the Gulf of Mexico) generally last only seven days. Approximately 70% of all hurricanes (known as Cabo Verde types) originate as embryonic storms coming from the W coast of Africa.

Fortunately, these natural disasters are comparatively scarce around Barbados and, since record-keeping began, only a few have wreaked havoc on the island. The most serious of these were in 1780, 1831, and 1898 and the most recent were in Sept. 1955, which damaged the S extensively. In recent years an invisible shield appears to be protecting the island and a number of hurricanes heading toward Barbados have diverted at the last minute.

Flora and Fauna

Plant Life

In order to appreciate the island's wealth of flora, one must dwell for a moment on what has vanished. The thick forests – once so close knit that they impeded agricultural cultivation – are a thing of the past. After colonization began, ship after ship bore away tons of fustic (a small tree yielding a yellow dyestuff), lignum vitae, and West Indian cedar. Others of their majestic species ended up as beams in greathouses or as fuel to fire cauldrons in sugar manufacturing plants. Both the population and sugar's value climbed, and the island's forests were ruthlessly pruned back until their thick, twisted tropical undergrowth gave way to smooth, rolling fields of cane. A 1671 report noted that "at the Barbadoes all the trees are destroyed, so that wanting wood to boyle their sugar, they are forced to send for coales from England." One particularly fine wood tree, the mastic, was driven to extinction. Today, reminders of the island's verdant past remain only at Foster Hall Wood and

Forest Hall Land, both near Hackleton's Cliff, and at Turner's Hall Woods, St. Andrew, in the Scotland District. Other still-verdant but secondary forest tracts are found in the gullies. Barbados has nearly 700 flowering plants but, as it is much drier than neighboring Dominica, St. Vincent, or Trinidad, it lacks their rich profusion of flora. One of the best places to see a sampler of island trees is in Bridgetown's Queen's Park (although it contains many exotic species). A better place (in terms of native species) would be Welchman Hall Gully.

TREES: The **mahogany**, indigenous to the forests of Honduras, was introduced sometime between 1780 and 1800. Surprisingly, it sheds its leaves in April and May. Watch out for its falling fruits! The majestic, heavily-branched **tamarind** (native to Indonesia) was imported around 1650, possibly via Mexico. Its pods are exported to Britain where they form one of the key ingredients in Lea and Perrin's Worcestershire Sauce. The low-lying **evergreen tree**, a common feature on sugar estates where it was planted for shade, stands with stately dignity – its thick horizontal branches spreading widely. Originally from India, it was introduced around the mid-18th C. and can still be found near the greathouses or dwellings, where it once provided shade for beasts of burden and a spot for slaves to take their siesta. The **casuarina** or "mile tree" (one of the taller trees, with an average height of 150 feet) waves gracefully in the breeze. It is a native of N Australia deserts where it flourishes and was imported to Barbados in about 1870. An extensive root system renders it immune from drought. It soon gained fame as an ornamental, although it was originally introduced as a windbreak. The **cabbage palm**, along with the casuarina, lines the sides of Bajan roads. Its name comes from its central bud in the palm which can be eaten as a vegetable. It is often confused with the royal palm, a Cuban species seldom found here. Graceful **coconut palms** frame the island's coastline and beautiful beaches. The most potentially useful tree here, its nut can provide food, oil, and soap; its fronds may be used in basketmaking, to make brooms, and to cover roofs. The "devil's tree," **African tulip tree**, or "Judas tree" – also known as the "Lent tree" because it blooms during the Lenten season – possesses nearly-circular dark green leaves and intricate blood-red flowers. The **baobab**, an import from W Africa, is found only in two places on Barbados – at Queen's Park in Bridgetown and in Warrens, St. Michael. Its jug-shaped trunk enables it to thrive in the dry savannah regions of its homeland. Rev. Griffith Hughes, one of the first chroniclers of the island's botany, maintained that the baobab at Warrens was imported from "Guiney" in around 1738.

UNIQUE NATIVES: The **Bajan**, ebony or "shak-shak" is found chiefly in gardens and is known as the "mother-in-law's tongue." This tree's long, straw-colored pods clatter in the breeze like a remonstrating mother-in-law and its wood, along with that of the fustic, has been used to make wheels for donkey carts here. Lovely white or green sweet-scented flowers appear in April or May. The **clammy-cherry** has twisted, horizontal branches that rise 30 feet into the air. After blooming in April and May, it produces a semi-transparent orange berry that schoolboys use as glue. The **sandbox tree**, large, symmetrical, strong, and stout, gets its name from its fruit; the ribbed peel, when seeded and flattened, was used to sprinkle sand used for blotting ink spilt on parchment. Its poisonous moon-shaped seeds fire off into the distance as the pods split open. A local legend insists that when this happens a lizard wedding has just taken place. The tree's acrid, milky sap irritates the skin and its trunk is covered with sharp prickles. This tree may rise as high as 100 feet. Possibly native, the **calabash** is heavily branched, deciduous, and has a flat crown. Its gourd-like fruit can be used as a utensil when dried and emptied. The **silk-cotton tree** is known as *ceiba* on Spanish-speaking islands. It was once believed by slaves to walk at night. The **West Indian almond**, a shade tree, has an edible but difficult-to-open fruit.

strangler figs: The indigenous **bearded fig** is found largely along gully walls or inland cliffs, where it perches precariously, aerial roots dangling from its branches. This impressive tree is common and is thought to have been behind the island's name. It has an absorbing natural history attached to it. Beginning life as epiphytes, some species of ficus and clusia send down woody, clasping roots that wind themselves around the trunk as they extend into the earth. As the roots grow, they meld into a trunk which surrounds the tree. These strangler figs are most likely to kill the tree, not through strangulation, but by robbing it of canopy space. They are also found in the ruins of buildings and are often the only trees left in an otherwise cleared tract of forest. There is little incentive to use their poor quality wood, but their spreading branches do provide shade. The holes, cracks, twists and turns in its trunk play host to geckos, anoles, ants, stingless bees, and scorpions, while bats, birds, and other fruit eaters flock above.

FLOWERING TREES: White and red **frangipanis** were introduced to the island in the early 1700s. They are closely related species. The white frangipani, better known as the "jasmine tree," bears bunches of leaves on forked twigs. At the beginning of the dry season, the leaves fall and are replaced by heavily-scented flowers. The frangipani's name comes from that of a legendary

European perfume whose scent was unparalleled at the time. Another species, the **red flamboyant,** has distinctive orange-red flowers unmatched by any other ornamental tree in the tropics.

FRUIT TREES: These include the mango, tamarind, coconut, guava, and the genip. It is believed that the **grapefruit** may have originated here, possibly as a natural hybrid between the shaddock and the sweet orange, both of which were introduced from Asia during the 17th C. Prominent deciduous fruit trees include the hog and Chili plum trees, golden apple, sugar apple, pomegranate, and soursop. Trees that flower and fruit irregularly include the gooseberry, cherry, sapodilla, and star apple. **Guavas**, thought to have been introduced by the Indians, contain five times as much vitamin C (by weight) as oranges.

FORBIDDEN FRUIT: The **machineel** – small, with a short trunk and numerous branches – grows near the sea. Its elliptical leaves possess a strange bright green sheen. The machineel secretes a fluid which may be deadly and it is said to be the original apple in the Garden of Eden. Biting into its innocuous-looking yet highly poisonous fruit will cause your mouth to burn and your tongue to swell up. In fact, all parts of this tree are potentially deadly. Cattle, standing under the tree after a torrential tropical downpour, have been known to lose their hides as drops fall from leaves. Other tales tell of locals going blind after a leaf touched an eye. Slaves (in the Virgin Islands to the N) wishing to do away with a particularly despicable master would insert minute quantities of juice into an uncooked potato. Cooked, these small doses were undetectable but always fatal if served to the victim over a long period of time. If you should spot one of these trees – which are not uncommon along the island's beaches – stay well away!

Another example of vicious vegetation is the "**poison tree**," a related species. Contact with its latex will result in swelling the next day. The "**cow itch vine**" produces lovely purple blooms which fruit into felt-covered brown pods covered with stinging hairs that can cause fierce irritation. Two types of nettles sting similarly.

ORCHIDS: A number of orchid species thrive in Barbados. Epiphytic orchids (those that grow on trees), have thicker leaves than other species and keep their stomata (tiny pores on their leaves that absorb carbon dioxide) shut during the day, storing the carbon dioxide for the next day's use. Nearly all orchids are pollinated by insects or hummingbirds, which are rife in Barbados. It is believed that many may only be pollinated by a specific one and, indeed, certain orchid blooms bear an amazing resemblance to specific bees or wasps. Aside from their aesthetic value, orchids are of little economic importance. They were once thought to have medicinal properties, but these claims have largely proven false and not a single species is used in modern medicine. Their only valuable product is vanilla, an extract obtained from the cured unripened pods of various species belonging to the genus *Vanilla*. Orchids were named by Dioscorides, a Greek physician who, noting the similarity of the tubers of one species he was examining to male genitals, named the species *orchis* (testicle). Orchids may be seen all over the island, but a particularly good place is Andromeda Gardens.

MANGROVES: Mangrove forests are found in greatly diminished numbers along the coasts. While the white mangrove is widely distributed on the island, the red mangrove is found only in Graeme Hall Swamp. These water-rooted trees serve as a marine habitat for sponges, corals, oysters, and other members of the marine community around its roots. Some species live out their entire lives here and many fish shelter or feed in and around them; lobsters use the mangrove environs as a nursery for their young. Above the water level, they shelter seabirds and offer important nesting sites. Their organic detritus, exported to the reef by the tides, is consumed by its inhabitants, providing the base of an extensive food web. Mangroves also dampen high waves and winds. The **red mangroves** act as land builders by trapping silt in their roots and catching leaves and other detritus which decompose to form soil. Eventually, the red mangroves kill themselves off by building up enough soil to form dry land, cutting off their water supply. It is then that the black and white mangroves take over. Meanwhile, the red mangroves have sent out progeny in the form of floating seedlings – bottom-heavy youngsters that grow on the tree until reaching six inches to a foot in length. If they drop in shallow water, the seeds touch bottom and implant themselves, but in deeper water they stay afloat until dragging across a shoal and lodging. Named after their light-colored bark, the **white mangroves** are highly salt-tolerant. If growing in a swampy area, they produce pneumatophores, root system extensions which grow vertically to a height that allows them to stay above the water during flooding or tides so they can carry on gaseous exchange. The **black mangrove** also produces pneumatophores as well as a useful wood. The buttonwood is smaller than the others and is not a true mangrove. It is found on the coasts where no other varieties grow.

OTHERS: Other trees include the "bead tree" or Barbados lilac, the continually-flowering willow, the lavender horse-radish, the bright green wild pine, and the lignum vitae – a hardwood whose name, "tree of life," refers to the medicinal qualities of its resinous gum. The trumpet or "pop-a-gun" tree is easily recognized by its large leaves which are divided into finger-like lobes; they are nearly white underneath. The phallic dildo cactus grows in the drier areas.

VINES, PLANTS, AND FLOWERS: The bright orange leafless stems of the parasitic love vine (dodder) are a frequent sight. At one time, people could be fined for having the vine on their property. Another vine is the clinging creeper golden shower. The climbing "**crab eye**" vine has poisonous black-spotted red seeds. The century plant, known locally as the "**maypole**," lives about 10 years, not the 100 its name suggests. The plant blooms only once (in its last year) and the canary-yellow flowers wilt and cast their seed to the winds. Its bouyant stems are used by fishermen as floats when they gather sea urchins. Leaving the stem to float above water, they tie a net bag on to it in which they place their harvest. Today, it's commonly found in the Scotland District, as is the columnar cactus. "**Pride of Barbados**" or "flower fence" (*Caesalpinia pulcherima*) is the national flower. It is colored a beautiful red with yellow borders and has protruding stamens that arch up like antennae. "**Khus khus**" is a hardy grass that can reach six feet in height. It can be used to make baskets, mats, and hats and once provided stuffing for matresses; its pulverized roots have traditionally been placed with clothing in order to imbue them with an attractive scent.

Animal Life

As with its flora, Barbados' animal population has been deeply influenced by human settlement patterns. Unlike mainland Guayana – where gargantuan primeval forests still maintain a universe for wildlife – Bajan fauna features your usual barnyard stuff: cows, pigs, horses, sheep, chickens, dogs, cats, mules, and goats. There are very few indigenous species. The most spectacular native species, the Bajan parrot, has been driven to extinction.

MAMMALS: On an island that is almost totally cultivated and so very heavily populated, only the most intelligent and the smallest of the wild kingdom have been able to adapt.

the green monkey: The most notable survivor is the Barbados green monkey (*Cepus Capucinus*). Widely distributed in W Africa, it measures some 16-18 inches, excluding its lengthy tail, and has a black face fringed with white hairs. They were probably introduced by sailors manning slave ships who brought them over for pets. Bajans regard the creature as an infernal nuisance. It ravages both vegetable patches and cane fields and there is a bounty out for its tail. One popular use for them is in medical research and the Barbados Wildlife Reserve exports them for this purpose. The modern era has actually assisted their continued survival: Because Bajans now cook with gas, the gullies are thick with brush – allowing the monkeys to thrive. There are an estimated 8-10,000 of them on Barbados.

blackbelly sheep: In contrast to the monkeys, blackbelly sheep are a welcome inhabitant and are the result of more than three centuries careful breeding between African long-hair sheep with European sheep. Since they have little fat but tender flesh, and are resistent to diseases, they are popular. Their numbers cannot, however, meet local demand and most lamb is still imported.

others: Other introduced animals include the hare and raccoon. Mongooses were imported from Jamaica (which had, in turn, imported them from India) to combat rats and now-extinct poisonous reptiles. They have propogated to the point where they too are a pest – attacking lambs, calves, and baby pigs as well as the reptile and bird population. The Barbados Legislature ordered its extermination in 1904, but it can still be seen darting among the bushes.

Camels in Barbados

Strangely enough, camels were brought to Barbados as pack animals. In *A True and Exact History of the Island* (published in London in 1657), Ligon relates that they were used to bring beer and wine to the plantations. There, they were laden down with sugarcane and returned to Bridgetown. The camels were unaccustomed to the terrain and diet so the industry came to an end shortly thereafter.

BIRDS: There are 24 species of resident birds, including brightly-colored wild parakeets, pelicans, and egrets; another 18 migrate each winter. Owls and hawks have become extinct, as have several other birds.

One of the most prolific birds is the yellow-breasted bananaquit, also known as the "sugar bird" or "yellow breast." This small, sooty grey-and-yellow-breasted creature, addicted to fruit juices and flower nectar, is often seen around flowers and fruit trees. Its white eyestripe and coral-red patch on its bill make it even more conspicuous. Another very attractive but rarely-sighted bird is the golden warbler, whose yellow mass is laced with streaks of dark chestnut (it may also have a green or golden tint). The Christmas bird, creatively colored in orange, black, and yellow, winters on the island. The thick-set wood (or Zenaida) dove is larger than the ground dove and combines a grey body with sprinklings of black, white, and cinnamon brown. Its soft cooing resembles a chant of praise so closely that Bajans have long maintained that it is uttering "Moses spake God's word." The Carib grackle or "blackbird" is a common bird that travels in flocks. It was once used as a fighting cock, made more threatening by the needles stuck through its legs. The grass finch, with its yellow breast and brown body, made its debut on the local scene only this century. when it arrived from South America. It resides in fields and savannahs. The cow bird, often confused with the blackbird because the male of the species is the same color, will deposit its eggs in blackbirds' nests. The nearly-black frigate bird, known as the "cobbler" or "man-o'-war" bird, swoops ominously overhead, occasionally veering down to the water to make a capture. The rarely-visiting brown pelicans fly in small flocks. Atlantic birds that winter on Barbados include the wood sandpiper, the Greenland wheatear, the alpine swift, the black-headed gull, and the ruff. There are two varieties of hummingbirds ("Doctor Booby"): the smaller, straight-billed Antillean-crested hummer and the larger, emerald-throat hummer or green-throated Carib, which has a curved bill.

You will see cattle egrets – also known as the common white heron – around cattle. They prey on insects wrested from their domicile as the cows move around and on newly-exposed grubs and insects in freshly-cut fields. The island's other birds include hawks, grey plovers, snipes, sandpipers, doves, sparrows (finches), thrushes, parakeets, yellow-breasted moustache birds, West Indian crows, wild pigeons, and canaries.

birding: While it lacks a large number of endemic species, Barbados attacts many migrants and is a fine place to birdwatch. The best place is Graeme Hall Swamp.

REPTILES AND AMPHIBIANS: The two species of snakes – the blind snake and a grass snake – are harmless. There are six varieties of lizards. Most notable (some might say infamous) of these is the "whistling frog," which frequently keeps you awake at nights with its piercing hum. The brown and yellow adult is one inch long (the female being the larger of the two). Unlike most amphibians, it has no tadpole stage and females do not return to the water to breed. Instead, 10 days after deposition, offspring emerge from their formative jelly ready to pump their lungs out. The "cock lizard," a male anole, displays its bright yellow throat fan as a warning. Two types of gecko are found. One of them, the harmless "poison lizard" or "woodslave," was introduced from Africa and is fairly common. The iguana has been driven to extinction.

The Crapaud

The giant toad or marine toad (*bufo marinus*) was purposely brought in from Guyana, S. America in 1835 and has made itself right at home. Known locally as a "crapaud," its glands contain toxins. Don't try to pick one up: it'll urinate on you! The marine toad, a predominantly nocturnal being, directs poison in a fine spray (that can be fatal to cats and dogs when ingested) through a gland between its eyes. An equal-opportunity eater, it will dine on anything from wasps to dog and cat food set out for pets. In Barbados it was traditionally used in *obeah* (magic). One practice by an *obeah* man in Speightstown was to take a police summons and stuff it into an unfortunate frog's mouth. He would then sew the mouth shut and, after the frog was dumped from a boat in the ocean, the petitioner would be assured that his or her case would be set aside.

INSECTS AND SPIDERS: These include the common house fly, the destructive cabbage white butterfly (one of 14 resident species), bees, wood ants, three different varieties of mosquitoes, and grasshoppers. The local centipede is known as a "fortyleg." One of the biggest miseries to many is the "merrywing," the local biting sandfly. Barbados has fewer of them than other islands, but they can still be found in "dead sand" areas which the tide does not cover. Butterflies here are called "bats," and what the Western English-speaking world calls bats are known as "leather bats."

Sealife

ECHINODERMATA: Combining the Greek words *echinos* (hedgehog) and *derma* (skin), this large division of the animal kingdom includes sea urchins, sea cucumbers, and starfish. They have in common the fact that they all move with the help of tube-feet or spines. Known by the scientific name *Astrospecten*, **starfish** (*estrella de mar*) are five-footed carnivorous creatures that use their modified tube-feet to burrow into the seabed. Sluggish **sea cucumbers** ingest large quantities of sand, extract the organic matter, and excrete the rest.

Sea Urchins

Seventeen species of sea urchins reside in Bajan waters and are one of the more infamous residents of the reef and flats alike. The sea urchin is protected by its brown, jointed barbs; it has a semi-circular calcareous (calcium carbonate) shell. It uses its mouth, protected on its underside, to feed by scraping algae from rocks. It will come as a surprise to those uninitiated in its lore that sea urchins are considered a gastronomic delicacy in many countries. The ancient Greeks believed they had aphrodisiacal and other properties beneficial to health. They are prized by the French and fetch four times the price of oysters in Paris. The Spanish consume them raw, boiled, in *gratinés*, or in soups, and the Japanese eat them as sushi. Bajans dub the white sea urchins "sea eggs" and have harvested them at the beach. They are traditionally either steamed or fried with chopped onions and sweet pepper until golden brown. Bajans believe them to be an aphrodisiac. Due to overharvesting, however, their numbers have been decreasing greatly and catching them is now prohibited. The black sea urchin is known as the "cobbler" and although a mysterious plague killed off 95% of them in the Caribbean in 1983, Barbados has recovered.

By all means avoid trampling on this armed knight of the underwater sand dunes. Sea urchins hide underneath corals. If a spine breaks off inside your finger or toe, don't try to remove it – it's impossible! You might try the cure people use in New Guinea. Mash up the spine under your skin with a blunt object so that it will be absorbed naturally. Then dip your finger in urine; the ammonia helps to trigger the process of disintegration. (Bajans urinate directly on the affected area or cover it with candle wax.) Avoiding contact in the first place is best.

sponges: Found in the ocean depths, reddish or brown sponges are among the simplest forms of multi-cellular life and have been around for more than 500 million years. They pump large amounts of water through their internal filters, from which they extract plankton.

jellyfish: Another marine creature to keep away from is the floating Portuguese man-o'-war, found mainly on the Atlantic side. Actually a colony of marine organisms, its stinging tentacles can be extended or retracted; worldwide, there have been reports of trailing tentacles as long as 50 feet! There are no regular jellyfish here.

crustaceans: The **ghost crab** (*Ocypode quadrata*) abounds on the beaches, tunneling down beneath the sand and emerging to feed at night. It can survive for 48 hours without contacting water, but must return to the sea to moisten its gill chambers as well as to lay eggs, which hatch into plankton larvae. It is known locally as a "**belly** (or **Betty**) **conscience**" and is used as fish bait. The "**scuttle**" (*Grapsus grapsus*) is a brown speckled crab commonly found near the water. The "**Shagguh**" (*Callinectes*), infamous for its nasty bites, is a swimming crab with a rough shell. The **hermit crab** carries a discarded mollusc shell to protect its vulnerable abdomen. As it grows, it must find a larger home and you may see two struggling over the same shell. The eight species of **freshwater shrimp** here breed in brackish water and are known as "**crayfish**."

Bajan Reef Fish

Reef fish are multicolored and diverse. Bajan fishermen place traps known as "fish pots" on the reef to catch grunts, porgies, and other fish. The pots are constructed by attaching wire mesh to wooden frames, which are then secured by ropes to buoys. Known elsewhere as parrot fish, the "**chubs**" differ in color between male and female. Bajans have given colorful appellations to many of the fish, the most vibrant of which is the "**our savior snapper**." This fish bears a dark mark just in front of the tail where Christ is alleged to have grasped it between his thumb and forefinger before tossing it back. The razor-sharp spines on its tail give the **barber** its name, and the **goggle-eye** has appropriately large eyes.

The Coral Reef Ecosystem

One of the least appreciated of the world's innumerable wonders is the coral reef. This is, in part, because little has been known about it until recent decades. A coral reef is the only geological feature fashioned by living creatures, and it is a delicate environment. Many of the world's reefs – which took millions of years to form – have already suffered adverse effects from human activities. One of the greatest opportunities the tropics offer is to explore this wondrous environment.

Corals produce the calcium carbonate (limestone) responsible for the build-up of offlying cays and islets as well as most sand on the beaches. Bearing the brunt of waves, they also conserve the shoreline. Although reefs began forming millenia ago, they are in a constant state of flux. They depend upon a delicate ecological balance to survive. Deforestation, dredging, temperature change, an increase or decrease in salinity, silt, or sewage discharge may kill them. Because temperatures must remain between 68° and 95°F, they are only found in the tropics and, because they require light to grow, only in shallow water. They are also intolerant of freshwater, so reefs cannot survive where rivers empty into the sea.

THE CORAL POLYP: While corals are actually animals, botanists view them as being mostly plant, and geologists dub them "honorary rocks." Acting more like plants than animals, corals survive through photosynthesis: the algae inside them do the work while the polyps themselves secrete calcium carbonate and stick together for protection from waves and boring sponges. Polyps bear a close structural resemblance to its relative the anemone. It feeds at night by using the ring or rings of tentacles surrounding its mouth to capture prey (such as plankton) with nematocysts, small stinging darts.

They are able to survive in limited space through their symbiotic relationship with the algae present in their tissues. Coral polyps exhale carbon dioxide and the algae consume it, producing needed oxygen. Only half of the world's coral species have this special relationship and these, known as "hermatypic" corals, are the ones that build the reef. The nutritional benefits gained from this relationship enable them to grow a larger skeleton and to do so more rapidly than would otherwise be possible. Polyps have the ability to regulate the density of these cells in their tissues and can expel some of them in a spew of mucus should they multiply too quickly. Looking at coral, the brownish algal cells show through transparent tissues. When you see a coral garden through your mask, you are actually viewing a field of captive single-celled algae.

A vital, though invisible, component of the reef ecosystem is bacteria, micro-organisms that decompose and recycle all matter on which everything from worms to coral polyps feed. Inhabitants of the reef range from crabs to barnacles to sea squirts to multicolored tropical fish. Remarkably, the polyps themselves are consumed by only a small percentage of the reef's dwellers. They often contain high levels of toxic substances and are thought to sting fish and other animals that attempt to eat them. Corals retract their polyps during daylight hours when the fish can see them. Reefs originate as the polyps develop, and the calcium secretions form a base as they grow. One polyp can have a 1,000-year lifespan.

CORAL TYPES: Corals may be divided into three groups. The **hard** or **stony corals** (such as staghorn, brain, star, or rose) secrete a limey skeleton. The **horny corals** (sea plumes, sea whips, sea fans, and gorgonians) have a supporting skeleton-like structure known as a gorgonin (after the head of Medusa). The shapes of these corals result from the way the polyps and their connecting tissues excrete calcium carbonate; there are over 1,000 different patterns – one specific to each species. Each also has its own method of budding. Giant elk-horn corals may contain over a million polyps and live for several hundred years or longer. The last category consists of the **soft corals.** While these too are colonies of polyps, their skeletons are composed of soft organic material, and their polyps always have eight tentacles instead of the six (or multiples of six) found in the stony corals. Unlike the hard corals, this group disintegrates after death and does not add to the reef's stony structure. Instead of depositing limestone crystals, they excrete a jelly-like matrix which is imbued with spicules (diminutive spikes) of stony material; the jelly substance gives flexibility. Sea fans and sea whips exhibit similar patterns. The precious black coral is a type of soft coral and is prized by jewelers. Its branches may be cleaned and polished to high gloss ebony-black and, in this state, it resembles bushes of fine twigs.

COMPETITION: To the snorkeler, the reef appears to be a peaceful haven. The reality is that, because the reef is a comparatively benign environment, the fiercest competition has developed here. Some have developed sweeper tentacles that have an especially high concentration of stinging cells. Reaching out to a competing coral, they sting and execute it. Other species dispatch digestive filaments which eat their prey. Soft corals appear to leach out toxic chemicals (terpines) that kill nearby organisms. Because predation is such a problem, two-thirds of reef species are toxic. Others hide in stony outcrops or have formed protective relationships with other organisms. The banded clown fish, for example, lives among sea anemones whose stingers protect it. The cleaner fish protect themselves from the larger fish by setting up stations at which they pick parasites off their carnivorous customers. The sabre-toothed blenny is a false cleaner fish. It mimics the coloration and shape of the feeder fish, approaches, then takes a chunk out of the larger fish and runs off!

CORAL LOVE AFFAIRS: Coral polyps are not prone to celibacy or sexual prudery. They reproduce sexually and asexually through budding and join together with thousands and even millions of its neighbors to form a coral. (In a few cases, only one polyp forms a single coral.) During sexual reproduction polyps release millions of their spermatozoa into the water. Many species are dimorphic, with both male and female polyps. Some species have internal, others external, fertilization. As larvae develop, their "mother" expels them and they float off to form a new coral.

EXPLORING REEFS: Coral reefs are extremely fragile environments. Much damage has been done to them worldwide through the carelessness of humans. Despite their size, reefs grow very slowly, and it can take decades or even centuries to repair the damage done in just a few moments.

BAJAN REEFS: The island's offshore reefs have played an important role in its history, acting as a natural barrier against conquest. Most common are fringing reefs close to shore, perhaps separated by a small lagoon. Elongated and narrow bank or ribbon reefs lie in deep water off the S and W coasts. Atolls and barrier reefs are absent. While the outer bank reefs are still in good condition, the fringing reefs have been severely impacted by sewage dumping and soil runoff.

ORGANIZATIONS: If you're interested in working to preserve coral reefs worldwide, contact **Coral Forest** (☎ 415-291-9877) at 300 Broadway, Suite 39, San Francisco CA 94133.

UNDERWATER FLORA: Most of the plants you see are algae, primitive plants that can survive only underwater. Lacking roots, algae draw their minerals and water directly from the sea. Another type of algae, calcareous red algae, are very important for reef formation. They resemble rounded stones and are 95% rock and only 5% living tissue. Sea grasses (plants returned to live in the sea) are found in relatively shallow water in sandy and muddy bays and flats; they have roots and small flowers. One species, dubbed "turtle grass," provides food for turtles. Seagrasses help to stabilize the sea floor, maintain water clarity by trapping fine sediments from upland soil erosion, stave off beach erosion, and provide living space for numerous fish, crustaceans, and shellfish.

FISH SPECIES: A kaleidoscope of fish include the doctorfish, grouper, cavalla, old wife ("ale wife"), one-eye, silver angelfish, sergeant fish, marine jewel, trunkfish, barracuda, sawfish, parrotfish, weakfish, lionfish, big-eye, bananafish, ladyfish, puffer, seabat, sardine, mullet, grouper, kingfish (wahoo), albacore (yellow-finned tuna), Spanish and frigate mackerels, red snapper, eel (the spotted moray is called a "conger" here), barracuda, and a variety of sharks. If one were to pick a "national" fish, it undoubt-edly would be the flying fish, which forms the national dish when served with "coo coo." Attracted by the plankton-rich waters sur-rounding the island and brought in by the warm water currents, their presence has given the island its nickname, "Land of the Flying Fish." The spiny lobster, another delicacy , resides 20-30 feet down in homes dug out under the reefs.

History

THE START: Barbados' beginnings differ from those of other Car-ibbean islands in at least one respect: Columbus never arrived to "discover" the island. Nor did he name it – some unknown Por-tugese or Spanish explorer did. The island may have been named for its "bearded" fig trees which send down aerial roots from their branches. Another theory is that the island is named after a tribe of bearded Indians, whose blood had mixed with that of ancient African explorers. Sixteenth-century variants of its name appear-ing on Spanish charts include St. Barbado, Barbudos, Bernardo, and even Barnodo. It is believed that those first to settle were members of the Saladoid/Barrancoid culture – named after the Venezuelan spot on the Orinoco River where their pottery was first unearthed. They may have arrived in Barbados as early as 2,000 years ago. Little archaeological evidence remains, but it *is* known that they were predominantly farmers and fishermen. Seven hun-dred or so years later these placid farmers and fisherfolk are thought to have already been supplanted by the Arawaks. Also hailing from the NE sector of the enormous continent to the S, the Arawaks brought along their crafts, including a simple pottery style. They lacked the implements and beasts of burden that would have made large-scale agriculture feasible and their cultivation consisted of literally "scraping by" – carving out meager plots in the bush. Armed with tools made from conch shells, they congre-gated near the ocean where they sought to supplement their lim-ited diet – cassava, maize, peanuts, squash, and papaya – with fish. The most likely explanation of the name "Arawak" is that it de-rived from Arucay ("jaguar island" in local dialect), a large settle-ment of the Lokono indigenous people, which was located on the W bank of the Lower Orinoco.

The Arawaks lived on Barbados until the 1200s when the fiercer, more nomadic Caribs are believed to have arrived. The Caribs – after whom the Caribbean is named – may have lived on the island for up to 300 years. They lacked the artisan skills of the Arawaks, but were master canoe builders. Their name comes from *caribal*, the Spanish word for cannibal – although it remains uncertain whether the Caribs actually ate human flesh. Indeed, little is known about all of these earlier inhabitants; grounds for their differentiation has been based on their various pottery styles. Similarly, the way we view the Caribs may be attributed to the fact that the Spanish had developed a friendly relationship with the Aracuay, traditional adversaries of the Caribs.

ENGLISH SETTLEMENT: Arriving to settle in 1627, the English found an uninhabited island of spectacular beauty. Where were the Caribs? While there are no historical records, it seems fairly certain that the usual scenario had taken place. In the best dog-eat-dog tradition of the Americas, they had been carted off to work in Spanish and Portuguese mines and plantations. Those left behind had succumbed to the White Man's dreadful diseases. This massive genocide happened between the first visits of the early 1500s by Spanish and Portuguese ships and the 1536 visit of Portuguese navigator Pedro a Campos. What happened in Barbados was replicated with variations all over the Caribbean. The only surviving Caribbean Caribs live in a small reservation on Dominica.

The major artifact left by the Indians on Barbados was a bridge over the arm of the sea at what is now Bridgetown. In July 1625, the *Olive*, the first English ship to dock, stumbled onto the island by mistake. The ship's captain, John Powell, reported the discovery to Sir William Courteen, his employer, who ordered him to go back to the island and start a settlement forthwith. After capturing a Spanish ship enroute, Powell returned to England and abandoned the expedition. Sir William Courteen was bent on having his own Caribbean island together with its profitable export crops, and sent out the *William and John*, which arrived at Holetown on Feb. 17, 1627. In a complicated series of crafty maneuvers popularly known as the "Great Barbados Robbery," the unscrupulous Earl of Carlisle stole Barbados from Courteen in 1629. Feuding between Carlisle and Courteen factions sapped the island's economic vitality; the mid-1630s were dubbed "the starving time."

In 1639, the nation's Parliament began when the House of Assembly was instituted by the infamously corrupt Gov. Henry Hawley as a representative rubber stamp. A new, more genteel rush of settlers arrived in the 1640s as the English Civil War progressed. Both factions, Cavaliers and Roundheads, peacefully co-existed through a system known as the "Treaty of Turkey and Roast Pork." Anyone who mentioned either "Cavalier" or "Roundhead" would have to provide a young hog and turkey for consumption at his house by all who heard him speak the forbidden words. However, the island's Cavaliers gained ascendency, and they proclaimed their loyalty to the Royalist cause on May3, 1650. In Feb. 1651, a fleet was dispatched to put down this insurgency. This "Barbados Fleet" arrived in Oct. of 1651. Even with the help of the "Virginia Fleet," which arrived subsequently, the English failed to occupy the island. A compromise emerged, however, and the Articles of Agreement (also known as The Charter of Barbados) was ratified by the British Parliament in 1652. It allowed for freedom of religion, no taxation without representation, a system of open ports, and a freeholder-elected Assembly. The controversial 4.5% duty on all exports was instituted by the Brits in 1663. Over the years this tax provoked frequent conflicts between the plantocracy and the British government.

The Carolina Connection

A little known fact of both Bajan and US history is the strong link that existed between South Carolina and Barbados. Shortly after the restoration of Charles II, wealthy Bajan planter Sir John Colleton petitioned the King for a land grant in the area that was to become Carolina. The first settlement (1664-1667) failed, but the second took root in present day Charleston in 1670. Many Bajans emigrated, lured by generous offers of land under "hire purchase."

Among these was Sir John Yeamans, a real estate speculator believed to have poisoned his partner in order to marry his wife. Yeamans led the second expedition to Carolina in 1665; it failed. He did, however, succeed in colonizing Charleston on a subsequent trip, after which he returned to Barbados. He went back to Carolina in 1672, was made governor again, and died in disgrace in 1674.

Even today, the connections are apparent. Parish names, street names, and Gullah (the dialect of Carolina's coasts and islands) all reflect the area's Bajan heritage. The "single house," a narrow and elongated home just a single room wide, is a Charleston archaeological specialty which tradition attributes to Barbados. For more information on the Barbados-Carolina connection, read the book of the same name by Alleyne and Fraser (published by Macmillan, 1988).

SLAVES AND SUGAR: Meanwhile, the colonists had wasted no time beating down the bush and planting cotton and tobacco. Their tobacco, however, paled in the face of Virginia's aromatic blend, and cotton could only be grown near the coast. At a loss for what to do, the colonists were saved by the introduction of sugarcane. This hardy, toothache-fostering weed was soon solely responsible for the deforestation of the entire island. By the 1640s the vast majority of the population consisted of indentured servants and English yeoman farmers. The mix included 10-15% African slaves.

Slavery was nothing new; it had come with the British. When the *William and John* arrived in 1627, she brought with her 10 slaves taken from a Portuguese ship captured enroute. Arawak Indians, brought as agricultural consultants from Guyana, were later treacherously double-crossed and enslaved. Even the whites were not immune: Indentured servants, in some cases political opponents of Oliver Cromwell, were shipped off to the island, where they subsisted under oppressive conditions. Some of them had been "barbadosed" – the 17th-C. equivalent of being shanghaied. One charming Bajan method of punishment was to string servants up by their hands and light matches between their fingers! They revolted twice; once in 1634 and again in 1639. But their numbers proved insufficient so the slave trade evolved and flourished. By the early 1650s, slaves outnumbered whites by two to one, and between 1640 and 1807, some 487,000 Africans were abducted and brought on crowded ships to Barbados. Many were resold to North America or other West Indian islands.

The immensely increased profitability of the land under sugarcane cultivation was directly responsible for this remarkable socio-economic transformation; the profits made the importation of slaves – despite the heavy initial investment – financially viable. Now, similarly high profits keep the duty-free zones giong. Sugar had first been introduced to the island by Dutchman Pieter Blower in 1637. He brought Brazilian cane which was used in brewing the first vats of rum. Going down to study in Brazil, the planters learned the ropes of cane growing. Underwriting this effort were the Dutch, who provided commodities; supplied cheap loans, insurance, and equipment; and introduced the Bajans to the wonders of the W. African slave trade. By 1684, the 60,000 slaves outnumbered the whites by four to one and white indentured servants by 30 to one! The first planned uprising h:d taken place in 1675, but it failed because a female slave informed on the conspirators. In retribution, the 17 ringleaders were executed; 11 were beheaded and six were burnt alive, with their beheaded bodies dragged through the streets. Other scares and plots were uncovered in 1683, 1686, 1692, and 1702 and similarly suppressed. On such a small, crowded and deforested island – with a majority of slaves kept in superstitious awe of the powers of their owners – it was nearly impossible for a rebellion to succeed. A dark cloud of misfortune cast its shadow over the last two decades of the 1600s. A fall in the price of sugar was coupled with a smallpox epidemic which decimated the population.

ENGLAND IN THE CARIBBEAN: Ironically, the cultivation of sugarcane brought about a remarkable transformation in appearance and the island came to resemble a "Little England" – though with warmer temperatures of course! As the decades wore on, it became the wealthiest and most profitable of the British Empire's New World possessions. Up until about 1700, Barbados was second only to Massachusetts in population among the colonies and settlements. Unlike the other British islands, whose planters lived in splendid comfort back in jolly old England, most of the Bajan planters chose to make the island their home. The island was of strategic military importance, holding down the easternmost upwind position. From the time of its founding it had a militia, the presence of which was largely responsible for the fact that the island never changed hands. It also sheltered imperial forces that were sent out from time to time to fight in the region. As the decades progressed the island becamed more "civilized" in the British sense of the word: A monthly packet ship carrying cards and letters began arriving in 1703; Codrington College was founded in 1710; construction of St. Anne's Castle was begun that same year; the *Barbados Gazette,* the island's first newspaper, began publication in 1731. Its editor, Samuel Keimer from Philadephia, had taught Benjamin Franklin how to use a press. Nevertheless, misfortunes continued. In 1760 swarms of sugar ants decimated the cane crop; two incendiary fires razed Bridgetown in both 1776 and 1777; and the hurricane of 1780 killed 4,000 and razed all but four of the churches. It was the worst in the island's history and damage was estimated to be £1,250,000.

THE END OF SLAVERY: The slave trade was abolished by the British Parliament in 1807. Under the sponsorship of the African Institution, a Slave Registry Bill was introduced in the British Parliament in June of 1815. The lively, antagonistic debate among the planters was picked up by the slaves who – misinterpreting the exchange of dialog – imagined that the bill would emancipate them. On Easter Sunday, April 14, 1816, cane fields and various trash heaps were set ablaze signalling the beginning of the insurrection. At 1:30 AM on Easter Monday, April 15, the firing of a cannon in Bridgetown sounded the planters' response. A great deal of damage was done before the revolt was suppressed. Plantations were burned and sacked and 20% of the island's sugar crop was destroyed. Property loss was estimated at £179,000. While only one white was killed, 176 blacks died. Another 214 were executed after a court martial. In 1823, the African Institution was absorbed by the Society for the Mitigation and Gradual Abolition of Slavery, which declared that slavery was "opposed to the spirit and precepts of Christianity as well as repugnant to every dictate of natural humanity and justice." A 10-point program of reform was circulated in the West Indies by the Secretary of State for the colonies. It met with a tepid response. The planters' love affair with authoritarian power was such that they could could not see the light of day, and conditions failed to improve. In 1831, the Great Hurricane struck the island, killing 1,591 and damaging more than £1,600,000 worth of property. The Emancipation Act, passed into law on August 28 1833, took effect on August 1, 1834. The slaves, however, were not freed immediately, but after a "period of apprenticeship," which was intended to last six years. In 1838, the 4.5% export duty – long viewed as onerous by the plantocracy – was repealed and replaced with a tax on essential imports. That same year, on August 1, the slaves were finally emancipated, two years ahead of schedule.

POST-ABOLITION BARBADOS: Despite the problems caused by competition with places like Brazil, Louisiana, and Cuba (where slave labor was still used) the cultivation of the sugar beet in Europe, and fluctuations in worldwide demand, the planters managed to stay afloat and even prosper. Indeed, with wages at 1 shilling per day during the harvest and 10 pence during the rest of the year, the laborers were little more than salaried slaves! The Masters and Servants Act of 1840 established the system of "Located Labor," which bound the ex-slaves as tenants on their former master's estate! In 1843, another milestone was reached when Samuel Jackman Prescod – the son of a white father and a black mother – became the first non-white member of Parliament. After helping to establish the Liberal Party, he retired in 1863. In 1871 there were 161,594 inhabitants, including 16,560 whites, 39,578 "coloured," and 105,904 blacks. In early 1876, Governor John Pope-Hennessy attempted to implement a Colonial Office plan which Bajans feared might pave the way for introducing the Crown Colony system of government and the end of the elected Assembly. Irish to the core, Pope-Hennessy sympathised with the lower classes and let them know how the plan would benefit them. The plantocracy, however, remained virulently intractable. Riots broke out in support of the plan from April 20-22. After 89 estates were attacked by about 1,000 people, eight people were killed in the ensuing suppression. The uprising's most startling feature was that rioters believed they had the Governor's blessing. Therefore, they had largely destroyed property rather than person. The affair's aftermath culminated with Pope-Hennessy's transfer to

Hong Kong. A major cholera epidemic, judged to be the worst disaster in the island's history, killed at least 20,000 in 1854. The late 1800s were marked by a decline in the sugar industry sparked by high European tariffs and irregular rainfall. The Franchise Act of 1884 opened up suffrage to a slightly wider segment of the population while still excluding the impoverished and landless majority. Mulatto William Conrad Reeves, considered to be almost single-handedly responsible for having rescued Barbados from the dreaded clutches of the Crown Colony system and with having pushed through the Franchise Act, was knighted and served as Chief Justice from 1886-1902. The hurricane of Sept. 10, 1898 devastated 18,000 houses and killed 80.

THE 20TH CENTURY: The new century had a very unpromising start. An epidemic of smallpox in 1902 was followed by one of yellow fever in 1908. Bajans began to emigrate in record numbers. About 20,000 males went to work on the Panama Canal and remitted "Panama Money" home. Some of this new-found wealth enabled the descendants of slaves to purchase land from indebted planters. Molasses exports to Canada helped compensate for the downturn in the sugar industry. Cotton became a substantial industry until WWI because it could be grown in drier areas of the island. When the war devastated Europe's beet sugar fields, the planters went back to sugar. The boom, however, did not last long. In 1920 the market crashed and sugar plunged from 146 shillings per hundredweight to 18 shillings per hundredweight. The market rebounded in 1923. The 20s saw a great deal of progressive legislation as well as the establishment of governmental departments dealing with public health, agriculture, and roads. Liberal crusader C. P. Clarke pushed through an income tax measure in 1921. Another prominent social crusader was *Herald* columnist Clennell Wilsden Wickham. Yet another was Charles Duncan O'Neal, a doctor who, following in Prescod's footsteps, founded both the Democratic League and the Workingman's Association. C. A. Brathwaite, the League's first candidate, secured a house seat in Dec. 1924. Although other candidates scored victories, O'Neal himself only secured a seat in 1932 – after his health and spirit had deteriorated. The Democratic League, originally modeled on the British Labour Party, promulgated the pioneering gospel of such progressive goals as universal suffrage, compulsory education, health and unemployment benefits, and workmen's compensation – ideals which took decades to bear fruit. The 1929 depression hit the Caribbean hard, but sugar was one industry least affected. Preferential assistance by Britain and Canada helped the industry, but the International Sugar Agreement of 1937 restricted growth.

The number of unemployed swelled as the population grew and emigration outlets had been cut off after 1929. Between 1928 and 1935, the world price of sugar was cut in half. As part of the general upheaval affecting the Caribbean in the mid-1930s, riots broke out in 1937. These began after a rally protesting the deportation of Trinidadian expatriate unionist Clement Payne. (Payne's parents, brothers, and sisters were all Bajan-born.) The Deane Commission investigated the riots and found that the Payne incident was merely a "detonator" and that the underlying explosive tension resulted from the desperately harsh economic realities of day-to-day existence. With a mere 2% of the population controlling 30% of the national income combined with a church that appeared to be still locked in the Middle Ages, the average Bajan had ample reason for discontent. Things just had to change!

Political Parties and Unions

Democratic Labour Party	DLP
Progressive Conservative Party	PCP
Barbados Workers Union	BWU
National Democratic Party	BDP
Barbados National Party	BNP
Barbados Labour Party	BLP
(former Progressive League)	
West Indian National Congress Party	

Given the breath of life as the BLP – a name to which it later reverted – the Barbados Progressive League was launched in Oct. 1938. Its first policy statement, released towards the end of the following year, delineated a policy of combining both socialist and democratic principles. The League advocated equal distribution of wealth and material resources in tandem with governmental control of production. The League's first success came with the passage of the Trade Union Act in 1939, and its first political victory was shown in 1940 when it secured five House of Assembly seats. The BWU, formed in 1941, had G.H. Adams and H.W. Springer from the League serving as President General and Secretary respectively. However, the League was hampered by the island's archaic representative system which still limited voting rights and access to public office to a tiny elite. Taking careful note of the failure of O'Neal's now defunct Democratic League, the Progressive League leadership realized that it must widen its base of supporters if the party was to achieve its goals. In order to do this, they introduced a bill that would have provided for complete suffrage as well as the ending of property qualifications which were *de rigueur* for admission to the House. Although the bill failed to pass, the League was successful in enacting both a minimum wage bill and one securing the collection of Death Duties (inheritance taxes). In a 1942 compromise, the income qualification for voters was reduced to an annual income of £20 and women were granted the right to vote and to be elected to the House. However, the League failed to eliminate the property requirements needed for entry to the House. The Legislative Council introduced an amendment making it obligatory for all election candidates to deposit £30 which would go to the Public Treasury should the candidate fail to win a certain proportion of the vote. One notable triumph that year was the passage of the Workmen's Compensation Act.

After the election of 1944, the League's representation doubled – from four to eight. Led by W.A. Crawford, the newly-formed West Indian National Congress Party, whose platform was similar to the Progressive League's, also gained eight seats. In the 1946 elections – because neither party gained a clear majority – the West Indian National Congress Party and the BLP joined in a coalition government which lasted until 1947. Adams was elected President of the Caribbean Labour Congress in 1947 and, in 1948, his party swept the general elections, capturing half of the 24 seats. The end of the 40s were marked by continued conflict between the more liberal Assembly and the reactionary Legislative Council controlled by the white conservative interests. Finally, the powers of the Council were reined in and those of the Assembly predominated. All Bajans became eligble to vote and property requirements for Assembly membership were eliminated in time for the General Election of 1951 (which the Labour Party also swept). One freshman Assemblyman was Errol Walton Barrow. The more conservative Walcott quarreled continually with leading leftist Barrow and the BWU. When the new ministerial system of government was introduced without any BWU or left-wing BLP members, a major schism occurred. Barrow quit, and the "Siamese twin relationship" between the two parties also came to an end. The DLP was formed in 1955. In 1956 election, the party won 15 seats, the DLP four, the PCP four, and Barrow lost his Assembly seat. The cabinet system of government was inaugurated in 1958 with G. H. Adams (later Sir Grantley) as Premier. When Adams was selected as the Prime Minister of the West Indies Federation later that year, his place was taken by Dr. Cummins.

THE WEST INDIES FEDERATION: Although Barbados had been represented at the 1932 Dominica Conference on West Indian Federation, Bajans were not passionate about the concept of federalism. The idea gained steam only in 1938 when they realized that only by joining together could the small islands of the British West Indies achieve independence and worldwide recognition. Negotiations began in earnest in Montego Bay in 1947, and the final decision was implemented in London in 1956. Initially, the concept was received with a bang. All of the British West Indian islands' political leaders were strongly in favor, and Grantley Adams led a torch-lit procession of 30,000 supporters through the streets of Kingston. However, as time elapsed, spirits cooled and differences emerged. Jamaica's Norman Manley stressed the need for an independent role for his island while Trinidad's Eric Williams preached the gospel of a strong federal government. The two leaders' diametrically opposed positions were one major factor in the Federation's demise, and it was further weakened right from the start by the failure of the leaders' parties in the 1958 federal elections! The Federation also had aspects of a puppet show – The Queen could legislate on behalf of the Federation in the realms of defense, finance, and external affairs, and the Governor General had the right to veto any legislation he disapproved of. Manley met with Williams and resolved their difficulties. The truce, however, was only temporary and the negotiations' secrecy had aroused the suspicion of other island leaders. By the time the curtain fell at the end of the Federation's final conference, held at London's Lancaster House in June of 1960, few of the major participants were still on speaking terms. Jamaica seceded in Sept. 1961; Trinidad followed suit in Jan. 1962. After the rest of the "Little Eight" fell down to five and then none, the capsized Federation was dissolved on May 31, 1962.

BARROW ON TOP: Having lost his seat in St. George in 1956, Barrow won a by-election in St. John in 1958. The DLP gained the support of the BWU, Barrow became the Chairman of the party and it swept the 1961 elections. Loaded with dynamism, the new government began a crash program of public works to create jobs for the nation's unemployed; instituted tuition-free education at all government-aided secondary schools; and inaugurated a system of school meals. The College of Arts and Sciences of the University of the West Indies (UWI) opened its doors in Oct. 1963. Additionally, tourism was expanded, 45 factories were built, civil servants' salaries were increased, and a system of national health insurance was introduced.

INDEPENDENCE: The next election was held on 3 Nov. 1966, just a few weeks before independence on Nov. 30th. The DLP won 14 seats, the BLP eight, and the BNP two. Independence Day passed as a matter of course. Barrow's DLP won an overwhelming victory in 1971 only to suffer defeat in 1976 when J.M.G.M. (Tom) Adams, Grantley Adam's son, grasped the reins of leadership.

POST-INDEPENDENCE POLITICS: The island's support for the 1983 US-led invasion of Grenada – for which Barbados supplied troops – strained its relationship with Britain and Trinidad. The latter claimed the decision to invade was made without proper consultation all around. Tom Adams died in March 1985 leaving H. Bernard "Bree" St. John to carry on. While said to be charismatically-deficient, he was competent nevertheless. After Adams' death, the government tilted briefly even more towards the US. In 1985 it was designated as the Center of the US-created Regional Security System (RSS). Barbados coordinated Eastern Caribbean military maneuvers that September.

THE 1986 ELECTION: The May 1986 elections saw the return of the sometimes bombastic Errol Barrow. He zeroed in on the economy's stagnation and the limited employment possibilities it presented. Other issues included high prices, governmental corruption, US foreign policy, and racism. Don Blackman, a prominent cabinet minister, quit the BLP and joined the opposition. He claimed that the BLP was not doing enough to stem white racism, possibly because of white influence in the party. The DLP's promise to lower energy rates and taxes proved popular. The election itself was quite a stunning upset. For the first time, one Bajan political party trounced another: the DLP netted 24 out of 27 seats!

Independent and strong spirited, Barrow was determined to keep the Caribbean free of superpower political maneuvering. His political positions put him at odds with the US, and he criticized the US-sponsored Regional Security System (better known as RSS). It is maintained that he inherited enormous problems: a huge national debt, strained relations within Caricom (the Caribbean trading community), an official unemployment figure of 19%, a heavy burden of taxes, and a developing drug problem. Barrow moved to abolish income tax on the first B$15,000 of earned income in order to spur consumer spending. On June 1, 1987 Barrow died of a heart attack at age 67. He was succeeded in office by the more conservative and less flamboyant Lloyd Erskine Sandiford, the 50-year-old Deputy Prime Minister.

THE SANDIFORD ERA: Sandiford's time at the helm proved turbulent, even though he was initially accused of being too nice, and his elevation split the party. Ritchie Haynes, the finance minister who was frustrated in his desire to cut taxes, quit the party to form his own National Democratic Party. Don Blackman, the BLP minister who defected to the DLP, announced that "for too long, poor black working-class Bajans have suffered at the hands of white businessmen. It is time for me to take up my cudgel and swing, and swing with malice." After Sandiford told him to cool it, he deserted the administration. Sandiford called elections for Jan. 22, 1991 in which his party triumphed.

Under Sandiford's administration crime and taxes rose and tourism declined, as did the budget deficit. On June 7, 1994, he lost a no-confidence motion by 14 votes to 12. Although his resignation was expected, he refused to resign and, as 15 of the 28 members were needed for his removal from office, an impasse was reached.

A minor highlight in the island's history was the United Nations Global Conference on Sustainable Development of Small Island Developing States, held in Bridgetown, May 1994. A "Barbados Delaration" as well as a 15-chapter "Programme of Action for the Sustainable Development of Small Island States" were produced, but the 120-nation-strong two-week conference only found the large nations of the North repeating the same promises without substance that were made at the Rio Earth Summit in 1992. Although Fidel Castro attended, Al Gore failed to show, and of the industrialized nations only New Zealand, Australia, Germany, and Canada sent ministerial-level representatives. The only beneficial outcome was a reinforcement of small nation solidarity.

THE 1994 ELECTIONS AND BEYOND: In the Sept. 1994 elections, the BLP took 19 seats, the DLP took eight seats, and the nation's third party, the National Democratic Party (NDP), took only the one seat belonging to its leader, Dr. Ritchie Haynes. Clearly, voters were ready for a change. The election's loss was directly attributable to Sandiford's failure to voluntarily step down after a no confidence vote and, if he had done so, the DLP would have been in a far stronger position. Owen Arthur, the new Prime Minister, was born in 1949 and was first elected senator in 1983-84; from 1984 to the present he has been the MP for St. Peter. Erskine Sandiford retained his seat, but David Thompson is now the opposition leader and shadow Prime Minister.

Important Dates In Bajan History

Before 1600: Various Indian tribes settle.

1518-early 17th C.: Portuguese and Spanish ships visit.

1529: Barbados makes its first appearance on map of the world.

1536: Arriving Portuguese captain finds Caribs vanished.

1625: *Olive Blossom*, first English ship, arrives by accident. Its report results in the formation of a colonizing expedition.

1627: The *William and John* arrives at Holetown.

1637-40: Sugarcane introduced from Brazil.

1639: Elected House of Assembly (House of Burgesses) convened.

1652: Charter of Barbados (Articles of Agreement) signed at Oistins. In exchange for guarantees of certain rights, the Bajans agree to recognize Oliver Cromwell's Commonwealth.

1663: End of the propietary system under which Barbados had been the property of and controlled by a private patentee. The island is now directly ruled by the British Crown. First postal agency is established.

1665: Dutch Admiral De Ruyter destroys buildings in Barbados during attack.

1668: Over 100 Bridgetown houses burn, causing an estimated £30,000 in damage. Drought ruins crops. House of Assembly petitions for "dominion status" for Barbados.

1675: Hurricane hits.

1722: Bishop of London extends his jurisdiction to include colonies.

1731: The *Barbados Gazette*, first newspaper, published.

1766: Fires destroy Bridgetown twice.

1780: Another hurricane hits. Bridgetown reduced to ruins.

1807: British Parliament abolishes slave trade.

1816: Major slave rebellion led by slave Bussa and mulatto Washington Franklin.

1818: Gun Hill Signal Station erected.

1827: First steamship arrives.

1831: Right to vote extended to include "free coloured men." However, the property ownership requirement remains in effect. Another "Great Hurricane" hits; over 2,000 are killed.

1835: British Parliament abolishes slavery.

1838: Slaves are finally freed.

1843: Samuel Jackman Prescod becomes the first "coloured" man to be elected to House of Assembly.

1845: Ten acres of Bridgetown destroyed by fire.

1852: First lighthouse erected at South Point. First postage stamps issued.

1854: Cholera epidemic kills 20,000.

1875: Bridgetown first illuminated by gas.

1924: Founding of Democratic League by Charles D. O'Neal, an organization fighting for social reform and widening political participation.

1934: Grantley Adams elected to House of Assembly.

1937: Riots in Barbados and the BWI spur foundation of the Progressive League, continuing the struggle begun by the Democratic League.

1950: Universal adult suffrage instated.

1954: Sir Grantley Adams becomes the first Premier under a system of ministerial government.

1955: The Democratic Labour Party (DLP) formed.

1958: Foundation of the West Indies Federation, a nation composed of five Caribbean territories, including Barbados. Sir Grantley Adams becomes its first Prime Minister.

1962: West Indies Federation dissolved.

1966: Barbados becomes an independent nation within the British Commonwealth. Errol W. Barrow is the first Prime Minister (Nov. 30).

1969: National government establishes control over local parish adminnistrations.

1971: Ernest Barrow becomes Prime Minister after the DLP wins a two-thirds majority in the election.

1973: The Barbados dollar replaces the East Caribbean dollar as the official currency.

1976: In upset victory, the BLP gains 17 seats in House of Assembly; J.M. G. Adams becomes Prime Minister.

1978: Exposure of mercenaries led by Robert Denard who were plotting takeover of the island. Establishment of the Barbados Defence Force.

1979: Grantley Adams International Airport opened.

1983: Barbados throws governmental support behind US invasion of Grenada. Oistins Fish Terminal is opened.

1984: Sir Hugh Springer replaces Sir Deighton Lisle as Governor General after the latter's death.

1985: H. Bernard St. John takes office as Prime Minister after J.M.G. (Tom) Adams dies. General Post Office opened.

1986: The DLP sweeps the elections, securing 24 of the 27 seats.

1987: Prime Minister Barrow passes on; he is succeeded in office by Mr. Lloyd Erskine Sandiford.

1994: Owen Arthur assumes Prime Ministership. Bajan soldiers, members of a Caribbean contingent, are sent to Haiti as part of peacekeeping forces.

Government

One of the oldest and strongest democracies in the Caribbean, Barbados – in keeping with the character of its people – is also one of the least contentious. Despite the short time univeral suffrage has been in effect, democracy and politics have become imbued in the island's psyche. Unlike other Caribbean nations such as Trinidad, Jamaica, and Guyana, Barbados was never controlled by the Crown colony system. It has the third oldest continuously-functioning legislature in the Commonwealth (ranking after Britain and Bermuda). It is not uncommon to hear Assembly members cite 17th-C. parliamentary precedents when defending their stand!

POLITICAL STRUCTURE: The 1966 Constitution reinforced a British parliamentary-style system. The Queen is the titular head of state and her interests are represented by an appointed Governor General. He or she, in turn, selects the Prime Minister, a minority of the Senate, and an advisory privy council. The council's functions are to hear appeals from civil servants and criminals on death row, and to consider appeals for remission from convicted felons. The Governor General acts upon its recommendations. Executive authority is vested in the Prime Minister and his cabinet, which must contain at least five ministers. The leader of the opposition receives a salary from the Crown. The bicameral legislature consists of an appointed Senate and an elected House of Assembly. Of the 21 members of the Senate, 12 come from the majority party, two are from the opposition, and seven appointees represent economic, religious, and social interests.

In line with the practice in other Commonwealth countries, the Senate's primary tasks are representation and debate; while it does vote on bills, introduction of financial legislation is left to the House. All Bajans older than 18 may vote. Since 1981, the island has been divided into 27 single-member constituencies. Elections for the House of Assembly are held every five years, but early elections may be called by the government or if the majority party should fail in a no confidence parliamentary vote.

THE COURTS: The judicial system is headed by a Supreme Court and includes a Court of Appeals and a High Court. The lower magistrates are appointed by the Governor General who follows the advice of the Legal Service Commission. He also appoints the Chief Justice after consulting with the current Prime Minister and the opposition leader. Barbados's judiciary system is among of the most impartial and nonpartisan in the entire world. In a celebrated libel case during the 1970s, the Supreme Court decided against *The Democrat*, the official paper of the then-ruling DLP which resulted in the publication's termination and in the removal from office (through bankruptcy) of the Speaker of the House of Assembly.

THE PARISH SYSTEM: The island's 11 parishes (modeled after those once controlled by the clergy), along with the Municipality of Bridgetown, are controlled by the central government. This hasn't always been the case. Two years after the arrival of the English settlers, the island was divided into six parishes. Then, under the 1645 revision, 11 parishes were established: St. Michael,

St. George, Christ Church, St. Philip, St. John, St. Joseph, St. Thomas, St. James, St. Andrew, St. Peter, and St. Lucy. Each of these was governed by a Vestry, composed of local property owners, whose chairman was the church rector (except in St. Michael whose chairman was the Dean of the Cathedral). Responsible for welfare of the poor and maintenance of the churches and roads, the Vestries levied property taxes to pay the cost. After the 1956 elections, the disestablishment of the church began – a process completed only on March31, 1969. In 1959, the island was re-divided into three areas: the City of Bridgetown, the Northern District, and the Southern District. Bridgetown was governed by Mayor and City Council; the other areas by their own District Councils. Council members were to be elected under universal suffrage for three-year terms. Although the Vestry system endured for three centuries, the Councils couldn't even hold up for a decade. In a complicated system of maneuvers, they were abolished in 1967 and, by 1969, their services had been transferred to the Central Government or to statutory boards controlled by the Central Government.

POLITICAL PARTIES: The slightly left-of-center Barbados Labour Party (BLP) holds power at present. The moderate centrist Democratic Labour Party (DLP), allied with the Barbados Workers Union (BWU), held power until Sept. 1994. Although there traditionally have been few substantive differences between the two, the BLP has adopted some right-of-center policies in recent years. Former BLP leader Henry Forde, who was succeeded by Owen Arthur in 1993, had announced that the party must be restructured into a "highly decentralized" organization featuring "mass democracy in the formation of policy."

There are three minor parties. Most successful of these is the National Democratic Party (NDP), which is represented in parliament only by its leader Dr. Richie Haynes who resigned from the DLP in 1989. The People's Pressure Movement (PPM), founded in 1979, is led by Eric Sealy. The left-wing Workers Party of Barbados (WPB), run by founder Doctor George Belle, dates from 1985.

Economy

As is the case with other Caribbean mini-state economies, Barbados has always had a rough time. Small fish in a big sea, they are seen by whale-like economies as krill for consumption. The West

Indies, once one of the most profitable and prosperous of Britain's possessions, had become the Empire's poorhouse by the late 1930s. A British government panel investigating the riots resulting from the economic hardships of the 30s had to withhold its report for fear that release would have damaged the Allied war effort. At the end of WWII, per capita income in Barbados was still well below US$200 per year and emigration was encouraged just to keep unemployment below double digits. The economy was still totally dependent upon sugar. Things improved tremendously from the period between 1965 and 1979, but the 80s were depressed. Between 1957 and 1980, Barbados developed one of the most advanced infrastructures of any Caribbean nation, and moved up from 11th to third place among Caribbean Basin countries. However, since 1980 it has become the fastest-borrowing nation in the Americas. Its external debt now stands at over US$600 million – scanty compared to the US$3.5 billion owed by Jamaica at the end of 1987, but still enormous for such a small nation with limited resources. In 1987 unemployment stood at 17.9% and per capita income was B$9,850 (it now stands at B$12,000,which ranks it fourth behind the US, Canada, and the Bahamas in the Americas). Since independence, Barbados has attempted to woo investment from abroad. However, as the island is learning, outside investment can be as fickle as tourism. Reflecting the nation's dependence on the US and UK, recession hit hard in the early 1990s with manufacturing, sugar, and tourism all earning less. Today, the island is becoming increasingly dependent upon tourism as golf courses replace sugarcane fields.

CARIBBEAN BASIN INITIATIVE: The CBI, much touted by former American President Reagan, has been perceived as a failure. Under this three-part aid-investment-trade agreement, originally promoted as a neo-Marshall Plan, non-military aid has been minimal, and few businesses have relocated or opened up subsidiaries. Although Barbados has invested substantial manpower and effort in promoting the plan and adopted its investment incentives, labor unions and political parties have resisted attempts to turn the island into a sweatshop like East Asia. The CBI was supposed to promote duty-free trade, but it excluded goods such as automobile accessories and clothing while permitting rum and tobacco into the US only under modified duties. Meanwhile, reductions in US sugar imports have nullified the program's benefits and, despite pledges to the Industrial Development Corporation, there has been little or no transfer of technology.

LIGHT INDUSTRY: Although it has the third highest per capita income in the Caribbean, Barbados offers comparatively low salaries, which have attracted export-orientated assembly and sub-assembly plants. In recent years, things have been grim for these manufacturers. Caribbean Services Incorporated, which made electrical components for Westinghouse, opened in 1986, only to shut in 1989. The Arawak Cement Plant, a joint venture with Trinidad that was a fiscal disaster, dominates Checker Hall, St. Lucy; it was sold in 1993. There are, however, over 150 factories that produce such items as soft drinks, biscuits, bread, ice cream, furniture, cement, and textiles for local consumption. Also, the island produces about 33% of its own oil needs.

TOURISM: The construction of the deep-water harbour during the 60s made it possible for cruise ships to dock, and the steady improvement in air service – the arrival of the jet airplane slashed the travel time from NYC down to four hours from eight – has increased tourism. Although it has superceded the sugarcane industry, this "new sugar" depends upon the whims of tourists as much as the original depended upon supply and demand.

OFFSHORE BANKING: Offshore banking, Foreign Sales Corporations (FSC), International Business Companies (IBC), and insurance are significant sources of income here. These businesses come to take advantage of tax exemptions offered upon their arrival. The government first started to court offshore banking in 1965 with the passage of the International Business Companies Act. It exempted international businesses (which are not trading locally) from certain taxes. The nation proceeded to negotiate tax treaties (involving double taxation and bilateral investment agreements) with the US, the UK, and other nations. Barbados is not a tax haven with nameplate-only operations, but rather a business center with more than 800 international business companies, 700 foreign sales corporations, 186 exempt insurance companies, and 16 offshore banks. These earn the island an estimated US$25 million annually in foreign exchange and employ some 2,500 people. Assets in offshore banks total some US$2.9 billion. Barbados currently ranks fourth worldwide as an insurance center and this is a fast-growing sector. Its 186 exempt insurance companies collected US$4 billion in premiums in 1991 while paying out $2.9 billion in claims.

DATA PROCESSING: Another industry that takes advantage of the island's relatively cheap but English-literate work force is data processing, in which Bajans receive data, process it, and transmit it back to the US. Beginning with simple work in the 1960s, operations now range from imaging to adjudicating insurance claims and airline ticket control. More than 20 local firms and 12 foreign ones operate here. Caribbean Data Services, owned and operated by AMR (parent company of American Airlines), began operating here in Dec. 1983. Known in the US as Data Management Services, it now has some 1,000 employees and, in addition to its work for American Airlines, does business marketing and insurance company claim processing.

Another company, Confederation Client Services (CCSI), was set up here in March 1991. As a subsidiary of Toronto's Confederation Life Group, it now processes 30% of the companies' dental and health claims. The latest company to open is a joint operation between Goddard Enterprises, a Bajan conglomerate, and Toronto's AJD Ltd., a data processing company. It will process market research information and credit card applications.

OTHER SECTORS: Although tourism, manufacturing, and sugar bring in the bulk of foreign exchange, they only provide employment for about a third of the workforce. The remainder work in retail and government service. The government civil service, which is said to be overmanned and underproductive, was once called an "army of occupation" by the late Prime Minister Errol Barrow. Although it is now much more difficult to emigrate to Britain and the US, the innovative Canadian Farm Labour Programme ships farm labor to Ontario and Nova Scotia; negotiations on broadening this program to include waiters, waitresses, and bus boys are now underway.

RECENT ECONOMIC HISTORY: As foreign exchange earnings evaporated in the late 1980s, the nation's fiscal deficit had expanded to 8% of the GDP by 1991's third quarter. With the intention of building up foreign reserves while reducing the deficit, the International Monetary Fund, in cooperation with the Barbados government, instituted an 18-month "stabilization program," which ended in March 1993. During this period the government slashed its payroll (laying off 2,000 workers) and re-organized agencies; shares in local industries (such as oil, dairy, telecommunications, and cement) were or are intended to be sold. While the deficit has been reduced to 1% of GDP, the human costs have been high: unemployment has hit 23%. The Throne Speech for the 1994-1999 Parliament, delivered by Governor-General Dame Nita Barrow, detailed the new government's commitment not to devalue the Barbados dollar and to keep inflation in single digits. Plans are to rehabilitate manufacturing and agriulture, focus on tourism development, and to cut some duties and taxes.

Agriculture

AREA: Out of a total land area of 106,253 acres, nearly 60% is used for agriculture; farmers and agricultural workers constitute 7% of the workforce. Sugarcane consumes over half the acreage, although 20% of these fields are rotated with other crops. The coral limestone has become fertile and loamy through the process of decay. Adding to this has been the infrequent but agriculturally significant deposits of volcanic ash from other islands. Sufficient rainfall also contributes to the island's fecundity, and a gently rising terrain makes transporting crops a breeze. Up to 80% of the surface area is planted with crops ranging from sugarcane to the "sour grass," which provides fodder for cattle. Agriculture is of such importance that buildings are seldom constructed on fertile land. Major export crops include cotton, sugarcane, coconuts and, more recently, bananas. Food crops are grown mainly by small-holders whose farms are rarely more than 10 acres (4 hectares); mechanization is practiced only on the large plantations which control the bulk of the land.

SUGARCANE: Barbados is so tied up with growing sugar that it has been called a city-state in which sugarcane grows in the suburbs. King Sugar's importance has diminished over the century, but it still plays a major role in sweetening the economic pot. Sugar is planted in nearly every area where the soil is more than a foot deep; it requires 16 months for a crop to mature. Fertilizers, such as ammonia and potash, are used to improve the annual yield, which stands at about 30 tons per acre. Approximately 30,000 farmers own their land, with the average being less than half an acre; most of the cane is still being grown on large estates. Crops are usually grown for four consecutive years, after which other crops (sweet potatoes, yams and taro) are rotated for one year. Although less important than in the past, the sugar industry is still a major employer. Harvesting sugarcane is one of the grimiest and most exhausting jobs, and the young pursue it only as a last resort. Consequently, despite the island's double digit employment rate, it's sometimes been necessary to import labor from other islands. It takes 8.5 tons of cane to produce one ton of sugar. The island's factories continue to be consolidated. Portvale was the largest remaining one, and on-island processing ground to a halt during the fall of 1994 with the demise of the Barbados Sugar Industries Limited; the Barbados Sugar Industry Restructuring Plan rose to replace it. A report by sugarcane consultants Brooker Tate, which called for factory closures, was challenged by the Sugar Industries Supervisors Association.

Production has continued to decrease in recent years; while 1988 saw a harvest of 80,000 tons, 1989 brought only 66,000. The 1993 harvest was slightly up on the previous year and reaped 48,372 tons. The government, which effectively controls 15,000 acres of land and the four operating sugar factories through the Barbados National Bank, is considering forming a company to assume control of the industry and to introduce foreign management – suggestions that have brought scorn from the sugar industry. Currently, sugar contributes about 7% of the GDP and earns over B$80 million in foreign exchange annually.

OTHER CROPS: Law provides that each sugar "estate" (defined as a farm of more than 25 acres) must devote 12.5% of its land to "ground provisions." Much of the food is grown by women. The lime in the island's soil, combined with inadequate rainfall and its exposed terrain, make fruit a scarce but, nonetheless, significant crop. Currently, 60% of the island's requirements are produced locally. Cotton has been unsuccessfully attempted as a major crop in the past. Another try is currently underway. Japanese textile company Nitto Boseki's Barbados factory began spinning yarn from locally grown Sea Island cotton in 1991. Corn is grown for local consumption and as cattle fodder. Other vegetables include peas, beans, beet, cabbage, carrots, cucumbers, lettuce, eggplant, pumpkins, peppers, squash, yams, sweet potatoes, shallots, onions, spinach, okra, and tomatoes. Finally, cut flowers are becoming a significant export crop.

ANIMAL HUSBANDRY: Barbados produces three million pounds of pork annually, and chicken and egg supplies are nearly sufficient for the island's needs. Beef, mutton, and veal are also produced. Although there are a few dairy farms, small farmers own the bulk of the island's livestock: cattle, pigs, sheep, and goats. Pine Hill Dairy is the island's sole commercial dairy producer.

The People

Caribbean culture is truly creole culture. The word "creole" comes from *criar* (Spanish for "to bring up" or "rear"). In the New World, this term came to refer to children born in this hemisphere, implying that they were not quite authentic or pure. Later, creole came to connote "mixed blood," but not just blood has been mixed here

– cultures have been jumbled as well. Because of this extreme mixture, the Caribbean is a cultural goldmine.

Brought over on slave ships – where differences of status were lost and cultural institutions shattered – the slaves had to begin from square one. In a similar fashion, but not nearly to so severe a degree, the European could not bring all of Europe with him. Consequently, African and European beliefs were merged and a new blend arose in language, society, crafts, and religion.

NATIVE INDIAN INFLUENCE: Although the Indians have long since vanished, their spirit lives on – in folklore, in the feeling of dramatic sunsets, and in the wafting of the cool breeze. Remaining cultural legacies on many islands include foods, place names, and words. On Barbados, names like Indian Pond, Indian River, and Indian Bridge remind the visitor of their presence.

AFRICAN INFLUENCE: This was the strongest of all outside influences on those islands with large black populations. Arriving slaves had been torn away from both tribe and culture, and this is reflected in everything from the primitive agricultural system to food preparation to the African influence on religious sects and cults, mirroring the dynamic diversity of W. African culture.

SPANISH INFLUENCE: Spain was the original intruder. The Spaniards exited Puerto Rico in 1898, after 400 years; other islands with a Spanish-influenced culture include Cuba and the Dominican Republic. Spanish continues to be the predominant language in the islands once controlled by Spain, although other European influences have also had a powerful effect.

AMERICAN INFLUENCE: The history of the US is inextricably linked with the Caribbean in general, and Barbados is no exception. American institutions such as television and fast food have their effect on the culture, as does tourism. Bajans who have returned home from North America also play their part.

The Bajans

Probably no people have ever had so many individual qualities and traits commonly ascribed to them. It is said that Bajans do not take offense easily; that they are down to earth, self-confident, and self-disciplined; and that they are always ready to oblige, but do not leave a feeling of obligation behind them. Their fellow West Indians find the Bajans peculiar, accusing them of being unruffled, reserved – seemingly know-it-all in their behavior – and of being smart-assed. Bajans have a firm sense of identity, one which might be envied by many coming from larger, more diverse countries. A number of factors have contributed to the development of this national consciousness. Among these are the island's compact size, its relative geographical isolation, its high literacy level, and its long tradition of legislative, judicial, and bureaucratic institutions. Acceptance of the latter has been spurred by the ongoing adaptation or "Creolization" of the society. Black and mulatto leaders from the early and mid-19th C. set role models, and the island's mass political parties and labor unions date from the 30s. One explanation for the extraordinary reserve possessed by Bajans may lie in the pattern of slave movements. Barbados was the first stop for the slave ships and the planters here were given first pick. Naturally, the ones whom they believed least likely to cause trouble were preferred. Thus, the spiritually-orientated Ibos – who had a reputation for being more peaceable than some of the other tribes – came to form the bulk of the slave population. However, it is getting more and more difficult to either characterize or stereotype the Bajan of today. Since gaining independence over two decades ago, Barbados has been in the process of forging a new society. Racial bars are crumbling and the once-isolated island is being influenced by expatriate returnees, tourists, TV, and cinema.

POPULATION: Barbados is estimated to have about 260,000 people and has one of the lowest growth rates in the world (0.4% based on an annual birthrate of 16.1 per thousand). Barbados ranks fourth in the world in terms of population density, with an overall density of 1,526 people per sq. mile (588 per sq. km). There are no uninhabited or sparsely populated areas. To keep the growth rate down, condoms and oral contraceptives are widely distributed, and abortions and sterilization operations are both legal (although abortion is technically restricted) and commonly performed in public hospitals. Still, the population is forecast to rise to 300,000 by the end of the century. One reason for this is that emigration routes have been blocked. From 1950-70, 25% of Bajans emigrated. This represents half of all the males and nearly half of all the females born betweeen 1931-1945. If they had not left, the current population would be over 370,000! The average Bajan male can expect to live 70 years; females live to the ripe old age of 75.4 on the average. Since the mid-70s, the infant mortality rate has plummeted dramatically – from 45 per 1,000 births to around 10 today. Barbados' babies are twice as likely to make it to their first birthday than those of Harlem, which has an infant mortality rate of 25 per 1,000.

Quality of Life

The 1993 Human Development Report, published by the United Nations Development Program, ranked Barbados first among all developing nations (worldwide) for the third year in a row. The Report, commonly referred to as the "quality of life index," evaluates and compares earning power, education, health, life expectancy, and other factors. Barbados ranked 20th among the 173 countries surveyed, right behind Israel (19) and in front of such industrialized nations as Ireland (21), Italy (22), and Spain (23). Barbados led all other countries in Latin America and in the Caribbean.

ETHNIC DIVERSITY: Over 70% of the population is black – direct descendants of those who survived the African diaspora. Another 7% are white – either "overseas" (pure) white or "Bajan" (mixed) white. A sizeable 20% chunk are varyingly described as "mulatto," "brown-skin," "light-skin," "fair-skin," "high-brown," or "red." The remaining 3% includes North and South American expatriate groups, Syrians, Lebanese, East Indians, and a smattering of Chinese.

"REDLEGS": The descendants of Scots, Irish, and Welsh who served as indentured servants are known as "red legs." The name comes from the sunburned skin on their kilt-exposed legs. These immigrants stayed at the bottom of the social ladder until the beginning of this century. Inter-marriage kept their bloodlines pure while having the deleterious effect of passing on inherited diseases. They are increasingly becoming subsumed in the evolving societal mass and will soon be indistinguishable from their fellow countrymen.

THE UPPER CLASS: The descendants of the approximately 200 families who dominated the island's economy for centuries are known as "high whites." Today, their monopoly on wealth has ended along with the tradition of racial exclusivity. Many families have left the island completely and the stereotypical "high white" may become a thing of the past. In myth, he has a pure West Country Bajan dialect tempered with a rich West Country brogue. He is passionately possessed with watching and/or participating in such sports as cricket, polo, golf, rugby, soccer, horseracing, and tennis. An avid Anglophile (without necessarily ever having set foot in the ancestral homeland), he is intensively supportive of the monarchy and the Anglican Church. His mark is evident on the linguistic landscape: Many of the island's houses, plantations and villages are named after ones in England. In fact, until Independence, "high whites" were notorious for supporting visiting English cricket teams over the local ones!

RACIAL STRATIFICATION: One cannot say that the color bar or class distinctions have disappeared. Only a relatively short space of time has elapsed since the effort to expunge racism began. Although the legislature is nearly 400 years old, the island has only enjoyed majority rule and universal suffrage for little over a tenth of that time. Despite the fact that 150 years have passed since Emancipation, it is only recently that jobs have begun to open up to blacks. Racial discrimination was openly practiced until comparatively recently in business, the civil service, and in sports. Blacks were relegated to the back of the Anglican Church until the 1930s. White-only clubs offering cricket, soccer, tennis, and bridge existed openly until 1970, when the last school was desegregated. Interracial marriage is still uncommon; although you may notice a number of mixed race couples, most involve foreigners. In 1989 a confrontation took place between the largely-white board of directors of Barbados Mutual, the nation's largest insurance company, and its black policy holders. Two thousand of the latter converged on a meeting which had been scheduled to elect two new directors and to change its deed of settlement. Whites, now the less-powerful minority, feel themselves to be beseiged at times; blacks sometimes feel that the true power due them has not been handed over.

MALE AND FEMALE RELATIONSHIPS: Barbados' matriarchal society has its roots planted in tradition. In some African societies, matrilineal by custom or otherwise, the sexes are independent of one another. African women and their children spend their lives separate from their husbands and fathers. Wives have their own hut or room and may own property individually. Hundreds of years of slavery have helped bring the present system of social relationships into effect. During the slave era, male slaves were allowed relationships with females only for the purposes of procreation. Prohibited from establishing long-term relationships, a male might be sold away without ever casting eyes on the child he'd fathered. As a consequence, children were largely raised by their mothers. This system of casual alignments continues to this day. The grandmother plays a vital role in the family. This came about during the days of slavery, when a mother might be sold without her children; the grandmother would then take over their care. Today, a grandmother may look after her daughter's children or even those of her son. If a daughter does not wish to be burdened with her children from a previous relationship, she may ask her mother to take care of them and, after a time, retrieve them. Sometimes the mother works so that the grandmother may remain at home with the children. This type of family pattern exists not only in Barbados, but wherever slavery has been in existence.

The Chattel House

Along with flying fish and the Bajan accent, the chattel house is one of the island's special cultural traditions. These attractive, one-storey homes are all over the island. Some are fronted by a pretty flower garden; others are in a state of disrepair and in danger of collapsing. Charming to the point of distraction, they are also small. As the Bajans have moved up the economic ladder, the houses have fallen into disfavor.

Emancipation found the former slaves landless and, although the Located Labourer's Act of 1840 allowed them to construct homes on less fertile plantation lands, land owners had the right to evict tenants at short notice. Thus, these homes were chattel (movable possessions) and were built in such a way that they could be taken down and moved to a new location by ox cart.

Typically symmetrical, their facades have a door placed dead center and windows on either side. These windows vary from glass sash and jalousie varieties to contemporary ones with aluminum frames. Over the decades, roof styles changed from the hip (four-sided style) to the gable (steep and low-sided) to the modern flat-top roof. Generally, homes are colorfully painted and each has its own color combinations; no two chattel houses look the same.

Houses were built in line with the owner's pocketbook. Thus a "one-roof" house, a single two-room building, was constructed, followed by a shed (or "shed-roof"), then a second roof and building was added, which made the home into a "two-roof house and shed." Sometimes, a third structure was added and a small kitchen built.

In the future, fewer Bajans are likely to live in chattel houses. Today, replicas are being used for tourist shopping minimalls, and older ones have been converted to bars and shops. But while you are in Barbados be sure to keep a sharp eye out for the originals!

FAMILIES: The average lower-class couple usually lives together for a long time before they get married, if in fact they get married at all. Contributing to this situation is the high cost of the wedding ceremony coupled with the fact that there is no tradition of formal marriage ceremonies. Consequently, 78% of all births occur out of wedlock; 35% of marriages end in divorce. Sex is considered to be a natural function which should not be repressed; male potency and female fertility are viewed as status symbols. A large percentage of births in Barbados occur among unwed teenage mothers, and the island population continues to grow. Having a child may be a way to insure a steady income; in many cases, a woman's sole income may come from child support. While in the "visiting union" a man will visit the woman at her house; in the so-called "keeper family" a man and a woman will live together. Thrown largely on his own resources, the Bajan male has had to use a combination of wits and trickery to survive. The woman may work and the man may not assert his authority as she can break away at any time. Under the "twin household" plan, a man may set up a second household with another woman where he is working.

CHILD REARING AND SOCIALIZATION: Children are raised by the mother and her female friends and relatives. Male relatives may sometimes serve as substitute fathers if the paternal father is absent. It is not uncommon for children to be farmed out to friends or relatives if a woman has too many children to handle. Indeed – because friends may address each other as "sis" or "bro" – it may be difficult for the outsider to establish exactly who is really related to whom. Raised in a matriarchal society, the young male Bajan views male absenteeism and multiple sexual partners as normal. He learns that he can expect to "settle down" in his 30s, if at all. Children frequently share a bedroom – often with more than one sibling and even with their parents. Schools socialize men for jobs and girls for housewifery or lower-paying positions of drudgery. Men occupy 85% of the top positions. While the male is brought up to be worldly, the female has traditionally been taught to find her place at home. When they are not at church, women are expected to cook meals, bear children and, above all, obey orders. Today, they are making great strides in playing an increasingly vital role in society. Men are made for "movin' around," "stepping outside," "firing" a shot of rum, and "slamming" dominoes. These days, common law marriage is legally recognized after living together for five years, and your partner is entitled to half of your property. However, in the case of paternity, DNA testing is not accepted; a man's child is his only if he acknowledges it as such. Although it is a fact of life, homosexuality is viewed with disdain – and often as a demonic sin – by both sexes. Abortion has been legal only since 1983 and attitudes towards it are ambivalent.

EDUCATION: Barbados has a literacy rate of 97% and the nation has a progressive educational policy. Children from 5-16 must attend school and education is free right through college. Major educational institutions include Barbados Community College, Barbados Institute of Management and Productivity, Codrington College, Erdiston Teachers Training College, Samuel Jackman Prescod Polytechnic, and the University of Education.

Social Organizations

FRIENDLY SOCIETIES: One of the more intriguing traditions on the wane here is the Friendly Society. The roots of this organization lie – as do so many other island institutions – back in jolly old England. In the Middle Ages, they were called guilds, and they acted as both trade union and insurance company. In Great Britain, a Friendly Society was legally defined around the turn of the century as a society whose purpose is to provide for the relief or maintenance of the members and their immediate families through a voluntary subscription and with or without the use of donations. Additional provisions covered loss of tools and loss by shipwreck. Today, in Britain, these societies have evolved into high-powered insurance companies. Barbados once had a peak of 161 societies with around 100,000 members, but the numbers have plummeted. Many of these societies were led by local schoolteachers. With a community standard bearer running it, a society's success would be assured. Customarily, the teacher would not occupy the position of president but that of secretary, because this gave the impoverished fellow fiscal control. A society's appeal lay in its inexpensive insurance rates, the "sick-relief," and the Christmas "bonus." Every society had its "Sick Visitor," whose task it was to insure that illnesses were legitimate. One reason for the demise of many of the societies was the fierce competition – each offered higher and higher bonuses until, eventually, they went under. Another was the increase in transport, which made Bridgetown the financial center of the island. Today, the largest societies – such as the Unique Progressive and the Civic – are based there. Sadly, the exclusively Bajan verb "to societ," meaning to associate on friendly terms, stands in danger of extinction.

THE LANDSHIP: Another deteriorating but extremely colorful institution is the Landship – the lower-class equivalent of the fraternal organizations (Elks, Masons, etc.) that the upper classes are so fond of. Ignoring this similarity, the Bajan white upper classes once tended to scorn the landships as stemming from a racial love for mimicry, pageantry, and a love for pet phrases. The most important of their tasks were the social heirarchy it created and its function as a mutual aid society. The heirarchy's structure provided order as well as incentive. With each rise in the ranks, access to new information was provided along with a medal and ribbon. Crews and officers paid a small weekly fee which partially indemnified them against the expenses of unemployment, sickness, and death and encouraged thrift.

Landships usually met in a small house with two "masts" (i.e., poles) on top. Ceremonial visits were often made between landships, each Admiral meeting the other with sword in hand. Funerals occasioned major turnouts with a squad of "blues" preceding the hearse, followed by a flock of "nurses," each of which had a pair of scissors hanging from her waist. The Lord High Admiral followed, walking alone, with the other officers behind him. The remaining landships are best known for their public performances which, although dead serious, are often found comic by onlookers. "Wangle low" consists of a limbo executed while marching in formation; their "center march" proceeds to the beat of an African rhythm. Known as the "engine," tuk band music accompanies performances which have titles such as "Changing of the Guard," "Sinking Ship," "Admiral's Inspection," and "Rough Seas." During the 1930s, the apex of its popularity, there were over 60 ships with some 3,800 members, and the movement even had its own magazine. Today, there are only six ships with 30-40 members.

Origins of the Landship

Although no one knows for sure, legend attributes the development of the Landship to one Moses Ward or Moses Wood in Oct. 1863 or 1868. Said to have been a Bajan who served in the Royal Navy, he strived to bring the order and camaraderie of the service to his home country by patterning his organization after the uniforms, ranks, and titles of the Royal Navy. When women were admitted around WWI and were dressed as nurses. Although there are some parallels with other West Indian organizations – the women associated with the "Big Drum" music in Nevis also dress in nurses' uniforms – the landship is unique to Barbados. Despite English organizational names such as *Rodney* or *Iron Duke*, the Landship employs African dance movements and is a perfect example of African-European cultural synthesis.

The Beach Boys

No visitor (save the visually impaired) can fail to notice the beach boys. Their local equivalent is found all over the Caribbean – indeed all over the world! Beach boys often hold the same jobs as their social equivalent on a much more prosperous island like Maui: water ski instructor, beach chair attendant, or surfing instructor.

MODUS OPERANDI: Like the hunter looking for traces of fur in the bush and rapidly scanning the sky for prey, the beach boy cruises the beach scouting his quarry. The beach is a large territory, and, in Barbados, access is legally guaranteed to all. A typical method is to go over to a lone female, strike up a conversation by asking for a cigarette or just sitting down and moving in. Nationality provides the first crucial clue: While *Quebecquoises* are considered to be particularly loose, American women may end an evening very frustratingly with a sweet but curt "thank you" at the hotel lobby – a lot of money blown on nothing. If she is lying on a towel marked with the name of an apartment hotel, it means that she is a better prospect than if she is staying in a hotel – which may have strict admission rules! Other clues, learned through past experiences, are to judge by suntan lotion, cosmetics, and reading material. Marital status is of no concern. The typical beach boy thinks nothing of brazenly asking a married woman, "Is your husband satisfying you sexually?" Since single women are a small minority of visitors, age or attractiveness are not necessarily of great concern – just a bonus. Because the beach is too public a stage for an erotic encounter, one typical move is to ask her to meet him later at her hotel. After several drinks – which she may have treated him to – she will be feeling less defensive. In order to defuse the racial barrier, he may ask her straight out if his color bothers her – especially if she appears to be rejecting his friendship. By buying drinks and paying for admission to a club (frequented by other beach boys), he molds his image as a companion. By having her pay for some things, he ensures that she will not feel in a subordinate role and, accepting his payment for others, ensures a feeling of obligation on her part. If she has fears about the acceptability of a fling, he will point out the other dancing interracial couples – all of whom are also beach boys, thus creating the ideologically acceptable but factually spurious line that there is no racial barrier in Barbados. The goal is always to prevent her catching on that he is "for sale." Unlike the female prostitute for whom it is socially acceptable to prowl for customers, he cannot be overt: to be forthright would blow the scene. He can't let on that he works as a farmer off-season for example. His target is likely accustomed to being treated by dates at home and this may be her first contact with a less "developed" society. Naive, the concept of "paying" may be foreign to her.

PSYCHOLOGY: The first-time tourist accepts the greetings of locals as a matter of course – as part of the mythical "welcoming society" that exists to serve his needs. The single woman may be looking for adventure. Feeling temporarily uncloseted from her society's stifling sexual straightjacket, she wants to have an "exotic" experience, and she may be already replaying in her head the tale she'll have to tell her friends back home. The myth of black prowess is firmly established abroad and, from her viewpoint, it may seem a physically and psychologically fulfilling interchange. From the beach boy's vantage point, he is entering another world: one in which he is accepted by whites thus enhancing his self worth. For many years Barbados clubs were the the exclusive domain of the whites and his conquest represents a dramatic and ironic historical about-face. Even today the color bar is strong for both races; inter-marriage and social contact between black and white are voluntarily restrained.

WOMEN TRAVELING ALONE: A large number of women come to Barbados alone or in groups, and the attitudes of some of them have led local males to assume that they are part of a woman's adventure in paradise. You should have no problems with men if you simply say "thanks, but no thanks" when you are offered the priceless chance to spend the night with their "big bamboo." Expect to be confronted and challenged aggressively by males even if you are with a guy. Part of the reason for the male chauvinist attitudes prevalent here is the state of male-female relations on the island. Another is the influence of Western movies and television programs. Traveling will be a relatively hassle-free experience as long as you exude a certain amount of confidence.

Language

ORIGINS: But Bajans speak English don't they? Yes, but it's not quite as simple as all that! Barbados, populated by African slaves from many tribes who had to learn English to communicate among themselves and with their overseers, has developed its own uniquely colorful dialect. In contrast to St. Lucia, where there are strong French influences in the native Creole, or Trinidad, which has Spanish as well as French influences, Bajan English has been predominantly affected by W. African languages.

GRAMMATICAL STRUCTURE AND LANGUAGE CONTENT: Both have been affected and shaped by the whims of historical circumstance. Africans learned English in the field directly from their overseers (no formal schooling was allowed under the slave system), thus creating a unique blend of African and British grammatical structures, language content and intonation. As an example, "d" is substituted for "th" as in "dat" for "that," and "de" for "the." Some aspects of intonation appear to be connected with Welsh as well, as in the dropping of the "w" sound in "woman" (pronounced "ooman"), the enunciation of "turtle" as "turkle," or the pronunciation of little as "likkle." Because of the immense distance from Britain, many words from Elizabethan English remain: jugs are still called goblets, small bottles are vials, and married women are still referred to as "Mistress" instead of "Missus." "Onliest," meaning "only," derives from Cheshire, England. Some words have been so transformed over time as to become virtually unrecognizable. The word virago (meaning "turbulent woman, vixen," or "a woman of extraordinary size and courage") was spelled "firago" in Shakesperean English. It survives today in the form of "fire-rage," meaning one side of a dispute, and is frequently used in the query "You going tek up she fire rage now?" (This translates as "Are you going to support her in this dispute?") The double negative, so dear to those living in Shakespeare's England, still finds a welcome home in the Bajan dialect. When something is running out, a Bajan will cry out "Somebody ain't going get none." Some words are simply mispronounced. "Hue and cry" has become "human cry," "spray" is now "spry," and "shrivelled" has been transformed into "swivelled." In other cases, the meaning of words has expanded – as in the case of "bare" which on Barbados also means "raw."

African influence is clear in the grammatical practice of duplication. "Fowl-cock" denotes the common rooster; and "sow-pig" refers to the female swine. Other like terms include "bull-cows," "boar-pigs," "ram-goats," "ram-sheep," and "hare-rabbits!" Fences have "gate-doors" and houses have "door-mounts." "Play-play" translates as pretence. Numerous words are of African origin. "Duppy" (or dopie, duppe), the word for ghost, derives from the Twi term *dupon*, which means the roots of a large tree. *Nyam* means "to eat." Probably also African in origin, "unna" or "wunna" is a personal pronoun meaning "all of you." The Bajan imagination has added many new colorful words to the language.

For example, the wonderfully expressive "tie-goat" describes a married person, "own-way" means stubborn, "stomach-bone" refers to one's chest, "push breadcart" denotes pregnancy. One of the more popular words is "lick." It finds new expression in such colorful terms as "lick away," "lick down," "lick out," "lick up," and "lick cork." One who kisses and tells is a "lick mouth." The phrase "to bite someone's hand" means to cuckold a close friend. There are also numerous types of pots: "coal-pot," "fish-pot," " pepper-pot," "co-hobble-pot," and "buck-pot" number among them. Even food items are imaginatively rendered with relish. Octopus are known as "sea cats," sea urchins as "sea eggs," and squid and cuttlefish as "ink fish." The island's language has also been adjusted to reflect social realities. The phrase "outside child" reflects the status of the illegitimate child in society – one which is less pejorative than the harsher term "bastard." The phrase "a certain way" is a vague filler used in conversation when a delicate situation is alluded to. A woman may be getting along with her boyfriend in "a certain way," a man may be "in a certain way" after stuffing himself at the dinner table, and one's pockets may be "in a certain way" after overspending. The "chupse," a sound formed by sucking in the air between one's teeth, may convey disgust, boredom, frustration, or a combination of all three. Some words even have biblical connotations. The cry "bassa-bassa" meaning "confused skirmish" in Bajan possibly comes from the Bassa mentioned in the first book of Esdras in the Apocrypha. He had 323 sons and, thus, a wildly prolific social life! Another, more likely, explanation is that it is the same word which in Yoruba means "nonsense."

VERB USAGE: Questions often appear as statements – that is, without inverting the subject and the verb. The raising of the voice at the end of the sentence indicates that it is a question. Even though they may be used as adjectives, verbs have no participle endings such as "-ed." The verb system also differs in that the present tense of a verb may be used to indicate past action. Instead of using simple present tense, Bajans usually speak of present actions as ongoing activity. Subject-verb agreements are also not of consequence in habitual action statements. "Got" is frequently used instead of "there is" or "there are." (For example, "they got a lot of boar-pigs on that farm.") Finally, expect to hear unusual patterns such as "must be can" and "must be could."

Bajan Dialect: A Capsule Vocabulary

above	on the right
acid	rum
across	means "along" when used in directions
again	now
all two	both
backra	white man
bad	super good
bare	raw, plain
bat	small moth or candle fly
beforetime	formerly, once upon a time
below	on the left
bite	to itch
black lead	pencil
bubbies	female breasts
bush	plant or shrub
caffuffle	confusion, to confuse
change	money
chat down	flirt with a girl
chupse	disgust, boredom, frustration
closet	privy
cool out	relax
de	the
duppy umbrella	mushroom
ever since	a long time ago (pronounced "every sence")
fast-fast-fast	very fast
fig	miniature banana or segment of an orange
fingersmith	thief
fire rage	quarrel
flash	fast
freeness	a giveaway (as at an opening celebration)
fresh	smelly
fuh	for
funny up	contorted, queer, odd, deformed
gap	entrance to a road, driveway, or short road.
grabble	to seize
hag	bother
hail	support
jook	stick or punch
jump up	dance
limin'	to hang out
malicious	inquisitive or nosy
mind	be careful, move or ignore
mistress	head of a household or superior

nyam, yam	to eat
onliest	only
pass by	to visit
put on some size	gained weight
rice	support, feed, maintain
sand side	beach
sea cat	octopus
sea egg	sea urchin
sea bath	swim
shagger	sea crab
sih	see
swing round	turn
swizzle	cocktail
t'ink	think
tie-goat	married person
unna	all of you
weather	bad weather
worm	pimple
yuh	you

Phrases and Expressions

break fives	shake hands
c'dear	exclamation expressing impatience, an appeal, sympathy, or delight.
De body is I	It's me!
dog dead	expression of finality
Don't hag me!	Don't bother me!
goat heaven	a state of bliss
gone cross	become pregnant
hold strain	take it easy
horn	to cuckold
huckum, hukkum	How come? Why?
indifferent	worthless, good for nothing
push breadcart	to be pregnant
pushing bread cart	become pregnant
Who de body is?	Who is it?

===

OTHER LINGUISTIC FEATURES: The sound "th" does not exist so either "k," "f," "v," "z," "t," or "d" will be substituted. Only one form of a pronoun may be used as subject, object, and possessive. (For example, "we know," "tell we," and "it is we house.") If numbers are used as adjectives before a noun, the plural "s" ending may be dropped, such as "two hill." The ending for two consonant words is also frequently dropped. Instead of using "very," as in "very fast," Bajans will repeat the adjective – "fast, fast, fast" – or emphasize the word.

PROVERBIAL BAJAN: Perhaps because of the importance of its agricultural roots; possibly because of its unique synthesis of Anglo and African; perhaps because the high population density lends transparency to human motives and foibles; and per chance for all of the above reasons, Bajans have a tremendous number of proverbs which are well grounded in common sense. A few of the more astute follow:

"De higher de monkey climb, de more 'e show 'e tail."
A rise in social status brings greater scrutiny (and therefore disclosure) of one's faults and shortcomings.

"Coconut don' grow upon pumpkin vine"
Children will inherit their parents' characteristics.

"One smart-dead at two-smart door."
The smarter you think you are, the more likely that you will be deceived by someone smarter.

"Pretty-pretty t'ings does fool li'l children."
The gullible and shallow are deceived by a show of style.

Religion

For many Bajans, religion is much more than just lip service to vague ideals; it represents a total involvement, a way of life. Some Bajans may literally eat, drink, sleep, and dream religion. As is true in poorer Third World countries, religion is very important because it is the only thing to provide respite from the constant difficulties and struggles of everyday life. For people living in acute poverty, anything which gives comfort or some small hope of rising from the surrounding squalor is welcome. Although Christianity forms the model for society, many African elements have crept in. The planters – concerned more with material than spiritual benefits – saw little incentive to introduce the slaves to the wonders of the Christian God. Although they were nearly all Anglican, planters defied criticism from clerics by maintaining that Christians could not hold other Christians as slaves. In keeping them out of church, it gave them the moral justification to keep them slaving away in the fields.

AFRICAN ROOTS: Owing to the mixture of African cultures, no single African religion was transported intact. The slaves, nevertheless, developed their own hybrid religious system in the absence of formal Europeon proselytizing – one which incorporated both disparate African elements and those copied through observation of Christian rites. The slaves' perception that the English were practicing a powerful form of witchcraft helped keep the slaves in a state of fearful subjugation. Although they are now dying out, some African practices and beliefs have survived. It was common up until recent years, for example, to plant the umbilical cord of a newborn infant near its birthplace to link the child's spirit with its new home.

A custom having its roots in both Anglo Saxon and African practice is that of the wake. However, the rationale for it is different in each culture. While the British custom has its roots in the desire to protect the deceased from evil spirits, the African version, accompanied by an ostentatious funeral, was designed to make sure that the *duppy* (ghost) would not return to haunt relatives. This fear of *duppies* is still widespread and it is common to splatter a few drops from a newly opened rum bottle on the ground to placate the spirits. There are ways to prevent a *duppy* from entering a dwelling: suspend various herbs from the windows and doorsill; leave one's shoes at the door; walk backwards into the house; or hang funeral clothes from a leeward window. Other actions, such as opening an umbrella in a house, will attract *duppies*. In a room containing a corpse, all mirrors must be covered or removed because a *duppy* will steal the soul of any person reflected. Food that you drop as you eat should be left in place – a *duppy* must have knocked it. If you find a piece of cobweb on you, it means that you are being followed by a *duppy,* and, if you get one on your face, someone is about to die. Scattering sand around the house compels the wandering soul to halt and count each grain – a task impossible to complete either because (depending upon the version) *duppies* can only count up to three and then must begin again, or because it will preoccupy them until daybreak, when they must return to the grave. A recently-widowed woman should sleep in navy blue bedclothes to deter her husband's *duppy* from visiting her and destroying her sex drive.

Duppies may take various forms, the most notorious of which is the *hag*. Customarily the wife of a planter, she would shed her skin nightly, transforming herself into a ball of fire in search of blood to consume. If one came across the temporarily-vacated skin, rubbing it with pepper or salt would prevent her re-entry and ensure her demise. *Hags,* however, are believed to be an extinct species today. The last one was exterminated some 70 years ago. The most famous example of possession by spirits is that of Conrad, a nasty and irritable ghost who squatted in a woman's belly. *Heartmen,* nasty buggers who kill children – offering their hearts to the devil for sacrifice or using them in brewing magic potions – appear to come and go with the sugarcane season. The *Baccoo,* a small man who inhabits bottles and is better known elsewhere in the West Indies, has a range of characteristics as wide as those of humanity. The *ballahoo* is a cow-sized spectral dog whose appearance is accompanied by the clinking of chains.

obeah: Other African beliefs continue to exercise influence. A form of magic, *obeah* (from the Akan word *abayi* meaning "sorceror") still enjoys an underground prestige. Today, as in the past, the practice of *obeah* relies both upon superstition and the effective use of herbs or "bush medicine." There are potions for success, for controlling one's rivals, for sexual attraction, and for leashing in an errant husband. Traditionally, these are served in *cou-cou* or coco tea. While many of the potions may have a purely fanciful effect, there is no doubt that some of these herbal remedies do have a consequence. In fact, some are thought to act upon the nervous system to produce a psychotic state. The power of others – such as the dreaded *duppy dust* (pulverized bones or grave dirt) – works by inducing fear. A matchbox containing a small dead lizard has been known to throw the receiver into a state of shock, as will the receipt of a small bottle of feathers or a vile-appearing liquid. It is widely belived that *obeah* men have the ability to "read up the dead," inducing them to enter the living. Practitioners have traditionally carried a bag of charms containing such "tools" as bits of broken glass, pieces of clay, feathers, and rusty nails. In theoretically Anglicized and Christianized Barbados, *obeah* is even recognized in the law courts. A statute giving the practice of *obeah* felony status is still on the books and, in the early 1960s, a man charged with the murder of his wife's lover had the charge reduced to manslaughter after claiming his actions were due to temporary insanity under *obeah.*

RELIGION TODAY: Although Barbados is frequently portrayed as a religiously fervent society, women make up the greater part of the believers. Over half the male population has no links with organized religion and the overall attendance rate is 60%. Men increasingly prefer the camaraderie of the rum shops to preaching in the pews. The type of bible-thumping fundamentalism taught on the island – full of restrictions and not geared to deal with life in modern day secular society – holds little appeal for today's young men.

Religious Sects

Despite the domination of religious life by the Church of England since Barbados was colonized, the number of religions has proliferated. Altogether, there are more than 140 religious denominations, including such diverse groups as Jews, Hindus, Muslims, Mormons, Bahais, and Catholics. Other churches include the Canadian Pentecostal, Seventh Day Adventists, Jehovah's Witnesses, the Church of the Nazarene, the New Testament Church of God, the African Methodist Episcopal Church (A.M.E.C.), and the Christian Scientists. The strength of belief is evident: The island's villages all feature "storefront" revivalist churches; the Sun. afternoon CBC TV program, *Time to Sing*, showcases a different choral group each week; and the weekly newspaper column "Gospel Bag" serves as a religious calendar which also publicizes new releases by local gospel groups.

Today, other than the 50% of the population who are Anglican, the Methodists, Moravians, and the Roman Catholics command the greatest support. Also growing in influence are the Jehovah's Witnesses; you might see their large plastic tents (which are moved from place to place) off the road.

The most prominent African-related sects are the Jamaican-rooted Rastafarians and the more traditionally-Christian, indigenous Tieheads. A survey of the historical influence and significance of each of these groups follows.

ANGLICANS: The Church of England (the Anglican Church), established for centuries as the official religion, has always enjoyed the widest following. Until its dis-establishment in 1969, it was *the* religion. As far as former British colonies go, Barbados was one of the few in which the Church of England remained so powerful. And, aside from Roman Catholic Malta, it was the only one where clergy were paid by the state. The first Anglican church was housed in a small, primitive structure in Bridgetown. It was replaced with the Church of St. Michael, consecrated in 1665. This church, destroyed in 1780, was replaced by the present structure nine years later, which became St. Michael's Cathedral in 1824. The parish churches were the core of rural life in past, but with the advent of TV and other entertainments, this is less true today.

CATHOLICISM: Formal practice was suppressed before the 1800s. Any priests landing on the island were promptly put on the next boat out and a 1650 statute prohibited any form of worship save that established in England. When Cromwell sent off Irish Catholic dissidents to work as "white servants" (read "slaves") for seven years, the priests sent with them were singled out for especially harsh treatment. In 1839, the first Vicarate Apostate was established in the West Indies, and a bishop was appointed and headquartered in Port of Spain, Trinidad. Construction was begun on the island's first church in 1840 but, owing to the poverty of the island's few Catholics, it was not completed until 1848. Fire destroyed it in 1897, and another was consecrated in 1899. Since then the Catholics have remained a small minority.

METHODISM: The first missionaries arrived in Dec., 1788. Finding only a few of their faith among the immigrants, it was a tough struggle to establish the faith in the face of repression. They encountered so much virulent hostility that they had to stick around Bridgetown and were given no opportunity to reach the slaves. In 1823, their new church was pulled down, its furniture destroyed, and proclamations posted about town stating that Methodism was to be exterminated. The believers resisted, led by Ann Gill. Persecution had died down by the time of Emancipation and the faith attracted many believers among the former slaves. Today, they have over 20 churches scattered across the island.

MORAVIANS: The first missionary arrived in 1765 and so began the sect's conversion efforts. They set up their first mission at Sharon in the Parish of St. Thomas. The Moravians' strong support for the slaves secured them safety during the 1816 slave uprising. Today, the congregations of the Church of the United Brethren are predominantly black.

Rastafarians

The most prolific of all the Caribbean's religious sects, Rastafarianism is also the most horrendously misunderstood. One reason for this is that its hip and cool posture – commercialized internationally through the exploitation of reggae music – fosters imposters galore. In fact, there are so many of these "wolves in sheep's clothing" that it is getting more and more difficult to find the genuine article. But dreadlocks alone do not a Rastafarian make. Although their appearance may be forbidding, true Rastafarians are gentle, spiritual people who really do believe in "peace and love." The name itself stems from Ras, the title given to Amharic royalty, combined with Tafari, the family name of the late Ethiopian Emperor Haile Selassie; the term Rastafarian thus denotes a follower of Ras Tafari or Haile Selasse. The great black nationalist leader Marcus Garvey set the stage for Rastafarianism when – speaking in a Kingston church in 1927 – he prophesied that a black king would be crowned in Africa. In 1930 Ras Tafari, the great grandson of King Saheka Selassie, was crowned Emperor of Ethiopia. Taking the name Haile Selassie ("Might of the Trinity"), he further embellished his title with epithets like King of Kings, Lord of Lords, His Imperial Majesty the Conquering Lion of the Tribe of Judah, and the Elect of God. The Ethiopian Christian Church, of which he was a devout member, considered their kings to be directly descended from King Solomon. In the midst of a severe economic depression, Jamaica in 1930 was ready for a new religion. Rastafarianism sooned gained currency among the island's rural and urban poor, promoted by early leaders such as Leonard Howell. It gained recognition and followers as it was publicized by the media during the early 70s through the 80s.

COSMOLOGY: Comparatively speaking, Rastafarianism may best be likened to a black version of messianic Judaism or fanatical Christian sects still found in the US today. The parallels are striking. Haile Selassie is the Black Messiah, and Ethiopia is the Promised Land. God is black, and Rastas are one of the lost tribes of Israel. They have been delivered into exile through the hands of the whites and are lost wandering in Babylon, this "hopeless hell," known to the world as Jamaica or Barbados or wherever the believer resides. The ultimate goal is repatriation to Ethiopia where they will live forever in Heaven on Earth. Neither Selassie's reputation as a despot, his death in 1975, nor his lack of support for Rastafarianism during his lifetime have fazed beliefs. Selassie is now customarily referred to with reverence as a living god who has simply moved on to another plane of existence. This follows a pattern typical of messianic cults throughout the world in which the leader lives on in the spirit after his death. Rastas generally regard Christianity with suspicion. Although some Rastas (notably the late Bob Marley) have become members of the Ethiopian Orthodox Church, the white Christian God is generally regarded as a dangerous deceiver because his religion denies blacks their rightful destiny (to rule the earth) and expects them to be humble while awaiting death and the passage to an imaginary heaven. For the Rasta, heaven is attainable in the here and now.

RITUALS, TABOOS, AND SYMBOLISM: Rastas are basically vegetarians. Vegetables, fruit, and juices are dietary staples. Fish less than a foot long may be consumed but shellfish, fish without scales, and snails are prohibited. Rastas prefer to eat *I-tal* (natural) foods and avoid cooking with salt and oil. They strongly object to cutting hair or shaving. Although Rastas are nonsmokers and teetotallers, their consumption of *ganja* (marijuana) is legendary. Its many names ("wisdom weed," "wisdom food," "the healing of the nations") reflect the Rasta reverence for the plant. The very act of smoking is considered a religious ritual. The pipe Rastas use to smoke *ganja* is known as a chalice, like the Catholic communion cup. Rastas usually pray to Jah Rastafari or recite variations on verses taken from Psalms 19 and 121 before smoking "the herb." They also cite other biblical passages which they believe sanction and sanctify the smoking of *ganja*. (Not all Rastas smoke *ganja*, however, nor is it necessary to smoke *ganja* to be a Rasta). They claim to suffer no ill effects even after decades of continued daily usage and, indeed, maintain that they are healthy *because* they use *ganja*. Dreadlocks are seen as connecting the Rasta with the Ethiopian lion, (although not all Rastas sport locks nor are all wearers Rastas); Rastas cite biblical passages (Leviticus 19, v. 27; Leviticus 21) to support this practice. The lion is a symbol of Rastafarianism and, as a representation of Haile Selassie, the Conquering Lion of Judah, it may be seen everywhere. Rastas represent the spirit of the lion in the way they carry themselves, in their locks, and in their challenging attitudes towards contemporary social values. Their colors – red, black, and green – are the colors of the Garvey movement; red represents the blood of Jamaican martyrs, black is the color of African skin, and green depicts Caribbean vegetation as well as the hope of achieving victory over the forces of oppression.

RASTAFARIANISM IN BARBADOS: Rastafarianism was introduced here in 1975 and spread through the island like wildfire. Unfortunately, the activities of deceitful dreadlocks and the presence of borderline psychotics in their ranks, draped the Rastas with a rapscallion image. But, as fashion faded so did the appeal of the dreadlocked facade and, today, most Rastas are sincere. Many of the island's sportsmen and artists are Rastas. Some of these include journalist and calypsonian Adonijah, poet and actor Winston Farrell, and calypsonian Ras Iley.

The Tie Head Movement
(Apostolic Spiritual Baptists)

The most colorful and flamboyant Christian sect, is also the only one indigenous to Barbados. Founder Granville Williams spent a 16-year sojourn in Trinidad. There, he met up with the Spiritual Baptists – revivalists with African roots. Upon his return in 1957, Adams spread the word that God had come to him in a vision and authorized him to preach the gospel. He began his Barbados career preaching outside at Oistins. Meeting a tumultuous response, he established the Jerusalem Apostolic Spiritual Baptist Church at Ealing Grove and then the Zion Sister at Richmond Gap. The sect's most distinctive feature is its dress; both men and women sport wrapped cloth turbans. Their colorful gowns are each symbolic of particular qualities. Red stands for strength and the blood of Christ; gold is for royalty, blue for holiness; silver-grey symbolizes overcoming; brown represents happiness; white stands for purity; green means strength; and cream symbolizes spirituality.

SERVICES AND RITUALS: As with other revivalist sects, the Tie Heads incorporate Christianized but African-like religious styles. Foot stomping, hand clapping, and dancing frequently accompany religious rituals. Even such stiff and sultry Anglican hymns as "Abide With Me" can be made danceable. Acceptance means that you must be baptized again. After a dipping in "living water," the novice adherents are schooled in doctrine. Devotees are then isolated in "The Mourning Ground," a section of the church devoted to prayer and meditation. After a week to 10 days, they emerge spiritually cleansed and revitalized.

MEMBERSHIP: The Spiritual Baptists are an up-and-coming sect, with about 7,000 adherents. Their membership is 40% male – a remarkable achievement on an island where men appear to do their worshipping in the rum shop on Sun. mornings while the women predominate in the pews!

Music

Bajan music has roots as deep as any island in the Caribbean, but – in light of its smaller size and anglophilic nature – it has developed less of a body of music than its larger cousins to the N and S:

Jamaica and Trinidad. Music is so much in the Bajan's blood it's said that a child can dance before he or she can walk. Barbados has some very fine calypsonians and a small posse of reggae musicians, along with some indigenous musical brews. While very much a domestic scene, the island's concert venues are occasionally enlivened by performers from abroad – brought in by individual promoters, the Barbados-Cuban Friendship Association, or during the Barbados/Caribbean Jazz Festival held each May.

ROOTS: The old Bajan work songs as well as the island's calypsos have deep African roots tempered by Caribbean colonialism. The ethos of musical expression in Barbados – indeed, in black music in the Americas as a whole – stems from the struggle of a people wrenched out of their own cultural milieu and thrown into unfamiliar circumstances with people of diverse cultural backgrounds. The only possession the Africans could bring with them was the space inside their heads; slave owners had no control over cultural memories. But even these, already dulled by the cruel voyage overseas and the horrors of slavery, were further confused by the mingling of various tribes. As is so often the case in the Caribbean, a cultural synthesis emerged which forged the old into the new. What the slaves could remember, they practiced – often in the face of prohibition (playing drums, for example). What could not be remembered – or only half-remembered – they improvised and expanded upon, often merging African and European elements. Barbados developed tuk music and calypso, while in Jamaica, indigenous forms like mento, ska, rock steady, and reggae emerged. Today, these share the island's music scene with imports like rock, reggae, soul, steel band music, and disco.

REGGAE: Reggae emanated from the steamy slums of Jamaica, but has now swept the world and gone international. No one is certain exactly where it came from, but it appears inseparably linked to the maturation of the Rastafarian movement. It is the synthesis of electrified African music coupled with the influence of ska, rock steady, and American rhythm and blues. Some give *The Wailers* credit for transforming reggae into its present format. No sooner had the band gained international fame in the early 70s, than its members went their own separate ways, with the band's major singer-songwriter, Bob Marley, changing the name to *Bob Marley and the Wailers*. Robert Nesta Marley had become an international superstar by the time of his death from cancer at the age of 36 in 1981. His influence remains strong to this day. There are a few reggae bands here and the music permeates the island, although it is not as strongly developed as you would think.

STEEL BAND MUSIC: This unique orchestra of Trinidadian origin has spread all over the Caribbean. It is now the darling of every tourist board, despite its low-life beginnings when it was a scorned child of the lower classes. Some orchestras have grown to as large as 200 members. Although it is often maintained that the instruments are the progeny of African drums, they have much more rhythmically in common with African marimbas. However, in truth, they are far removed from either. The *pan* – as the individual drums are known – are made from large oil drums. First, the head – along with six inches to a foot of the side – is severed. Then, the top is heated and hammered until a series of large indents emerge. Each of these produces a musical note. Each *pan* is custom designed. The bass *pans* have only three or four notes, while others produce many that carry the melody. Bands are now divided into three major sections: the "ping pong" (or soprano *pans*) provide the melody using 26-32 notes; the larger *pans* ("guitar," "cello," and "bass") supply the harmony; and the cymbals, scratchers, and drums add the groundbeat. A contemporary steel drum orchestra in Trinidad generally contains 20 or more *pans*; those found on Barbados commonly have considerably fewer.

TUK BANDS: From the start, slaves on Barbados suffered from musical repression. In 1675, the code against the beating of drums was enforced after an uprising and, as of 1688, drums or any other loud musical instrument would be burned if discovered. But the impulse to drum still survived and resulted in the onomatopoecally-named tuk band – named after the "tuk tuk" sound of its large log drum. The tuk band has provided the rhythmic foundation for every major celebration for the past 125 years or so. While reminiscent of British military bands, its base is African. A pennywhistle player sets the tune and tempo; the snare drummer (playing the "kittle") changes the movements and style; and the bass drummer throbs along in time. The tuk band operate independently, although has been closely associated with the Landships, for which it provides the "engine." When a band appears, villagers may dress as bears or donkeys – swaying lasciviously in time with the music. Men sometimes don dresses, stuffing them with rags in imitation of pregnancy. These characters have been given colorful names such as Donkey Man, Stilt Man, and Mother Sally. Today, the island's foremost practitioner is the Rose Hill Tuk Band.

MARCHING BANDS: At public functions you might notice a colorful band of musicians wearing red caps with white brims and long gold tassels along with red vests with gold trim. These musicians, the Zouaves, are the official band of the Barbados Regiment. Their uniform is that of the Zouaves, a detachment of French Colonial Light Infantry constituted from members of Algeria's fierce Zouaoua tribe. Legend has it that Queen Victoria was reviewing troops around 1855 when she spotted the Zouaves. Craving such a regiment for her own, she instructed the British Army to create similar uniforms for one of its regiments. The West India Regiment, then deployed in the Ashantee Wars, was chosen, and the troop continued to don the uniform after their return to Barbados in 1858. The Corps of Drums of the Barbados Volunteer Force (the precursor to the Barbados Regiment) adopted the uniform after the regiment was disbanded in 1926. The uniform was worn by the Barbados Regiment's marching band in 1987 to commemorate the island's 21st anniversary of independence.

Calypso

Perhaps no music is so difficult to pinpoint, and none is quite so undefinable as calypso. Next to reggae, it is the best known music to come out of the English-speaking Caribbean. Its rhythm is Afro-Spanish: sometimes the Spanish elements dominate, sometimes the African. Call-and-response is employed frequently. It *is* strikingly African in the nature and function of its lyrics. The tunes don't vary a whole lot – there are some 50 or so – but the lyrics *must* be new! And, without exception, they must also pack social bite. Calypso is a political music, like reggae, and one which, more frequently than not, attacks the status quo, lays bare the foibles of corrupt politicians, and exposes empty programs. The songs often function as musical newspapers, providing great insight into society. Calypso is also a very sexual music – as even the briefest listening will reveal. One of the most frequent themes is the wrath of a scorned woman focused on an unfaithful male partner.

ORIGINS: No one can say precisely where or when calypso began, and – although there are many theories – no one knows the origin of the label "calypso." Each island claims it for its own, and certainly all of the islands had music similar in style. In fact, some of them were also called calypso. However, these styles were all influenced by Trinidadian calypso. This was partly because of the popularity of Trinidadian calypso and partly because the same businessman who had the island's calypsonians under contract owned a group of record stores on the other islands. The famous Trinidadian calypsonian Atilla the Hun (Raymond Quevedo) maintained that it was "undoubtedly African." According to

Quevedo, the first calypsos were sung by *gayap* – a group of organized communal workers which has equivalents in W. Africa. These work songs – which can be found in every African community in the Americas – still exist. Their more ribald counterparts, which served to spread gossip concerning plantation folk, paralleled modern day calypso. However, it is more likely that they were merely an influence. The true origins of calypso remain shrouded in mist. Certainly, there are many African elements present in the music, including the use of dynamic repetition, call-and-response patterns, and the rebuking of socially reprehensible behavior – a frequent theme in traditional African songs.

Whatever its roots, calypso seems to have reached its stylistic maturity in the 1870s. It was originally accompanied by rattles, a scraper (called a *vira*), drums, and a bottle and spoon used like a W. African gong. During the 40s and 50s, calypsonians first began twisting words – executing swift ingenuity – to contrive rhymes that also produced a wide range of rhythmic effects in the vocal line. Lines that vary in length as well as short phrases or cries, juxtaposed between the lines of verses, serve to enliven the music's spirit. Calypso music has incorporated elements of jazz, salsa, Venezuelan, East Indian, and R&B music. But – like all great musical forms – it has been strengthened rather than swamped by their influence.

RISE IN POPULARITY: Calypso was first recorded in 1914, but it was not recognized in the US until American servicemen were stationed in Trinidad during WWII. After the war, the Andrews Sisters pirated and popularized Lord Invader's *Rum and Coca Cola*. Harry Belafonte recorded a calypso album in the 1950s which, because he clearly pronounced the words, made the music more accessible to the rest of the English-speaking world. Lord Kitchener recorded a number of albums in England and Sparrow began pumping them out on the home front. In the 1980s and into the 1990s, a new trend began to emerge. Growing technical advances made musical composition more important, and calypsonians now record with gifted arrangers and the best studio musicians. Soca, a merger of soul and calypso, has given the music a new level of popularity. It is, in effect, a more danceable and commercial form of calypso. The most famous soca singer is *Arrow* whose *Hot, hot, hot* is set to become a timeless classic. Even the first woman to capture the calypso crown, Calypso Rose, has recorded an album entitled "*Soca Diva.*"

THE CALYPSONIANS: As with other contemporary popular styles, the music focusses on the singer. The calypso kings are sexual objects, like the American and British rock stars. One quali-fication for this position is to be unemployed – the image of the witty indigent – bordering, but not entering, criminality; another is to be very dashingly and wickedly attractive to swooning women. The calypso singer lives through donations, like the *griot* musicians of W. Africa. Flamboyant titles – whether it be the Mighty Sparrow or Atilla the Hun – serve to reinforce the high-and-mighty image. Crowned in a tent, he becomes masculine prowess incarnate.

EARLY BAJAN CALYPSO: The influence of Trinidadian calypso began spreading in Barbados during the early years of this century, but it was decades before it attained any degree of popularity on the island. To Bajans preoccupied with trying to be as properly British as they could, an indigenous musical form like calypso appeared to lack class and culture. The average calypsonian wan-dered from bar to bar strumming a guitar. The best known calyp-sonians in the 30s included Frank Taylor, Da Costa Allamby, and Mighty Charmer. Only the latter made much of a splash, with his hit *My Dear Mammy* in 1947. The local stuff, however, seemed to lack appeal compared to the Trinidadian variety. So Mighty Charmer made the pilgrimage to Trinidad and hit it big there with his tune *Flying Saucer*. His lyrics grew more and more satirical, influenced by the Mighty Sparrow (Francisco Slinger). Charmer was succeeded in the tradition by the Merrymen – the Bajan Beatles. Developing a trademark beat called the "Caribeat," the Merrymen, led by Emile Straker, began by recycling old calypsos like *Sly Mongoose, Millie Gone to Brazil,* and *Brudda Neddy.*

CONTEMPORARY BAJAN CALYPSO: Calypso finally started to catch on in the early 60s. Its popularity mushroomed with the advent of radio and a larger number of performers arriving from Trindad for shows. By the mid-60s, the pool of talented performers had grown to include the Mighty Gabby, Mighty Viper, Lord Deighton, Mighty Dragon, and Lord Summers. The years 1968 and 1969 saw major competitions. In the early 70s, however, calypso was eclipsed and sent into retreat by a new music called spouge. This reggae-calypso hybrid, introduced by its inventor Jackie Opel, a former calypsonian who had developed the style while in Ja-maica, dominated the music scene from 1969 to 1974. Although Opel died in an auto accident in late 1970, groups such as the Blue Rhythms Combo, the Draytons Two, Sandpebbles, and the Outfit continued the short-lived tradition. Calypso began to grow once again after the 1974 revival of the Crop Over Festival. Today, more than half of the songs deal with political issues. Bajan calypso has truly matured.

THE MIGHTY GABBY: Gabby, foremost practitioner of Bajan calypso, holds out in his tent, Battleground, and expounds on favorite topics, including the foibles of island politicians. He has won the Crop Over Festival competition in 1968, 1969, 1976, and in 1985. His real name is Tony Carter and he has been singing since age 6, competed in a calypso contest as a teenager, and spent time in New York from 1971-76. Some of his more famous songs include *Jack*, which deals with the controversial concept of limiting beach use; *Miss Barbados*, which concerns the Canadian selected to represent Barbados in an international beauty pageant; and 1985's *Culture*, focussing on the threat posed by the imported "trash" coming over the airwaves. *Chicken and Ram*, one of his most recent tunes, deals with the infamous Mrs. Ram, who allegedly sold diseased chickens to restaurants. Infuriated by the tune, Mrs. Ram sued and lost. Gabby dances and sways expressively in concert – swinging his mike like a bat on *Hit It* and folding his arms and jumping like a chicken during *Chicken and Ram*. He is a protest folksinger of note and was voted Folksinger of the Year in 1977, 1978, and 1979. Gabby has two solo albums out, *One In The Eye* and *Across the Board*, on the Ice label.

Ice Records

Based in Barbados, London, and New York City, Ice Records is the label of producer, arranger, guitarist, and singer Eddy Grant. It offers solo works by local artists Gabby and Grynner as well as superb albums by calypso greats such as Lord Kitchener and the Mighty Sparrow. These come with lyric sheets so you can better understand what you are hearing. Soca afficionadoes will appreciate the eminently danceable compilation, *A Taste of Soca*, which brings together 12 different artists ranging from Calypso Rose to Black Stalin to Gabby to Eddy Grant. *Soca Trinity*, released in 1993, features Gabby, Grynner, and Bert "Panta" Brown in a combined effort, and 1994's *Fire in De Wave* exemplifies the Bajan "Ring Bang" dance style of soca. Its highlights include Gabby's *Fire in De Wave* and *Ring Bang Soldier* by Bajan Viking-Tundah.

THE CURRENT CROP: Tops among Gabby's rival today is Red Plastic Bag. His claim to fame is *Mr. Harding Can't Burn*, which won him his first calypso crown. Another song, *Holes*, laments the miserable condition of the island's roads. Other prominent performers include Romeo, Bumba, Viper, and Grynner (pronounced "Grinder"). The latter often tours with Gabby. His album on Ice, *King of the Road March*, is a greatest hits compilation. It includes his most famous composition, *Leggo I Hand*, the story of a band of Rastafarian musicians accosted by the police.

The Arts

Theater and Dance

DINNER THEATER: Supper shows, entirely formulated and produced for the tourist trade, provide the visitor with sheer entertainment rather than a feel for the island and its history. They all include a buffet dinner, drinks, and transportation to and from your hotel. **"1627 and All That Sort of Thing"** is presented on Sun. and Thurs. evenings outdoors under open tents at the Barbados Museum. During the show, the Barbados Dance Theatre dramatizes the lifestyle of a Bajan village. The bright costumes really help the presentation; this is an excellent opportunity to explore the museum – which is open before and during the show – at night. **Barbados by Night** (☎ 428-5048/2986, fax 420-6317) held in the garden of the Plantation Restaurant, presents an evening of song and dance in a garden setting with white tablecloths. On one stage to the right, a steel band provides entertainment; the theater stage is to the left. Spice & Co. perform and there's also fire eating and limbo dancing. **"Barbados, Barbados,"** held Tues. nights at Balls, an old sugar estate, is a musical comedy based on the life of the semi-mythologized whorehouse manager Rachel Pringle. The **Easter Opera in Barbados,** held annually since 1993, consists of Verdi and Mozart extracts performed by London's Opera Interludes.

OTHER DRAMA: Try to catch a performance by the **Green Room Players** or **Stage One Theatre Productions**. Watch for shows at Queen's Park Theatre, the Steel Shed, Combermere School Hall, and The Auditorium (on George St.). Throughout Feb. and March during the **Esso Arts Festival**, performances of the island's three best current plays are staged; and the **Farley Hill Concert**, held in the park atop Farley Hill, and **Cohobblopot**, held at the National Stadium, both offer dramatic productions during Crop Over.

DANCE COMPANIES: Dance on the island is ebullient yet disciplined and combines African zeal and exuberance with European conservatism. All types of dance troupes – from ballet to avant garde – flourish on the island. The foremost ballet schools are the Penny Ramsey and Sheila Hatch schools. Mary Stevens single-handedly introduced modern dance to the island when she founded the **Barbados Dance Theater Company** in 1968. It has drawn on African roots – introducing a new version of W. African spider-hero *Anansi* and the *Hag*. The latter is a mythical woman who sheds her skin nightly – transforming herself into a ball of fire in search of blood. The **Rontana Dance Movement**, formed by the 1975 merger of the Rontana Dance Company and the Awade Drummers, presents dance to percussion. The **Yoruba Dancers**, a semi-professional company formed by the revolutionary late-60s theater group the Yoruba Yard, give occasional performances. The **Dance Experience** – a group of young dancers who incorporate jazz, folk, and modern techniques in their performances – were founded in 1981 and are frequently accompanied by the **Wesahh Singers**. Yet another group is the **Country Theatre Workshop**, founded by Patrick Cobham. It performs regularly at the Plantation Spectacular. In addition to the regular hotel gigs, many companies strut their stuff during the Esso Arts Festival and at the Farley Hill Concert (see above).

Art

Barbados is a wellspring of artistic talent. Most of the island's early art reflected the needs and values of the colonial power structure – and, like the planters themselves, most originated in England. The most famous early sculpture is that of Admiral Nelson, which stands in Trafalgar Square, and the island's most renowned painting is one by Benjamin West, which hangs in the St. George Parish Church. The liberated slaves, struggling to survive, had little time for artwork initially but, after a while, the art movement began to grow. Formation of Barbados National Arts Council in the mid-50s was a milestone in the island's history. Tourism has contributed to the art boom by its constant supply of patrons.

MURALS: Mural art has flourished on the island, as it has all over the Americas. On Barbados, mural painting originated with the works done on the exterior of shops on Baxter's Road and Nelson St, which were colorful advertising billboards in Bridgetown. Similarly, vendors' carts still display cute, often cartoonish ads. In 1981 Barbados hosted the Caribbean Festival of Creative Arts (CARIFESTA), and this form of art began in earnest. During the festival, the murals that festoon the Barbados Community College, the Springer Memorial School, and the Eagle Hall Post Office were created.

PAINTERS: Many painters seek to record fast-disappearing aspects of Bajan life such as windmills, greathouses, donkey carts, and chattel houses. One of the finest artists of the latter is Fielding Babb. Other painters of traditional Barbados include Oscar Walkes, Briggs Clarke, twin brothers Omowale and Sundiata Stewart, Kathleen Hawkins, twin sisters Winifred and Harriet Cumberbatch, and Adrain Compton. Artist Ena Power specializes in painting flowers. David and Indira Gall use local images to project symbolic messages.

MUSEUMS: The Art Collection Foundation (ACF) has recently launched the **National Art Collection**, at Barbados National Bank on Broad Street. Older treasures, including prints, may be viewed at the **Barbados Museum**.

ART GALLERIES: Foremost among these are the **Barbados Arts Council Gallery** at Pelican Village, ☎ 426-4385, and the monthly rotating exhibits at the National Cultural Foundation's **Queen's Park Gallery**, ☎ 427-2345. The **Barbados Gallery of Art**, opened in 1995, is on the Turf Club premises at Bush Hill here. **Fine Art Framing** (☎ 426-5325) and the **Studio Art Gallery** (☎ 427-5463) in Bridgetown also hold exhibits occasionally. **Origins** (☎ 426-8522), on the Bridgetown waterfront, contains both paintings and "wearable" art. The **Verandah Art Gallery**, on Broad Street (☎ 426-2605) sells a wide variety of both island and Caribbean art. Ras Akyemi and Ras Ishi sell their artwork in their **Art Animal's Gallery** at #6 Pelican Village. **Fairfield Pottery & Gallery** (☎ 424-3800), Fairfield Cross Roads, sells pottery produced by the Bell family as well as other artwork. **Medford Craft Village**, at Barbarees Hill in St. Michael (☎ 427-3179) sells mahogany-crafted items. **Omowali Stewart** (☎ 424-3561) is a prominent figurative painter whose works adorn the lobby of the Barclays Bank on Lower Broad St. (call for an appointment). You can visit his studio in Clermont Gardens, St. Michael. **Ras Akyemi Ramsay** (☎ 423-1022, 10-6), on St. Hill Rd. in Tweedside, St. Michael, produces spiritually-centered expressionist paintings; call for an appointment. In Brittons Hill, St. Michael at **Obajuiu**, Horn's Development, Arlette St. Hall (☎ 450-8547, 429-4262, 426-3913) is a painter, printmaker, and collagist; call for an appointment. **The Barbadoes**, located inside the Sandy Lane Hotel in Sandy Lane, exhibits arts and crafts such as jewelry, hand-painted silk, batik, ceramics, and paintings. In Prospect, at the corner of Hwy. 1 and Batts Rock Rd., **Portobello** (☎ 424-1687; B$5 admission) has a formerly-private collection of Haitian paintings that are now for sale.

In St. Peter, **Kay Fedel** (☎ 422-2128) is a painter, collagist, and cloth sculpturist; call for an appointment. **Coffee and Cream Gallery** – in St. Lawrence Gap, Christ Church – represents about 40 island artists, including jewelers. It doubles as a coffeeshop and bar and is open from 11-5:30 Tues. to Sat. **Talma Mill Gallery** (☎ 428-9383) is open by appointment only. It is set in the ruins of an old mill at the home of Barbados Art Council founder and painter/papermaker Norma Talma in the S coast village of Enterprise. **Bertalan Gallery** (☎ 427-0414) is set in a garden in Christ Church's Marine Garden. It showcases William Bertalan's metal sculptures. Also in Christ Church, watercolorist **Corrie Scott** (☎ 436-8377) has her studio at 17 Pavilion Court in Hastings.

Painter and ceramicist Golde Spieler (☎ 425-0223) operates out of **Earthworks Pottery**, her workshop complex, at Shop Hill in St. Thomas. Jill Walker is another painter who sells her work at her chain of "Best of Barbados" shops found islandwide (see chart). **Gail Hermicks Contemporary Sculpture Studio** (☎ 433-1246) operates out of Cliff Plantation in St. John. She creates whimsical sculptures using objects found in sugar plantations. **Analee Davis's Studio** is also here. **Ras Ishi Butcher** (☎ 423-1022), is also in St. John. His studio at Sealy Hall is open 10-6; call for an appointment. Outdoor arts and crafts displays are found at the annual Crop Over Holetown festivals.

Best of Barbados Shops

Best of Barbados Sandpiper Inn Holetown	Best of Barbados Cruise Ship Terminal Bridgetown
Best of Barbados Mall 34 Bridgetown	Best of Barbados Quayside Centre Rockley
Great Gifts Da Costas Mall Bridgetown	Best of Barbados Andromeda Gardens
Gift Shop Mt. Gay Visitors' Centre Spring Garden Highway St. Michael	Best of Barbados Sam Lord's Castle
Walker's Caribbean World St. Lawrence Gap	Best of Barbados St. Lawrence Gap

Literature

The island's literary culture is rooted in oral tradition. It began with the legends and folklore that developed with the combination of transplanted European and slave cultures. Most of the works originally published about the island were written by outsiders. Richard Ligon's *A True and Exact History of the Island of Barbadoes* was the first to be published in 1657. It took hundreds of years for the local literature to evolve and gain acceptance. The first publicity indigenous literature received was on the 1940/50s BBC program, *Caribbean Voices* and through the literary magazine, *Bim*, which began publication in 1942. Much of Bajan literature deals with cultural identity and racial strife. Famous Bajan writers include Oliver Jackman, Geoffrey Drayton, Austin Clarke, and John Wickham. One of the most important writers – not only in Barbados but in the entire Caribbean – is George Lamming. He refused to give heed to conventional plot and characterization. His novel *In the Castle of My Skin* is a masterful account of village life, one which should be required reading for any visitor. One well known poet is H. A. Vaughn. Edward "Kamau" Braithwaite, a former lecturer at the Dept. of English at the University of the West Indies, is an internationally known poet. He won the prestigious Neustadt International Prize for Literature in 1994 and is recognized as one of the most important living poets. Braithwaite employs an interweaving of "voices" and much of his work deals with the African diaspora and its cultural repercussions. Barbados named him Companion of Honour in 1987. He is presently a professor of Comparative Literature at NYU.

Festivals and Events

Holidays

1 January	New Year's Day
1 May	May Day
30 November	Independence Day
25 December	Christmas Day
26 December	Boxing Day

Christian holidays observed are Good Friday, Easter Monday, and Whit Monday. Other holidays are Caricom Day in early July and United Nations Day in early October.

THE HOLETOWN FESTIVAL: This February festival celebrates the arrival of the first settlers. It has been held since 1977 and commences with a week-long celebration. Although the date commemorated (February 17, 1627) may be incorrect, this festival really swings regardless. You may hear medieval hymns in the churches and experience the sights, sounds and smells of the carnival held at the fairgrounds. The St. James Parish Church is filled with exotic blooms and displays its antique silver. Evening activities include a performance by the Royal Barbados Police Force band and the Mounted Troop with torches blazing on their lances. Other features are food stalls and folksinging and dancing.

OISTINS FISH FESTIVAL: This two-day festival in April celebrates the island's fishing industry. Contests are held in fishing, boat racing, fish "boning," and crab racing – all to the clamor of steel bands. There are food stalls galore as well as arts and crafts booths. The Coast Guard even puts on an exhibit.

CROP OVER FESTIVAL: This all-island festive explosion is the highlight of the summer and takes place from mid-July through early August. It is a version of an earlier island festival that celebrated the sugarcane harvest – a Caribbean version of Thanksgiving – and was revived over two decades ago. Calypso music rings out from the performers' tents and the sweet smell of Bajan cooking permeates the festival grounds.

Features include the "Bridgetown Market," a delight for epicures; the "Cohobblopot," a pastiche of dance and drama which frames the crowning of the King and Queen of costume bands; and the "Pic-O-de-Crop Show," when the year's King of Calypso is revealed. The climax comes with "Kadooment Day" (Bajan slang for a "fuss" or an "important occasion") on Aug. 1. From 8 AM, costume bands parade before judges at the National Stadium. The flurry of costumed performers and bands then take to the streets, parading the three miles to the Spring Garden Hwy. The road is closed off and there are lots of stands, some of which have their own sound systems. The day climaxes with bursts of fireworks illuminating the night sky at around 8-9 PM.

THE NATIONAL INDEPENDENCE FESTIVAL OF THE CREATIVE ARTS: Each Nov., contests are held in the fields of music, singing, acting, dancing, and writing. Winners are announced on November 30, Independence Day.

Cultural Calendar

JANUARY
National Trust Open Houses (Sun.)
Barbados Horticultural Society, Open Gardens
Barbados International Jazz Festival

FEBRUARY
Barbados Horticultural Society, Flower Show

APRIL
Holder's Easter Season: Polo, Shakespeare plays, opera at Holder's House

MAY
Gospel Festival (first weekend)
Cultural Heritage Week

JUNE
Environment Week

JULY
Crop Over Festival
Summer Program at Barbados Museum

AUGUST
Aug1: Kadooment

OCTOBER
St. Lawrence Music Festival

NOVEMBER
Independence Celebrations

DECEMBER
Fine Craft Festival (first Sat.)

Food and Drink

A limited variety of produce combined with a skimpy household budget mean that Bajans have always been cautious and resourceful when cooking – a set of conditions which has produced innovative culinary delights. Bajan cooking has been influenced by a number of different cuisines, including W. African, English, French, Spanish, Amerindian, Indian, Chinese, as well as recipes from other Caribbean islands. Meat is a luxury item (although many Bajans raise their own pigs and chickens), and the staple food is rice supplemented by sweet potatoes, yams, and beans. Those who can afford to, rely on dairy products, imported salt beef, codfish, and pork, local pork and mutton, and imported frozen beef for protein.

The Hotel Association sponsors the "Bajan Table," an annual culinary exhibition held in early Oct. Hotels, restaurants, and individuals are awarded prizes for dishes in different categories. The National Independence Festival of Creative Arts (NIFCA) is a celebration of indigenous culinary skills that awards highly-regarded bronze, sliver, and gold medals on Independence Day (Nov. 30). American fast food has also made its indelible mark on the Bajan culinary psyche, but it has yet to take the place of "home cooking" in the hearts and minds of locals.

SNACKS: Street vendors sell a wide variety of tasty, deep-fried snacks. Dried and salted codfish, likened to "slabs of wood," had traditionally been imported from N. America to feed slaves. People used to view it with disdain as "slave food," but it has now lost that stigma and codfish balls and cakes are considered culinary delights. They are made by mixing boiled and finely-minced salted dried cod, boiled pumpkin, grated raw yam, beaten eggs, milk, butter, salt and pepper, which is then fried in boiling lard. They are often sold one or two in a bun in rum shops. A *cutter* is a French roll (known as a salt roll) with a slice of meat, ham, a fried egg, or cheese inserted. Pastries include the *lead pipe* (coconut bread), jam puffs, and turnovers. Roasted corn is a roadside treat. *Conkies* consist of corn meal, coconut, pumpkin, sweet potatoes, raisins, and spices mixed and steamed inside a banana leaf. Their name derives from an African dish called *kanki* or *kenke* in Ghana and *dukunoo* (the name by which it is known in Jamaica) among the Ashanti. Traditionally, housewives prepared *conkies* on Guy Fawkes Day, a celebration held on Nov. 5th that commemorated a failed attempt to blow up the Houses of Parliament in England. That celebration was abolished, and *cokies* are now made for Independence Day. *Travellers* are syrup-covered snowballs sold by pushcart vendors. Sweets or "sweeties" include guava cheese, coconut sugar cakes, tamarind balls, sugar cocks, nut cakes, glass cakes (peanut brittle), ginger-flavored sweetie boots, and shaddock rind. One unique dessert is stewed guava eaten with ice cream or evaporated milk. Guava jam and jelly are also made.

LOCAL SPECIALTIES: A dietary mainstay here is peas and rice. One or several different types of peas (such as blackeye, pidgeon, green, cow peas or lentils), are combined with cooked rice that has been flavored with salted pig tails or salted meat. Macaroni pie (macaroni and cheese) and sweet potato pie are similar accompanying side dishes served in local restaurants. Cornmeal and okra pudding is directly related to African culinary staples such as *foo foo* or *kush kush*, *cou cou* (or *coo-coo*). It is customarily served with gravy and salt fish or with flying fish and is sometimes jestingly referred to as "organ dust," because its grainy texture resembles the debris left by the wood ant. *Jug* or *jug-jug* is a mixture of guinea corn and green peas cooked with salt pork and beef. One account maintains that its name is a corruption of the Scottish dish *haggis*. When Scots were exiled in Barbados after the 1685 Monmouth Rebellion, they brought with them their favorite dish – a mixture of oatmeal, well seasoned and steamed like a pudding, with minced liver and suet mixed in. Bajans substitute whole grain millet for oatmeal; salted or fresh meat, peas, fat, and herbs are minced and blended with the grain. Naysayers point out that sheep organs were an important traditional component of *haggis*, but that no sheep are used in *jug-jug*; thus, it is more likely a Bajan invention. It is a traditional Christmas dish. *Cohobblopot* or *pepperpot* is a very spicy stew made with different meats and casareep (see Vegetables). *Calalu*, another island dish with African origins, is a crab and okra stew made with dasheen leaves, pork fat, and grated coconut. *Roti* (meaning "bread") was originally from the Indian subcontinent and consists of a *chapati* (a stovetop-baked, circular unleavened bread) wrapped around curried meat. Vegetarian versions are also available. Many dishes are supplemented with the ubiquitous hot sauce, a mixture of peppers, vinegar, mustard with onions, tumeric, and other spices.

Sea urchins: White sea urchins, known locally as "sea eggs," have traditionally been gathered at the beach. The roe of several urchins are combined into one emptied shell and, topped with a sea grape, they are ready for market. Traditionally, they are either steamed or fried with chopped onions and sweet pepper until golden brown. Bajans believe them to be an aphrodisiac. Harvest is currently prohibited because of greatly decreasing numbers.

Pudding and souse: This is one of the island's oldest and most legendary dishes. Its preparation is almost an art form. First, white "pudding" is prepared using grated sweet potatoes, thyme-seasoned pumpkin, sweet marjoram, and shallots. To create black pudding, pig's blood is then mixed in. The resultant pudding is salted and stuffed into pig intestines that have been rinsed with lime juice. The puddings are tied at both ends with strings and suspended in pots of boiling water. They are rotated continually until cooked. "Souse" is made by placing the chopped and boiled head and feet of a young pig into a bowl of brine with hot red peppers and lime juice. It is customarily served with chopped onions, cucumber slices, and cut peppers. It is a traditional Sat. night meal and is often fried up as breakfast on Sundays.

Other pork dishes: It is said that the only part of a pig that the Bajans cannot turn into a dish is the hair. *Stew food,* devised to cover the mid-week days when funds and fresh food might be short, combines ground provisions (roots such as yams and breadfruit plus greens) with finely chopped pig heads, trotters, snouts, and tails. For another dish, several pounds of pig is "corned" (pickled) in a stone urn along with saltpeter, sea salt, spices, and water. It is removed after several weeks and desalted through soaking before being combined in a stew with onions, butter, gravy, tomatoes, white beans, parsley, thyme, and pepper.

Flying Fish

Flying fish (*Hirundichthys affinis*) are one of the island's staples and are served fried, steamed, or baked. Barbados is so identified with these creatures that it is known as the "Land of the Flying Fish." They were formerly caught during the season and frozen or dried for later in the year. Today, better boats with a longer range ensure a year-round harvest. During the May spawning season, fishermen can gather them with only a dip net. A special seasoning used in their preparation (they may be served steamed, fried, or baked) incorporates onion, garlic, black and red pepper, parsley, thyme, paprika, lime juice, salt, and other spices. One prime local delicacy is flying fish "melts" (male sex organs) – a word derived from the now obsolete term "milts," referring to the roe or spawn of fish.

These seven-to-nine-inch flying fellows travel in schools as small as 50 and as large as 1,000 members. The fish does not actually "fly," but rather leaps from the water. It can glide quite a ways by using its two pectoral and ventral fins, and is propelled by its tail fin. It has been timed at speeds reaching 55 kmh and may leave the water for as long as 13 seconds. There are 13 species of flying fish in Bajan waters, although only one variety is caught. Gill nets are used, and "screelers," bundles of cane trash, attract the fish; the fish are lured because they lay their eggs on bouyant objects.

In addition to flying fish, Bajans also consume tuna, dolphin (not the mammal), kingfish, red snapper, bonito, chub, and smaller fish such as jacks, sprats, and fray.

VEGETABLES: A surprisingly large variety is available. These include roots such as yams, sweet potatoes, and white eddoes (taro). Cassava is a tuber introduced by the Indians. Although it has traditionally been used to make a type of bread, (called "bammy" in Jamaica), Bajans chiefly use it for processing into casareep, a preservative used in cooking pepperpot. Other vegetables include cabbage, okra, spinach, cristophenes (a type of gourd), onions, and tomatoes. Breadfruit was introduced from Tahiti by British sea captain, Captain Bligh, in 1792, and has become an island staple. It is covered with a bright green skin and has a white starchy pulp which may be boiled, fried, or pickled. It is actually a number of fruits in one: each polygon on its surface is a single fruit forming from a flower; all coalesce to make the whole fruit. The breadnut is a close relative of the breadfruit, although its skin is covered with fleshy prickles and it has less pulp. When roasted or boiled, the edible seeds taste similar to chestnuts.

Vegetable prices are surprisingly high. Cabbage can range from B$2-$3.50/lb., tomatoes from B$3.50-$5/lb., carrots from B$3.50-$6/lb., and sweet potatoes from B$1.50-$3/lb.

FRUIT: Since Barbados can't grow enough of its own, much must be imported from other islands. Fruits found include the mango, mammee apple, pomegranate, genip, avocado, grapefruit, shaddock, Chinese orange, tangerine, guava, lime, sapodilla, golden apple, dunk, sugar apple, soursop, custard apple, and Barbados cherry. The latter has the highest vitamin C content of any fruit in the world: just one cherry has the full daily requirement! The melon-like paw paw (papaya), containing the digestive enzyme papain which is used as a meat tenderizer, is one of the world's most delicious tropical fruits. The sour pulp of the Indian tamarind tree, extracted by sucking, is a delicious treat. The hogplum is pleasant smelling but slightly sour tasting and is often been used to fatten up hogs and cattle.

FRUIT DRINKS: Coconut water is a popular drink which is often served by Rastas on streetcorners. Lemonade is made using fresh limes. A variety of punches are made with mangos, guavas, papayas, passion fruit, tamarind pods, cherries, soursops, golden apples, and gooseberries.

OTHER BEVERAGES: Mauby was once dispensed by the then ubiquitous but now extinct mauby lady. It is a drink made using a bitter tree bark which – after boiling with spices – is strained and sweetened. It may also be brewed to make a non-alcoholic beer. Ginger beer is made in a similar fashion. Sorrel, prepared from the fresh or dried red sepals of this colorful plant, is a Christmas drink and is also packaged commercially. It is often mixed with rum. Soft drinks include the non-alcoholic Giant Malt and Ginseng Up from St. Kitts, Coca Cola, Joe's beverage (carbonated concoctions), Plus Action Drink, alcohol-free Tiger Malt, and Barbados Bottled Water. Locally brewed Banks Beer and Stallion Stout are available in every bar. Imports – including brews from Trinidad and Jamaica – are widely available. Dark and Stormy is a 30-proof canned mixture of rum, ginger, and quilaia bark extract.

HERBAL REMEDIES: These are legion in number. Local knowledge derives from combining African, indigenous, European, and creole discoveries over the centuries. *Sea moss*, a red seaweed used to manufacture agar-agar, is claimed as an aphrodisiac and a dessert and beverage (Irish Moss) are made from it. Other alleged aphrodisiacs include *gully root* and *hug-me-close*. Young men rub *tim-tom bush* on their bodies to attract women. The *chawstick*, a woody vine, can be used as a toothbrush, aphrodisiac, and as a remedy for gonorrhea. The *Christmas candle* will treat various skin maladies.

Rum

The name of this premier Barbados beverage probably comes from the archaic term "trumbullion" – a drunken tumult resulting from drinking, or from *saccharum*, the Latin word for sugar. Barbados produced the first and finest rum in the world. By the mid-18th C. it had developed a thriving trade selling to other W. Indian islands, N. America, England, and Ireland. Rum was even brought to W. Africa where it became a very popular barter item for slaves. For hundreds of years the British Navy dispensed a daily rum ration, a blend including Barbados rums; this practice ended in 1970. Barbados became one of the exporters of the new light-bodied rum at the end of the 19th C.

MANUFACTURE: There would be no rum without molasses. Molasses is what remains after most of the sugar has been extracted from sugarcane juice. It is distilled in American white oak wooden pot stills to form dark rum. As the wood adds color and flavor, the longer they are aged the better. A small amount of caramel (burnt sugar) is also added. Light rum is aged for a shorter time in modern metal stills.

MARKETING: Because of the sugar glut, most Caribbean islands strive to prop up their fragile, import-dependent economies with rum exports. Barbados has no special access to the US market, unlike the US-controlled Commonwealth of Puerto Rico (whose brand Ron Rico is nearly synonymous with the word "rum" itself), but the island's major exporter, Mount Gay, strives to make up for this deficiency with its elite appeal. It pushes hard to have its Eclipse brand be the choice of the American sailing set. And –quite amazingly considering the wealth of varieties available to the imbiber – it has succeeded. Recently, it has been joined in competition by Hanschell Inniss, Ltd. with its Cockspur brand. Mount Gay has the clear advantage (because of its distinctive packaging which incorporates a map of Barbados on the label), although both brands taste nearly identical. The vagaries of historical circumstance have set distillers competing with each other in unusual ways. The local taverns, panicking in the face of overwhelming competition from Mount Gay and West India Rum Refinery, impelled the legislature to pass the Rum Duty Act of 1906. It forbade the two refineries from selling rum in anything smaller than 10-gallon containers. Accordingly, both refineries have built up separate companies for bottling. Thus, local brands may be aged by Mount Gay but bottled by West India!

Malibu, brewed by the West India Rum Refinery, is a rum and cream liqueur chiefly exported to the US. Sales in 1994 totalled some US$3 million from export of 15 million bottles. A competitor is Crisma ("cream" in Latin), which is brewed by Huncol.

RUM ON BARBADOS: No fluid has such a socially solidifying an effect anywhere in the world as on Barbados. Not only do the island's inhabitants consume an ungodly 250,000 cases per year, they also do so in an enviable atmosphere of conviviality. For the female Bajan, church is equivalent to social life; men invest their Sun. morning spiritual endeavor inbibing spirits in that second pillar of the community – the rum shop. Rum is "fired" on social occasions, including at all rites of passage: births, christenings, marriages and funerals. It is drunk either straight from the bottle, using a small "snap" glass, on the rocks, mixed with water, or with a chaser. A small bottle is called a "midi," and a larger one a "flask." Politicians are notorious for trading rum in exchange for votes, the traditional practice being to supply a repast of rum and corn beef to voters both before and after elections.

RUM SHOPS: Most Bajans eat at home and usually only snack at other times. A major place for both snacking and socializing is the rum shop. The shop, often doubling as a general store, displays buns, pastries, and other goods inside glass cabinets and on the counter. Food is generally eaten inside. Men usually buy a "mini" or a "flask" of rum, ask for some cold water to dilute it, and swallow it right down. If music helps your digestion, you won't go wanting here. Jukeboxes sport an incredibly eclectic selection of music, including R&B, Prince, calypso (Gabby, Grynner, Red Plastic Bag), Country & Western, and more.

MIXED DRINKS: A rum punch is made with four parts water, three parts rum, two parts of falernum or other syrup, and one part lime juice – otherwise known as "one of sour, two of sweet, three of strong, four of weak." This is supplemented with a dash of Angostura bitters, a few grains of nutmeg, and a sprig of mint. A planter's punch has identical ingredients; the difference lies in the glass and decoration. The latter is adorned with chunks of mango, papaya, or other seasonal fruit and is served in a long glass. An orange slice and a toothpick-stabbed cherry are added for decoration.

The name "punch" was taken from the large puncheons or casks used to hold up 120 gallons of liquid. *Corn and oil* is a mixture of rum and falernum. Falernum was a discovery of Bajan Henry Parkinson who combined ground almonds, brown sugar, clove powder, and ginger root, with crushed limes. Parkinson's descendant, Arthur Stansfield, registered it in 1934. A famous local concoction is *sangaree*, a longtime favorite of the upper classes. It is made by adding a wine glass of sherry, Madeira, or port to a half-pint tumbler of cracked ice along with a half-teaspoon of both port and Curacao or Dom. Soda water, a slice of lime and a sprinkle of grated nutmeg finish it up. The *Barbados bombshell* is a cocktail made from rum, Pernod, freshly-pressed lime juice, and Grenadine syrup. Drinks such as piña coladas and banana daiquiris were developed especially for the tourist trade. Piña coladas are made with cream of coconut, pineapple juice, rum, and crushed ice.

Dining

DINING OUT: Many tourist restaurants are in the B$60-70 range; the best generally come to B$140 including tax and service, but not wine or other beverages. If you have a prepaid package at a luxury resort such as the Coral Reef Club, you may be able to take advantage of "exchange dining," which allows you to dine at, for example, Cobbler's Cove. Most dinner shows and buffets have an all-you-can-eat policy, but you are limited to "firsts" on the meat, fish, or chicken. Generally, a 5% tax and 10% service charge are added on top of the base price (except in the case of fixed-price buffets). If in doubt, ask. A number of restaurants – from fast food to gourmet – are listed in the travel section.

☞ Traveler's Tip
When a 10% service charge is applied, it's not necessary to tip. Otherwise, tip 10-15% in restaurants and give taxi drivers 10% on top of the fare, room maids B$2-4 pd, bellboys B$1 per bag (not less than B$2), and airport porters B$1 per bag.

BUDGET DINING: There are a small number of local restaurants in Bridgetown with some food (but mostly cutters) for sale in rum shops islandwide. Restaurants offering counter service are generally less expensive. Snackettes have the most reasonable food and some of the minimarts serve take-out items. All prepared food in Barbados is supposed to have a 5% tax added, even if it's a take-out item, but the local restaurants usually include this in the price. A variety of food is sold on the street, including the popular drinking coconuts. These are young coconuts which the vendor opens with a machete. He hacks off a piece from the edge which, after you're finished eating, serves to scoop out the soft white creamy jelly inside. If you want more water than jelly (or vice versa), just tell the vendor and he'll hand pick for you. Since much of the island's food is imported, supermarket prices are guaranteed to shock.

FAST FOOD: Junk food emporiums have increased in numbers. The most popular establishment is Chefette's. Interestingly enough, you won't find a Big Mac because the one McDonald's set up here failed to attract sufficient business and folded.

TIPS FOR VEGETARIANS: This is definitely a carnivorous society, so the more you compromise your principles, the easier time you'll have. In many cases, rice and peas are flavored with pork, and there is no plain rice available. If you're a vegan (non-dairy product user), you're in trouble unless you're cooking all of your own food! Vegetables in general, and salads in particular, are near non-existent outside of the tourist restaurants and the Chefette chain of fast foods. Since the bulk of the vegetables go to feed hungry tourists and a large number are also imported, prices tend to be very high. Locally grown fruits, such as papaya, when purchased from hucksters, are much more reasonable. If you do eat fish, you should be aware that locals eat it fried and that it may have been cooked in lard or in the same oil as chicken or pork. Cheese *cutters* will serve you well in a pinch, as will saltfish cakes on a bun. Macaroni pie (macaroni and cheese) is widely available and may serve as a main course. If you eat a lot of nuts, plan on bringing your own because those available here are expensive. The same goes for dried fruits. Finally, bear in mind that – outside of tourist restaurants – fish may be in short supply at times. **Note:** Places serving vegetarian food are frequently listed in the text.

Practicalities

WHO SHOULD COME: Barbados has always striven to attract an upscale sort of traveler. If you have a fondness for luxury hotels and gourmet restaurants, it has some of the best in the world. Those on a budget can expect to pay what they might at a comparable location in Canada, the US, or Europe; there really aren't any exceptional bargains. What Barbados provides is an attractive island with modern facilities and reasonable roads. While it lacks the cultural glamor of Jamaica, Jamaica's often-evident harrassment is also largely missing. Barbados, while not rich, has a much higher standard of living than many other Caribbean nations. Health and educational standards are also relatively high. These factors make things in Barbados more expensive than poorer locales such as the Dominican Republic.

On the whole, Barbados is not a place for low-budget travelers. There is no camping and only limited low-cost accommodation. The best you could do here would be in the range of US$30 pp, pd. And you could easily spend much more.

You can get practically everywhere on the island by public bus, everyone speaks English, it is reasonably safe to walk anywhere, and there are plenty of good places to hike. Bajans are quite friendly and hospitable.

WHEN TO COME: The winter season is the most popular time and for good reason. Most people want to get away from snow or, at least, cold weather. The "rainy season," is no longer quite so rainy in Barbados these days. A drought in 1994 was the worst in 106 years! During the off-season, prices drop and everything becomes more available, but there may be a less active social scene at your hotel.

Basics

MONEY: Monetary unit is the Barbados dollar, which is divided into 100 cents. Notes are issued in denominations of 1, 5, 10, 20, and 100; coins are minted in amounts of 1, 5, 10, and 15 cents, and $1.

changing money: Current exchange rate is US$1= B$1.98. There is no black market. Most banks have a service charge of B$1-$2 plus stamp duty of 10 cents per check. You may evade the service charge by changing a larger amount of money. Cash brings slightly less than traveler's checks. It's always better to use cash and to change your money at a store or a restaurant where the rate will be two-to-one and your change will be dispensed in B$. You must produce an air ticket and identification to change your money back to foreign currency. This can be done at the airport or bank: you loose around 2-3%. The bank opens at 8 AM so, if you have an early morning flight, be sure to do it the evening before.

credit cards: Although American Express is the nation's "official credit card," other major cards are accepted by banks, shops, and restaurants. **advances:** Visa cards may be used to obtain cash at 24-hr. ATM facilities at Broad St., Rendezvous, Wildley, and Sunset Crest (near Holetown) locations. Royal Bank of Canada's ATMs accept Visa cards and "PLUS" bank cards at their locations at the airport, on Broad St., in Collymore Rock, Hastings, St. Lawrence Gap, and Sunset Crest. **problems:** Call 431-2433 for American Express, 431-0186 for Diners Club International, and 431-5151 for Discover, Barclaycard, Visa, and MasterCard.

BANKS: Banks are open 9-3 Mon. through Thurs., and Fri. 9-1. Barclays is open Mon. to Thurs. 8-3, Fri. 8-1 and 3-5. Barbados National Bank (at the airport) is open 8-midnight daily. Money can also be changed at your hotel at a slightly lower rate.

MEASUREMENTS: The metric system is used; gasoline and milk are both sold by the liter. Road distances are given in kilometers, but speed signs and car speedometers use miles per hour. Land elevations are expressed in meters. The island operates on Atlantic Standard Time, which matches Eastern Daylight Time during the summer.

VISAS: Citizens of the British Commonwealth and the following nations do not require visas for stays of up to three months: Austria, Belgium, Columbia, Denmark, Finland, Germany, Greece, Iceland, Republic of Ireland, Israel, Liechtenstein, Luxembourg, Netherlands, Norway, Peru, San Marino, Spain, Surinam, Sweden, Switzerland, Tunisia, Turkey, USA, and Venezuela. (American citizens may enter with a passport, driver's license, or voter's registration card.) Citizens of most other countries (except Communist ones) may stay without visas for 21 days providing they have onward tickets. All others must have visas; applications should be accompanied by two photos and a letter from a travel agent on letterhead that certifies the booking. Business travelers should have a letter from their company giving details of their business and confirming financial support for the applicant. If you are arriving from South America, you may be asked to produce a yellow fever vaccination certificate. In order to extend your stay, you must apply at Customs House at The Wharf in Bridgetown, ☎ 426-9912.

HEALTH: Water is safe to drink everywhere and has become renowned for its purity worldwide. Medical care is usually on a first-come, first-served basis. Bridgetown's 600-bed Queen Elizabeth Hospital (☎ 436-6450) is the main hospital; eight health centers and 10 other health clinics are scattered across the island. Bayview Hospital (☎ 436-5446) is private and is the one most often used by visitors. It's on St. Paul's Ave. in Bayville. The Queen Elizabeth Hospital does not accept overseas health insurance, but it does take American Express credit cards. The Bayview may or may not accept foreign insurance; the same applies to the remaining clinics and health centers. Although the quality of medical and dental services is among the highest in the Caribbean, it's not quite up to US standards. **alternative health:** The Ash-Phil Health & Herbal Corner (☎ 436-1169) is at El Dorado in Black Rock. The Herbal Apothecary and Acupuncture Clinic (☎ 431-0459) is in the St. James Fort Building on Hincks St. The Colon Hygiene Centre (☎ 437-3593) is at 16 George St. in St. Michael. Yin & Yang Natural Health Clinic (☎ 435-0107) is in the Barbados Hilton at Needhams Point.

Selected Island Pharmacies

Bridgetown

City Pharmacy, Lower Broad St.	426-5191
Collins Ltd., Broad St.	426-4515
dispensary	426-4246
Connolly's Pharmacy Ltd., Hadley House, Lower Broad St.	426-4045
Gill's Pharmacy, Chapel St. near Tudor St.	427-2654
Jones Drug Store, 8 High St.	426-3241
Neil's Pharmacy, 35 Roebuck St.	427-5762
Peoples Pharmacy, Swan St.	426-4373
PPS Pharmacy, City Centre	431-0580
Walkes Pharmacy, 47 Tudor St.	426-3707

St. James

Jamestown Pharmacy Ltd., Holetown	432-5599
Knights Pharmacy, Sunset Crest	432-1290

West Terrace Pharmacy	424-9658
St. Peter	
Pharmaco, Speightstown	422-1908
Roach Noel & Sons, Speightstown	422-2112
Christ Church	
Elcourt Pharmacy, Maxwell Main Rd.	428-5323
Grants Drug Mart, Oistins	428-9481
Hastings Pharmacy, St. Matthias Gap, Hastings	429-8932
Joe's Pharmacy, Hills Plaza 4, Oistins	428-6025
St. Philip	
Cosmopolitan Pharmacy, Six Roads	423-6640
Eastern Pharmacy, Church Village	423-2828

PHOTOGRAPHY: Film isn't cheap here so you might want to bring your own. Kodachrome KR 36, ASA 64, is the best all-round slide film. 100 or 200 ASA is preferred for prints, while 1000 ASA is just the thing underwater. For underwater shots use a polarizing filter to cut down on glare; a flash should be used in deep water. Avoid photographs between 10 and 2 when there are harsh shadows. Photograph landscapes while keeping the sun to your rear. Set your camera a stop or a stop and a half down when taking photos of beaches; this will prevent over-exposure from glare. A sunshade is a useful addition. Keep your camera and film out of the heat. Replace batteries before a trip or bring a spare set. Do not subject your exposed film to the X-ray machines at the airport: hand carry them.

FILM DEVELOPING: Sun Colour Limited has one-hour photo developing and printing at their Cave Shepherd (Broad St.) and Sunset Mall (St. James) stores. Their Windsor store in Hastings is open 24 hours. Shep's Photo Centre is in Mall 34 on Broad St. in Bridgetown. Photo Finish is in the Royal Plaza on Broad St. and also in Worthing. True Colour Photo Lab is in Quayside Centre in Rockley.

THEFT: This should not be a problem if you're reasonably cautious. Don't flash money or possessions around and, in general, keep a low profile. Don't leave anything unattended on the beach and keep off deserted beaches at night. Never, never leave anything in an unoccupied vehicle. Remember that locals who form sexual liasons with foreigners often do so with pecuniary gain in mind and, if you give one of them access to your hotel room, it's a bit sticky to then go to the police and make a charge!

The Barbados Heritage Passport

The Barbados Heritage Passport offers discounts to a number of the island's attractions, including shops, publications and videos. The Full Passport (B$70) offers discounts to over a dozen places of interest, and the Mini Passport (B$24) comes in three different packages and gives 50% discount to five or six different specified sights. Up to two children (under age 12) are admitted free if you are passport holders. Sights include Gun Hill Signal Station, Morgan Lewis Sugar Mill, Welchman Hall Gully, Villa Nova, St. Nicholas Abbey, Andromeda Botanical Gardens, the Barbados Museum, the Bridgetown Synagogue, Harrison's Cave, Sunbury Plantation House, the Sugar Machinery Museum, Francia Plantation House, Grenade Hall Signal Station, Oughterson House, Codrington College, and Francia Plantation House.

WHAT TO TAKE: Bring only what you need. It's easy to wash clothes in the sink to save lugging around a week's laundry. Laundromats ("laundermats") are available at selected locations; a wash is around B$3.50. Remember, simple is best. Set your priorities according to your needs. With a light pack or bag, you can breeze from one town to another easily. Confining yourself to carry-on luggage also saves waiting at the airport. See the chart for suggestions and eliminate unnecessary items.

What to Take

CLOTHING
Socks and shoes, underwear, sandals or thongs, T-shirts, shirts (or blouses), skirts/pants, shorts, swimsuit, hat, light jacket/sweater.

TOILETRIES
Soap, shampoo, towel, washcloth, toothpaste/toothbrush, comb/brush, prescription medicines, Chapstick/other essential toiletries, insect repellent, suntan lotion/sunscreen, shaving kit, toilet paper, nail clippers, hand lotion, small mirror.

OTHER ITEMS
Passport/identification, driver's license, travelers' checks, moneybelt, address book, notebook, pens/pencils, books, maps, watch, camera/film, flashlight/batteries, snorkeling equipment, extra glasses, umbrella/poncho, laundry bag, laundry soap/detergent, matches/lighter, frisbee/sports equipment, cooking supplies (for apartment hotel living).

Transport

BY AIR: Shop around for the best deal on airfares. A good travel agent should scan for the lowest fare; if he or she doesn't, find another agent, or try doing it yourself. If there are no representative offices in your area, check the phone book – most airlines have toll-free numbers. In these days of airline deregulation, fares change quickly, so it's best to check the prices well before departure and then again before you go to buy the ticket. The more flexible you can be about your dates, the easier it will be to find a bargain. Whether dealing with a travel agent or with the airlines directly, let them know clearly what you want. Don't assume that because you live in Los Angeles, for example, it's cheapest to fly from there. It may be better to find an ultrasaver flight to gateway cities like New York or Miami and change planes. Fares tend to be cheaper on weekdays and during low season (mid-April to mid-Dec.). The most prominent carrier serving the Caribbean from the US is American Airlines, with flights arriving daily from Miami and San Juan. From either of these hubs, convenient connecting flights are available to and from virtually every major city. If you need to change your reservation while in Barbados, a reservation counter is located inside the Cave Shepherd Department Store on Broad St., right in the heart of downtown Bridgetown. American flies to approximately 180 destinations worldwide and serves 108 cities on the US mainland. Their AAdvantage Travel Awards Program, the first frequent flyer program, has 23 million members.

BWIA flies direct from Baltimore, Miami, New York, and Toronto as well as to Frankfurt, London, and Zurich on its European routes. Air Canada and BWIA fly nonstop from Toronto, and Air Canada has one flight per week from Montreal. British Airways flies nonstop from London and offers a Concorde flight from NYC in conjunction with the European Management Travel Group (☎ 800-992-7700); other British charters also offer quite inexpensive packages. Check the travel sections of your newspaper and the London Yellow Pages. **flying times:** From New York, 4 hrs. 20 min.; Miami, 3 hrs. 40 min.; Toronto and Montreal, 5 hrs; San Juan, 1 hr. 30 min.; Caracas, 2 hrs. 30 min.; Rio de Janeiro, 8 hrs.; London, Frankfurt, and Brussels, 9 hrs. **from the Caribbean:** Barbados may also be reached by air from everywhere in the Caribbean. LIAT and BWIA are the most prominent inter-island carriers. Aeropostal stops in Margarita and Caracas. Sunrise, a new regional carrier which will be partially owned by British Airways, is expected to begin operations in 1995.

ARRIVING BY AIR: Immigration cards are dispensed on the plane and stamped upon arrival. Retain yours and reserve B$25 for the air departure tax. (Cruise ship passengers are exempt.) Be certain to request more time than you think you'll need. If you wish to stay longer than 28 days, you will have to extend your visa, a time consuming process requiring money and photos. You will be speeded through customs if you have nothing to declare. Among the forbidden goods are meat and frozen foods, flowers, plants, fruits, guns, and any pets.

☞ Traveler's Tip

Although a passport is preferable, US visitors will be admitted with a birth certificate or papers of citizenship along with a photo ID, such as a valid driver's license, a university or school ID, a work ID, or a senior citizen ID.

BY SEA: Although there's no regular passenger service between Barbados and other major Caribbean islands such as Jamaica, and none at all from North America, the *M/V Windward* (☎ 431-0449/0937/0451, fax 431-0452) sails between St. Lucia, Barbados, St. Vincent, Trinidad, and Isla Margarita or Guiria (alternating weeks) in Venezuela. There is no regularly scheduled alternative to the cruise ship – which, in addition to costing more than flying, allows only a very limited stay and often isolates you from locals. Cruise ships serving Barbados include P&O Lines from Southampton; Hapag and Lloyd from Bremen; Royal Cruise and Royal Viking from San Francisco; Sitmar Cruises from Fort Lauderdale; Royal Caribbean Cruise Lines and Cunard Line from Miami; and a host of others from San Juan, Puerto Rico. These only stop at the island for a day or two.

One rewarding opportunity if you can afford it is to sail your own yacht here and travel independently. It's possible to crew on a boat coming from Europe; most head for the southern Caribbean.

PACKAGE TOURS: All that glitters is not gold. This cliché may be old but certainly pertinent when it comes to package tours! If you want everything to be taken care of, then a tour is the way to go. However, there are at least two distinct disadvantages: Most things have already been decided for you, which takes much of the thrill out of traveling; and you are more likely to stay in a large characterless hotel (where the operators get quantity discounts), rather than in a small inn (where you get quality treatment). Think twice before you sign up. Read the find print and see what's *really* included. Don't be taken in by useless freebies that gloss over the lack of paid meals.

HITCHHIKING BY YACHT: This can be easy if you have the time and money to wait and are at the right place in the right season. The best time is about mid-Oct., just before the boat shows and the preparation for the charter season. The marinas on St. Thomas (at Red Hook and Charlotte Amalie), along with those at English Harbor on Antigua, have the greatest concentration of boats and the most competition for work. Many times it's easy to get a ride from one island to another; just hang around the docks or pubs and ask! Working on yachts is hard, with low wages and long hours, and you must have a real love for sailing and the sea. You are usually doing something from early morning until late at night, although this varies from boat to boat. Check out *Sail* or *Yachting* magazines for the addresses of charter companies. Most people are employed on the spot, though, and writing may be a waste of time.

GETTING AROUND: Transport Board buses (blue with yellow stripe) and yellow private minibuses cover all paved roads, but you'll need patience! Allow plenty of time.

Bus service is inexpensive but painfully slow: an example of slothful government bureaucracy at its worst. As Bajans put it, "we complain and complain until we are blue in the face, but things don't improve." Buses are packed during peak hours (7-10 AM, 4-7 PM) and traffic is near gridlock in and around Bridgetown at these times. It takes an hour from Bridgetown to Bathsheba under normal circumstances, and about half that from Bridgetown to Speightstown. The fare is $1 (exact change) regardless of distance. Tokens are available in the bus terminal at the information windows. **routing:** The major routes are: No. 1 travels along the West Coast from Bridgetown to Speightstown and on; No. 2 goes to Rock Dundo; No. 3 runs to Turner's Hall via St. Andrew's Church and Hillaby; No. 4 goes to Shorey Village via Welchman Hall Gully, Harrison's Cave, and Flower Forest; No. 6 runs between Bridgetown and Bathsheba; No. 7 runs to Bowmanston via Gun Hill; No. 7A goes to Sergeant Street (village) via Gun Hill station, Bridgetown, and Codrington College; No. 12 runs to Sam Lord's Castle and the Crane Beach Hotel; No. 13A goes to Silver Sands via the S coast. All of the buses lead to or from Bridgetown except those on the Speightstown to Bathsheba (once every two hours) and the Speightstown to Oistins (hourly) routes. The latter is notoriously unreliable; avoid it during rush hour. Bridgetown has three terminals – the largest is on Fairchild St. and the other major terminal is at Speightstown. Otherwise, buses stop at round signs marked "TO TOWN" or "OUT OF TOWN" depending on direction.

Yellow private minibuses, with reggae music flooding their interiors, ply the nation's roadways. Just like the houses, they are

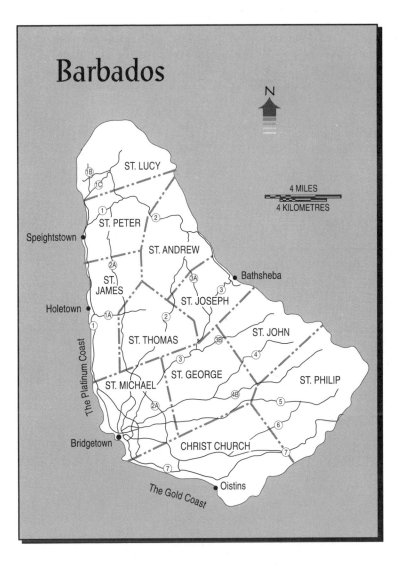

named, and have unique slogans and paintings on their rear ends. Generally, they run over the most heavily populated (and therefore profitable) routes; destinations are marked in the window. Shared taxi vans (also B$1) now cover some routes (such as Bridgetown to Christchurch). Their destination isn't marked so you'll need to ask.

Jitney buses, owned and operated by hotels, shuttle tourists to and fro for free or for a small charge. Local taxis, identified by the letter "Z" on their license plates, are expensive, whether shared or not. Be sure to agree on the price *before* getting in.

Taxi Fares

Per hour rate is B$32. Rate per mile or 'part thereof' should not exceed B$2.50. Rate per km should not exceed B$1.50

Between Grantley Adams Airport and

Atlantic Shores	B$16
Bathsheba, Cattlewash	B$36
Belleplaine	B$42
Bridgetown Harbour	B$30
Callenders	B$16
Coverley	B$8
Crane Beach	B$20
East Point	B$26
Garrison	B$24
Gibbs	B$42
Holetown	B$38
Long Beach/Silver Sands	B$16
Oistins	B$16
Pollards	B$22
Porters	B$38
Prospect, St. James	B$34
Providence	B$12
Rockley	B$22
Sam Lord's Castle	B$22
Speightstown	B$48
Trafalgar Square	B$28

Between Bridgetown/ Bridgetown Harbour and

Airport	B$30
Bathsheba	B$38
Callenders	B$24
Cattlewash	B$38
Crane Beach	B$34
East Point	B$40
Grand Barbados Resort	B$12
Gibbs, St. Peter	B$25
Grand Barbados Resort	B$12
Harrison's Cave	B$30
Hilton	B$12
Holders	B$16
Holetown	B$25
Long Beach	B$24
Oistins	B$24
Paynes Bay	B$16
Paradise	B$12
Porters	B$25
Rendezvous	B$16
Sam Lord's Castle	B$38
Sandy Lane	B$25
Silver Sands	B$24

Speightstown	B$30
St. Albans	B$25
St. George's Church	B$38
St. John's Church	B$36
St. Lawrence, Dover	B$18
Welchman Hall Gully	B$30

Between Sandy Lane/Glitter Bay and

Harrison's Cave	B$27
Sam Lord's Castle	B$55
St. John's Parish Church	B$40
Bathsheba	B$45

Between Bridgetown Harbour and

City Centre/Deacons Road	B$6

Between Sandy Lane and

Oistins	B$35
Rockley	B$30

Between Glitter Bay and

Oistins	B$35
Rockley	B$30

Between Glitter Bay and

Oistins	B$37
Rockley	B$35

RENTING A CAR: Avis and Hertz rent from the airport. If you show a valid US or International driver's license, a temporary Barbados license will be issued for B$10. This is available from Hastings, Worthing, and Holetown Police Stations and at the Licensing Authority offices at Oistins, Christ Church; the Pine, St. Michael; and Folkestone, St. James. The best choice, however, is to get it at the police window in the airport. Car rental companies can also make arrangements. A permit is required for motorbikes (70 -90 cc maximum available) or mopeds; helmets are required by law. You must be able to show either a motorcyle license or a driver's license with a motorcycle endorsement.

Expect to pay from B$400 per week for a four-passenger "mini-moke" (a hybrid between an Austin Mini and a jeep) to B$650 for a six-passenger automatic saloon. A mini-moke, resembling a low-slung, half-sized jeep, lacks windows or doors and has a cloth convertible top. You have to hike one leg over and jump in. Most companies require a rental of three days or longer. Produce a credit card or face paying a substantial deposit. Smaller companies frequently offer better deals. An important consideration is insurance.

If you are not covered, you must pay the first B$600 in damages if you have an accident. Even if it's only a scratch, it could easily amount to this much. It costs about B$10 per day extra for insurance; keep in mind that this only covers the insuree(s) who is (are) renting the vehicle. It is illegal for someone else to drive the car. Likewise, if you rent from a private party you may save, but you'll receive no insurance coverage. Gasoline – an astronomical B$1.54 per litre (for premium and unleaded) – is extra. As you should do everywhere, read the contract thoroughly – especially the fine print. Ask about unlimited mileage, free gas, late return penalties, and drop-off fees.

RENTAL AGENCIES: For a full list of the car rental companies, check the yellow pages. Some of the more prominent are listed here.

In St. Michael's: **Hill's Garage** (☎ 426-5280) offers free pickup and delivery to and from the airport; **Barbados Rent-A-Car** (☎ 425-1388, 428-0960/3737); **Express** (☎ 428-7845); **P & S Car Rentals** (☎ 424-2050/2907); **Hills** (☎ 426-5280, 433-1892 after hours); **Courtesy** (☎ 420-7153, 431-4160); **Auto Rentals Limited** (☎ 428-9085); **Jones** (☎ 426-5030, 431-9029); **National** (☎ 426-0603); **Premier** (☎ 424-2277); **Corbin's** (☎ 427-9531); **Coconut** (☎ 437-2097); **Regency** (☎ 427-5663); **Leisure** (☎ 420-6564); **Willie's** (☎ 428-7500); **Direct Rentals** (☎ 428-3133). **Johnson's** (☎ 426-4205) has locations in Hastings and in Bridgetown. Also try **Dear's** (☎ 429-9277, 427-7853); **Thompson** (☎ 428-7500); **P & S Car Rentals** (☎ 424-2052) in Pleasant View, Cave Hill, St. Michael; and **Sunny Isle** (☎ 435-7979). **Sunset Crest Rent-A-Car** (☎ 432-1482) rents mini mokes as well as four-door automatics.

other wheels: For scooters and motorbikes try **Lynn's Rentals** (☎ 435-8585). Finally, don't forget the alternative of renting a bicycle, one of the most economical and ecologically-sound ways to get around. Outlets include **M.A. Williams** (☎ 427-1043/3955) in Hastings and **Fun Seekers Inc.** (☎ 435-8206) in Rockley.

DRIVING IN BARBADOS: Don't forget that you drive on the *left* side of the road! The island's 830 miles (1,280 km) of public roads are poorly marked, so getting anywhere can be an adventure in itself! The greater part of the road system was laid out with 17th-C. donkey carts in mind, so there are a number of blind corners. Potholes reflect poor maintenance. Barbados has one of the most extensive road networks of any island its size, but it also possesses the largest quantity of poorly paved surfaces. Drivers frequently disobey the speed limits so exercise caution. Limits are usually 35 kmh (21 mph) in town and 60 kmh (37 mph) in the countryside. A notable exception to this is on the Spring Garden Highway, which connects Bridgetown with St. James. The speed limit there is 80 kmh. Keep in mind that "highway" here means an ordinary country road stateside. You will notice coral outcrops on either side that were left when they dug out the land to construct the road. When approaching a roundabout, remember to give way to traffic from the right. Be aware of special island vocabulary when taking directions. "Gap," for example, may signify an entrance to a road, a driveway, or a short road. Barbados's numbered routes all lead to or from Bridgetown. Parking in Bridgetown is denoted by blue "P" signs. Once parked, you will find entrepreneurs offering to either wash your car, "mind" your car, or both. Street parking is scarce, but there are several parking lots. It's usually easier to catch the bus into town as congestion and the confusing one-way streets can ruin the trip.

Tours and Excursions

One option for visitors without a great deal of time or with a yen to savor a few different experiences is to take a tour. Many of these include hotel pickup and drop-off in their prices. In addition to those listed, large resorts like Sam Lord's Castle offer their own tours for guests. **by taxi:** An ideal to really experience the island on a more personal level is to take a trip with a taxi driver. One reliable guide is Samuel Farley (beeper 436-1420, pager 0710). Check with your hotel desk or the tourist bureau for others.

BREWERY AND DISTILLERY TOURS: Banks (☎ 429-2113) offers tours of their beer brewery at Wildey, St. Michael on Tues. and Thurs. at 10 and 1. Admission is B$6 adults, B$3 children; proceeds are donated to charity. A chattel house on the premises has been transformed into a souvenir shop. **Cockspur** (☎ 429-8369, 426-0038) also offers tours of their rum plant. **Mt. Gay Distilleries** (☎ 425-8757) is set on Spring Garden Hwy. and offers a 30-40-min. tour of its distillery along with tastings. It's open Mon. to Fri. from 9-5; admission is B$8 adults; children under 12 are free. A **Best of Barbados** sales outlet is also located here.

INTERNAL AIR TOURS: You can tour Barbados via a number of small airlines, despite the lack of an internal flight system. **Acro Services** (☎ 428-8628/9) is at the airport. **Skytours** offers a 30-min. air tour (☎ 428-5010/7101), which includes a buffet, rum punch party, and transport to and from your hotel. **by helicopter: Bajan**

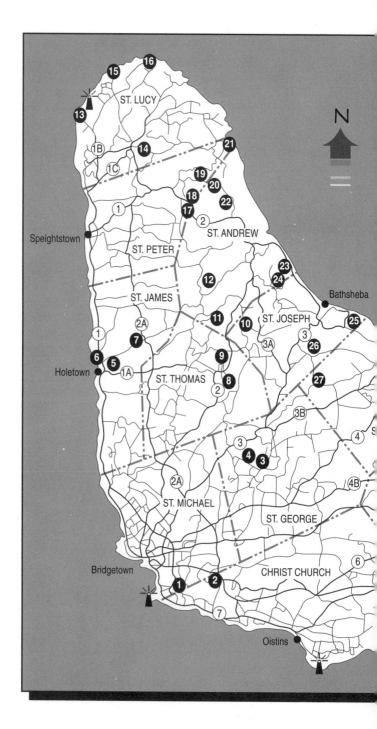

Historical & Natural Sights

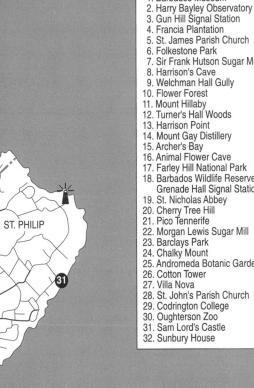

1. Barbados Museum
2. Harry Bayley Observatory
3. Gun Hill Signal Station
4. Francia Plantation
5. St. James Parish Church
6. Folkestone Park
7. Sir Frank Hutson Sugar Museum
8. Harrison's Cave
9. Welchman Hall Gully
10. Flower Forest
11. Mount Hillaby
12. Turner's Hall Woods
13. Harrison Point
14. Mount Gay Distillery
15. Archer's Bay
16. Animal Flower Cave
17. Farley Hill National Park
18. Barbados Wildlife Reserve and Grenade Hall Signal Station
19. St. Nicholas Abbey
20. Cherry Tree Hill
21. Pico Tennerife
22. Morgan Lewis Sugar Mill
23. Barclays Park
24. Chalky Mount
25. Andromeda Botanic Gardens
26. Cotton Tower
27. Villa Nova
28. St. John's Parish Church
29. Codrington College
30. Oughterson Zoo
31. Sam Lord's Castle
32. Sunbury House

ST. PHILIP

4 MILES

4 KILOMETRES

Helicopters (☎ 431-0069) leaves from the heliport near downtown (follow the signs). It offers air-conditioned rides in five-passenger Astars over the island. A 20-min. flight is B$130; a half-hour trip is B$200. While the longer flight takes you around the island from top to bottom, the shorter brings you past the St. James resorts, over Flower Forest, and down over the E coast, dipping in over the rocky crags, and then back to Bridgetown. The views are spectacular and really give you a splendid overview of the island. The pilot exercises common courtesy: you fly offshore and don't buzz the resort hotels. If you've always wanted to go up in a helicopter, this may be a good time to try it.

BY SUBMARINE: The most unusual activity on the island is an underwater voyage on the *Atlantis Submarine* (☎ 4368929/8932). This US$3 million recreational sub is the brainchild of Canadian Dennis Hurd. It is one of a small fleet deployed at tourist concentrations throughout the world; the others are at Kona and Honolulu (Hawaii), St. Thomas, Grand Cayman, and Guam. A videotape orients you before a launch takes you out to the 28-passenger sub. It only goes down 150 feet (50 m) for 45 min., so there's no need to worry about mishap. Besides, the 49-ton vessel holds food sufficient for three days. The *Atlantis II* cruises over the purposely-sunk wreck of the *Lord Willoughby*. A running commentary provides information on all of the corals, sponges, and fish that pass. Fishfinder and coral-finder charts are conveniently located onboard. Dives run from day until night, but the best times to see fish fans are early in the morning and from 3-4 PM. After your voyage, the center awards you a dive certificate. Three tours are offered: The Atlantis Odyssey, the Atlantis Expedition, and Atlantis by Night. Trips on the *Atlantis Seatrec*, an a/c semi-submersible boat, enable you to see the reef as snorkers do without actually getting wet. Children 4-12 are charged half-price and must be over three feet tall. To book, call 436-8929/8932 or 1-800-535-6564 (Caribbean Appetizers) stateside.

GREATHOUSE TOURS: During the winter season (mid-Jan. to early April), tours are conducted of a selected greathouse every Wed. by the **National Trust** (☎ 426-2421, 436-9033). Homes are open from 2:30-5:30 PM; admission is B$10 or B$28 with bus tour and welcome drink.

GROUP TOURS: Sightseeing taxi tours are available; a six- to seven-hour tour costs around B$150 for a group of 1-4 people. The most established sightseeing bus tour operator is **L.E. Williams** (☎ 427-1043/6006/6007/2257) who, on their "80-mile tour," offer free drinks along with lunch at the Atlantis Hotel. Some of the more notable sights include Animal Flower Cave, Cherry Tree Hill, and St. John's Church. **Sunflower Tours** (☎ 429-8941) offers a variety of tours ranging in price from B$45-B$100. Their tours run to Harrison's Cave, Flower Forest, and other sights. **Remac** (☎ 422-0546) offers three different tours. **VIP Limo Services** (☎ 429-4617), run by Sally Shearn, is another alternative. It offers custom-designed limo tours; charges run from around B$60 ph for a car seating up to four. **historic tours:** Call 431-2094 or 424-8140 (after hours), or fax 436-1643 for information about this tour (B$50) which leaves from Cave Shepherd on Wed. The "Hop a Tour" also leaves Cave Shepherd at 10:30 and 2:30. Contact Barbados Activities Hub (☎ 431-2094; 424-8140 after hours, fax 436-1643). **by bus:** If you have patience, you can create your own tour using the local transport system. For example, take a bus along the S coast to Oistins, then hop on a College Savannah bus to the E coast and return to Bridgetown. Alternatively, take the bus from Bridgetown to Oistins, then another to Speightstown, and go on to Bathsheba before returning to Bridgetown. In any event, it's good to allow plenty of time. The travel section contains many useful suggestions regarding bus routes and travel.

RUM TOUR: One of the more unusual tours is **"Where the rum comes from"** (☎ 435-6900), which combines a tour of the Spring Garden Highway Mt. Gay rum plant with a buffet lunch. Drinks are dispensed gratis as a warmup and a four-man steel band plays under the shelter of a green and white canopied tent. Lunch – set out on tables under a green corrugated zinc-roofed pavilion – offers a choice of chicken, stew, macaroni pie, rice, salad, plus coffee and desert. The short but informative tour illustrates the distilling process.

HIGHLAND ADVENTURE TOURS: This operator is centered at a scenic outlook at Canefields, St. Thomas and is unique to the island (☎ 438-8069, fax 438-8070). Horseback riding (B$100 adults and children), a jitney tour (B$50 adults, B$30 children), and hiking (B$140 adults, B$100 children) are offered here. (Prices include pickup.) Hiking is an all-day affair every Wed. For horseback riding, you get up on a step and mount your steed, which has been selected to suit your ability and size. You are led through fields and get to see the working cattle ranch; adorable calfs – unaware of the butcher's knife indelibly etched into their horoscope – lie next to their mothers. Heading through secondary forest, you pass breadfruit trees and cecropia as well as a lime kiln and the ruins of an abandoned brick factory. Circling around, you return to your starting point with its splendid views. The entire tour takes about 1.5 hrs, and you get a drink and a juicy skewer of freshly barbequed beef. The jitney tour takes you through a still-working plantation. The hike takes you across Mt. Hillaby, through Gregg Farm, and down to the old Spring Plantation enroute to Turner Hall Forest. **Note:** Activities here are still in flux. Check with your hotel desk or with Highland Outdoor Tours to see what is happening when.

AIR EXCURSIONS: Caribbean Safari Tours Ltd. (☎ 427-5100, fax 429-5446) offers one- or two-day air excursions to neighboring islands (such as St. Vincent, Dominica, Martinique, St. Lucia, Grenada, the Grenadines, and Tobago). It's located in the Ship Inn Complex in St. Lawrence Gap. **Chantours** (☎ 432-5591, fax 432-5540) is at Sunset Crest Plaza II and offers similar trips. **Grenadine Tours** (☎ 435-8451), 26 Hastings Plaza, offers one-day tours to Mustique and the Grenadines. A final alternative is **Palm Tree Tours** (☎ 437-1230, fax 437-2202).

A Different Spin on Barbados

Here are some suggestions for activities that the typical visitor doesn't think about doing...

Take a hike, either on your own (using the suggestions in this book) or with the National Trust.
Spend a few hours or an entire afternoon wandering around Welchman Gully and studying the flora and fauna.

Visit the Henry Bailey Observatory on a Friday night.

Head to Bottom Bay near Sam Lord's Castle and have a picnic.

Observe the House of Assembly when it is in session.

Feast on a traditional Bajan buffet for Sunday brunch.

Accommodations

The cost of lodging is high – from around US$35 d to $500 or more per night. The 5% room tax along with a frequently applied 10%

service charge makes it even more expensive! It's cheapest to visit here between mid-April and mid-Dec. The major resorts have three or four rates: winter, summer, shoulder, and (sometimes) Christmas. Camping is forbidden. Hotels range from beefy 300-roomers to small guesthouses. In addition to luxury resorts, there are apartments with kitchens plus furnished villas and cottages. The majority of the structures are designed to blend with the landscape. Hotels, guesthouses, condos, and other places to stay are listed in the back of this book. It's a good idea to get the current rates from the tourist board. If they don't have the rates, it's because the hotel in question hasn't supplied them, so use the address or phone number listed in the chart. There are also rental agents on the island. The Board of Tourism has offices to help you in both the airport and the harbor. Finally, while reservations may not be needed for the large hotels (except during the season), it would be prudent both to reserve and send a deposit to the smaller establishments to ensure your booking. Otherwise, your vacation could cost you substantially more than you had counted on.

ALL-INCLUSIVES: All-inclusive hotels are a recent introduction here and are growing tremendously in popularity. They differ from ordinary hotels in a number of ways. At "normal" establishments you will pay for every meal and every drink and have to tip; all-inclusives allow you not to worry about handling money during your stay. You have a wide range of options available, some of which (such as a "clothing optional" beach and spa facilities) may not be offered elsewhere. Facilities are generally well maintained and the resorts are attractive. If your idea of travel is basically relaxation and escapism, this may be your cup of tea.

There is, however, a down side to the all-inclusives. They may deprive you of the motivation to sample other restaurants – local as well as touristic – because they include all meals. Most prohibit outsiders from entering the grounds. The "games" and other programs can be rather irksome at times, as can the fawning, slurpy honeymoon couples – unless you happen to be one of them of course! You should be someone who will take advantage of what the resort has to offer. Vegetarian teetotalers can find better values elsewhere. On the other hand, if you do windsurf, scuba, enjoy expensive alcoholic beverages and gourmet French cuisine, you will be hard pressed to do better. Should you choose to stay in an all-inclusive, do get out and explore the island, if only for a day.

Barbados's first major all-inclusive resort was the upscale **Almond Beach Club**. It offers a Bajan restaurant, tours and fitness facilities. It has another branch at Almond Beach Village (the former Heywoods resort) that has been sold to the Jamaican Sandals chain. **Sandal's**, built on the site of the former Paradise Village Beach Club at a cost of B$42 million, is now the island's foremost luxury all-inclusive resort. Set on 45 acres of land, it has 300 rooms, five restaurants, five swimming pools, nine bars (including two swim-up bars and a piano bar), a sports complex and fitness center, and a theater.

All-Inclusives

NAME	TEL.	FAX	800#
Almond Beach Club	432-7840	432-2115	425-6663
Almond Beach Village	422-4900		425-6663
Club Rockley Barbados	435-7880	435-8015	
Island Inn	436-6393	437-8035	US: (800) 221-6509 UK: 071 995-8211 Can: (800) 424-5500
Mango Bay Club	432-6044	432-5297	
Sandals Barbados	428-0888 424-0889	425-1384	SANDALS

OTHER PLANS: Some hotels offer MAP (Modified American Plan), which includes two meals, generally breakfast and dinner. EP (European Plan) means that all of your meals will be on your own tab. CP (Continental Plan) includes breakfast. AP (American Plan) covers all meals. The best way to decide what plan to take is by considering both your appetite and the hotel's location. If it's within walking distance of other hotels and restaurants, it's worthwhile getting EP.

APARTMENT AND CONDOMINIUM RENTALS: Located at Derricks on the St. James coast, **Alleyne, Aguilar,** and **Altman** (☎ 432-0840) have a large list of villa rentals. If calling from abroad, you may try **Island Hideaways** (☎ 202-667-9652, 800-832-3202/2303, fax 202-667-3392), which has a number of attractive villas available. Others include **Caribbean Home Rentals**, Box 710, Palm Beach, FL, ☎ 305-833-4454; **Villas and Apartments Abroad**, 19 East 49th St., NY, NY 10017, ☎ 212-759-1025; and **Travel Resources**, Box 1043, Coconut Grove, FL, ☎ 305-444-8583.

Nightlife and Entertainment

Few locations of similar size rival Barbados's scope of nightlife. While the island has the usual plethora of Caribbean pseudo-cultural events comprising limbo dancing, belly dancing, fire-eating demonstrations and dancing on broken bottles barefoot, it also features high-quality theater performances. There are discos, English-style pubs, rum shops, and local dances with sound systems.

DINNER ENTERTAINMENT: Marriott's Sam Lord's Castle offers a special eight-course dinner in its antique dining room. The meal commemorates the banquet served to Queen Elizabeth II during her visit and is served on the Queen's china complemented with Waterford crystal. The **Shipwreck Party** features an outdoor buffet (flying fish, steak, chicken, salad, baked potatoes, etc.), a steel band, Egbert the fire eater, a flaming limbo duo, and Roslyn "the Golden Girl" calypso dancer. Yet another Sam Lord production is **Bajan Fiesta Night.** A "village" is created in the pool area with each hut offering a different speciality; a floor show follows. A **Night of the Buccaneers** takes place on Thurs. evenings at the Barbados Hilton; it showcases a performance by the Country Theater Workshop. The Ocean View features the seasonal **Xanadu Follies.** For other dinner and entertainment, see the "Theater" section.

ENGLISH-STYLE PUBS: There are a number of these, including the Mill Pub and Restaurant, The Windsor Arms, and the Cricketeers at Coconut Creek Hotel on the W coast.

CLUBS: The **Warehouse** was rebuilt after a devastating 1989 blaze and features an open-air terrace with the lights of Bridgetown gleaming in the background. It has live bands on its bandstand below. The **Waterfront Café** (similarly destroyed and rebuilt) is set right on the water's edge at the Careenage. It features entertainment focussing on jazz and folk almost every night. **Harbour Lights** (☎ 436-7225; open 9:30 PM-4:30 AM) – set right on the beach overlooking Carlisle Bay – offers dancing to live bands under the stars. The bands are on two to five nights per week; unlimited drinks (B$18 cover) are dispensed on Wed. There's a mostly youthful crowd here and a selective door keeps out hustlers; shorts and vests are prohibited. **13 Degrees**, on the beach at Hastings, offers bands and caters to a younger set.

The liveliest area on the island for nightlife is in St. Lawrence Gap. **After Dark** (☎ 435-6547) is unquestionably the island's classiest as well as its most iconoclastic club. The twin bars feature rows of hanging sparkling crystalware and fine mahogany and pine walls and counters. There are also beautiful chandeliers and plenty of mirrors. A passageway leads to the bar, which has comfortable stuffed armchairs. Open 5 PM-5:30 AM, After Dark caters to an older crowd and, unlike other clubs, it has a large local clientele.

To one side of After Dark is **The Reggae Lounge** (☎ 435-6462), a delightful outdoor bamboo-style disco frequented by beach boys and their clientele. This is a great place for people-watching. Karaoke is featured early on. Ladies are admitted free until 11 PM on Thurs. Cover (B$10) can be applied against your bar tab.

On the other side, the **Ship Inn** (☎ 435-6961) features bands nightly. Unfortunately, they play inside and the only dancing area is the narrow path right in front of them. Although it's another big beach-boy hangout – lotsa cool young dudes done up in dreads and gold chains. You might see tourists inside. The restaurant/bar area has a unique nautical atmosphere with eclectic displays of sea-oriented paraphernalia. Like the Reggae Lounge, the cover is redeemable in drinks. Some 400-500 people circulate here on Fri. and Sat. nights. Right around the bend, the **Watering Hole** has live music on weekend evenings. **Tapps** also has live music and karaoke. **B4 Blues** (☎ 435-6560) has live blues, generally on Thurs. night. The **Divi Southwinds Resort**, just down the road, has a floor show and buffet on Tues. nights.

The **Bagatelle Great House's restaurant** in St. Thomas converts into a sophisticated nightclub after hours. **The Beach Club** (☎ 432-1163) features a different band nightly and is the liveliest club in St. James in Holetown. In Paynes Bay, the **Coach House** (☎ 432-1163) has karaoke and jazz as well as other bands.

☞ Traveler's Tip
The Visitor Information Network (☎ 426-5017) provides taped information on cruises, clubs, shopping, tours, shows, and more.

LOCAL DANCES: These gatherings are one of the best ways to enjoy yourself and are found easily through posters and in the newspapers. Generally, they occupy small rectangles spread over a full page in the *Weekend Nation*. Each notice has picture(s) of the sponsor(s) along with their name(s), occupation(s), and where the dance will be held. The sponsors rent the place for the night, jack up the drink prices slightly, and charge B$3-5 admission. Attendance is the key to profit and, while a dance may lose money, it can make up to B$600 or so. The dances are divided into certain categories. A "dance" usually plays reggae, oldies, spouge, and calypso. A "grand dance" simply has a more impressive title. A "splash down" is frequently a more informal event, and a "supa fete" caters to a younger crowd and includes more dub music.

MOVIES: Kung fu, sex, and violence. This thematic threesome dominates the fare at the island's cinema, a hole-in-the-wall found in Bridgetown. Award winning films arrive on occasion, but *only* on occasion.

OTHERS: Baxter's Road is always fun and is known as "the street that never sleeps." It may be difficult *not* to hang out in local bars as there are an estimated 1,000 or more rum shops on the island. The Henry Bailey Observatory (see pages *) in Clapham opens its doors to stargazers every Fri. night. Church socials, listed in the paper, are a good way to meet locals.

CONCERTS: The major hall in Queen's Park is the Steel Shed. Inside, swirling ceiling fans hang from the rounded corrugated iron roof. The comfortable green upholstered chairs can be moved across the red painted concrete floor. The Queen's Park Theatre, in Queen's Park House just a bit farther on, shows plays on occasion. The Frank Collymore Hall, named after the eminent writer and linguist, is inside the Central Bank Building.

Sports and Recreation

Sports lovers can play golf, tennis, or ride horses, and there's a wealth of spectator sports too. Get a copy of the *Sports and Cultural Calendar* published annually by the Ministry of Tourism.

Water Sports

BEACHES AND SWIMMING: There are over 70 square miles of beaches that range from virgin white to coral pink in color. Seas are rougher along the Atlantic on the N and E coasts and you should exercise caution while swimming here. On the lee side, the W and S coasts are generally calm.

Don't swim after eating and don't allow your kids to swim unsupervised. Legally, all the island's beaches must have unrestricted access, but you can expect to pay for the use of beach chairs.

Selected Beaches

Accra Beach - A great place for socializing and peoplewatching. A car park is right at the beach. Food and rentals are available.

Casuarina Beach - A decent-sized beach at St. Lawrence Gap. Good windsurfing. Eat at Casuarina Beach Hotel.

Church Point - The Colony Club's beach. To get here, take the left turn N of St. James Church alongside Heron Bay to the Colony Club Hotel; park outside. Food is available at the Colony Club's beach terrace bar.

Crane Beach - Good bodysurfing at this beach which has cliffs and dunes. Park either at the Crane Beach Hotel or at the opposite end of the road. If you come by bus, it's a long walk. Steps lead to and from the hotel which charges an admission that may be applied to food or drink.

Foul Bay - Situated along a rugged stretch of coast, this long, wide beach has a number of fishing boats. Bring all your own food and drink. Great place to have a picnic.

Mullins Beach -This beautiful beach has blue water, good snorkelling, easy parking (on the main road), and the popular Mullins Beach Bar.

Paynes Bay - An attractive beach with good snorkeling and water sports. Park opposite the Coach House or by the Bamboo Beach Bar.

Sandy Beach - This attractive lagoon has calm, shallow water. Park at the public car park on the Worthing Road or go down one of the side roads next to the hotels. Ideal spot for families. Plenty of places to eat; weekends are lively.

Roman Miami Beach - Set at Oistins, this wide and very attractive beach is quite popular with locals.

Silver Sands Beach -Near the island's S point. It offers premium conditions for intermediate/advanced windsurfing.

Bottom Bay - This idyllic cove is a great picnic spot. It is to the N of Sam Lords. Park on the top and bring everything down.

Bathsheba/Cattlewash - Here, along the island's untamed Atlantic coast, you find miles of untouched beach. Surfing is great at Bathsheba. Swimming, however, is dangerous anywhere along this stretch. Food (and a car park) are available at Barclay's Park.

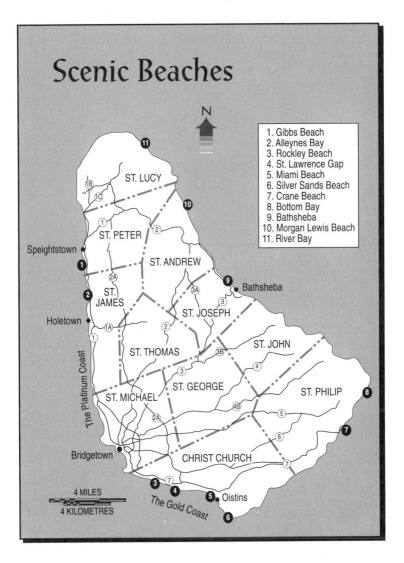

Scenic Beaches

N

1. Gibbs Beach
2. Alleynes Bay
3. Rockley Beach
4. St. Lawrence Gap
5. Miami Beach
6. Silver Sands Beach
7. Crane Beach
8. Bottom Bay
9. Bathsheba
10. Morgan Lewis Beach
11. River Bay

ST. LUCY

Speightstown

ST. PETER

ST. ANDREW

Bathsheba

ST. JAMES

Holetown

ST. JOSEPH

ST. JOHN

ST. THOMAS

ST. GEORGE

ST. PHILIP

ST. MICHAEL

The Platinum Coast

Bridgetown

CHRIST CHURCH

Oistins

4 MILES
4 KILOMETRES

The Gold Coast

SCUBA AND SNORKELING: Barbados is an exceptionally fine place to do either. A large number of companies offer instruction/rentals with PADI and/or NAUI certified teachers. If you're inexperienced in diving, expect to train for a few days in a swimming pool before heading into the open sea. Plan to spend about B$60-70 per one-tank dive, including boat fee. Gear is loaned out free of charge on excursion cruises. Other snorkelers would do well to bring their own equipment because gear rents for B$8-10 per hour. (Snorkeling gear is provided *gratis* on day-boat excursions.)

Locations for renting snorkeling and scuba equipment are numerous. **in St. Michael:** Dive Boat Safari (☎ 427-4350, 426-0200 ext. 395, after hours: 429-8216) at the Hilton on Needham Point has rates from B$70 for one dive (B$60 if you   have your own gear) and introductory and certification courses; The Dive Shop (☎ 426-9947) is near the Grand Barbados Beach Resort; Willie's Water Sports is at Colony Club (☎ 422-23350) and at Sunset Crest (☎ 432-7090). A PADI 5 Star training facility, Exploresub Barbados (☎ 435-6542, 428-7181 ext. 349, fax 428-4674) is in St. Lawrence Gap as is Scuba Barbados (☎ 435-6565). **in St. James:** Shades of Blue (☎ 422-3215, 432-2068) operates out of the Coral Reef Club; Blue Reef Watersports (☎ 422-3133) is at Glitter Bay; Sandy Lane Watersports is at the Sandy Lane Hotel (☎ 432-1311). **in Hastings:** Hazell's (☎ 426-4043, 436-5726 after hours), inside the Sandy Bank Complex, offers rentals and sales; Underwater Barbados (☎ 426-0655) offers five-10 dive packages. **excursions:** *Heatwave* (☎ 436-9060, 423-7871), a 57-ft. catamaran, offers day trips, as do *Tiami* and *Wind Warrior* (☎ 427-7245, fax 431-0538); the latter two offer lunch cruises as well as afternoon snorkel cruises. The *Why Not* (☎ 427-1043, 429-8580 after hours, fax 427-6007) will also take you snorkeling.

Free Spirit Cruises and Water Sports (☎ 420-3286/0890) has two locations (Pebbles Beach and Carlisle Bay Center) and offers one-day packages for B$80. These include snorkeling, windsurfing, Hobie cat and sunfish sailing, and glass-bottom boat trips.

The ruins of the deliberately-sunken freighter *Stavronikita* lie at the Folkestone National Marine Reserve. For information on scuba diving there, call Brian Stanley at the Barbados Subaqua Club, ☎ 427-5190.

SURFING: The E coast is famous for its waves. Surfing spots include Bathsheba, just inland from Bow Bells reef off South Point; Gravesend near the Hilton; Rockley Beach (on the SW coast between Worthing and St. Lawrence); and Enterprise Beach near Oistins.

WINDSURFING: Conditions are said to be among the best in the world. Try the Watersports Centre (☎ 436-3549) at the Hilton; Club Mistral (☎ 428-7277, fax 428-2878); Benston Windsurfing Club (☎ 428-9095); Silverrock Windsurfing Rentals (☎ 428-2866) at Christ Church; and Jolly Roger Water Sports (436-6424) in St. James. Steady breezes at Maxwell, Silver Sands, and Round Rock offer perfect conditions. Expect to spend around B$90 pd or B$360 pw to rent a board.

FISHING: Some of the best fishing is off the N and S coasts. The prize catch is blue marlin. Offshore anglers can reel in yellowtail, snapper, mackerel, jacks, small barracuda, snook, and tarpon.

DEEP-SEA FISHING: Yellowfin tuna, dolphin (dorado), mackerel, bonefish, sailfish, barracuda, yellowfish, blue marlin, and wahoo are common here. Charters (available for half- or full-day) include *Bill Fisher II* (☎ 431-0741; Bridge House Wharf, Bridgetown); Blue Jay Charters (☎ 422-2098); Dive Shop Ltd. (☎ 426-9947); Cannon Charters (☎ 424-6107; St. James); Jolly Roger (☎ 436-6424); *Loisan II* (☎ 427-5485); Sandy Lane (☎ 432-1311); Cap'n Jack (☎ 427-5800-02 / 428-2793); Southern Palms (426-7171); *La Paloma* (☎ 427-5588 / 429-5643); Challenge (☎ 436-5725); the *Barracuda* (☎ 426-7252 / 7898); and Pakis Water Sports (☎ 426-9947, 4262031 after hours) in St. Michael. You'll pay between B$300 and B$450 per half-day.

SEA EXCURSIONS: Many boat trips are available. Most include lunch and or cocktails as well as transportation to and from your hotel. *The Bajan Queen* (☎ 436-6424) offers water cruises, as does the *Jolly Roger* (☎ 436-6424). Both have a party atmosphere, a buffet meal, a live band, and free use of snorkeling gear. The *Jolly Roger* serves free booze. *The Bajan Queen* has a rope by which you can drop right into the water. Sailboats and yachts (see below) offer more intimate excursions.

NIGHT CRUISES: These are usually party, party, and more party. With unlimited free booze and a live band, a good time is had by all. *The Bajan Queen* (☎ 436-6424) caters to a mixed crowd and features a live reggae band and a Bajan buffet dinner. Her sleek red and white hull leaves at 6 PM. Transport is provided to and from your hotel. The *Jolly Roger* (☎ 436-6424) appeals to the college set and features the renowned local group The Merrymen on Thurs. nights. The *Irish Mist* (☎ 436-9201, 436-7639 eve.) offers a sunset cruise, as does the *Why Not* (☎ 427-1043, 429-8580 after hours, fax 427-6007).

GLASS-BOTTOM BOATS: This type of trip is best on the W coast with its calmer sea. There are a number of private firms on the beach offering trips. Try Blue Reef Watersports (☎ 422-3133), Dive Shop, Ltd. (☎ 426-9947), Jolly Roger Watersports (☎ 432-7090), and Sandy Lane (☎ 432-1311).

SAILING: Conditions are excellent and huge catamarans and yachts are available for charter. Catamarans include the 52-ft. (17-m) *Irish Mist II* (☎ 436-9201), the 42-ft. (14-m) *Wind Warrior* (☎ 436-5725), and the 60-ft. (20-m) *Tiami* (☎ 427-SAIL). Also, try the luxury yacht *Carib Girl* (☎ 427-1655); the 56-ft. (18-m) yacht, *Station Break* (☎ 426-9502); *Carie-Dee* (☎ 422-2319); and *Sin-Bad* (☎ 425-9346). Call the Barbados Cruising Club (☎ 426-4434) and the Barbados Yacht Club (☎ 427-1135/427-7318) for information on others. Both clubs sponsor regattas from Jan. to May. Hobie craft and other small fry may be rented on the beaches; venues include those at the Hilton, Royal Pavilion, Sandy Lane, and Paradise Beach hotels.

PARASAILING: Ever hung suspended over water 200 feet up in the air by a parachute? Here is your chance! It costs about B$50-60 for a five- to 10-min. lesson and is surprisingly safe.

REGATTAS: Several yacht races are held each year. The highlight is the Atlantic Rally for Cruisers (ARC), which attracts over 200 yachts from Gran Canaria for the dramatic climax. Many of these stay for the Mount Gay Regatta which is held around Christmas time.

Land Sports

GOLF: The Rockley Resort Hotel's greens (☎ 435-7873, fax 435-8268) were originally opened as a nine-hole course in 1946. They were re-designed to form an 18-hole course later on. It's now known as the **Rockley Golf and Country Club** and is open 7-3 on weekdays and on weekends by prior arrangement. The **Sandy Lane Golf Club** (☎432-1145, fax 432-2954/2462) is just outside Bridgetown in St. James and has an 18-hole course that is in the process of being expanded to 36. Hole # 7 is said to be one of the prettiest in the world. Stars who have played here include Frank Sinatra, George Harrison, and Ringo Star. Politicos gracing the course have included Gerald Ford and a host of Lords. The three-day Sandy Lane Open, the Barbados Golf Association's main annual event, is played here in Nov. The **Royal Westmoreland Golf and Country Club** (☎ 422-4653) is owned by Pemberton Resorts and opened in 1995. Its 27-hole course sprawls over 100 acres in the hills overlooking the Pemberton hotels of Royal Pavilion and Glitter Bay. It cost US$30 million to build and was designed by Robert Trent Jones, Jr. Facilities include a clubhouse and restaurant; 300 luxury villas border the course. Another nine-hole course is at the former Heywoods Resort in St. Peter, now called **Almond Beach Village**. The course is open only to its guests as well as those of sister resort Almond Beach Club. **Belair** (☎ 423-4653), in St. Philip near Sam Lord's Castle, is a par 3, 18-hole course that charges B$40 for 18 holes; club rentals and weekly memberships are available.

Finally, five more courses on the island's S coast are planned. Check with the Tourism Authority regarding their status.

Major Sporting Competitions

JANUARY
Race-walking: Annual Carlton and A-One 5000 Safari.
Soccer: Barbados Football Association's Preliminary, Shell Caribbean Club.
Horseracing: Asia International Jockey Championship, Barbados Turf Club.
Squash: Barbados Squash Rackets Association, Mutual Inter-Club League.
Cricket: Barbados Cricket Association, Red Stripe Geddes Grant Regional Cricket series.
Yachting: Mount Gay Atlantic/Barbados Challenge.

FEBRUARY
Squash: Barbados Squash Rackets Association Mutual Inter Club League.
Cricket: Barbados Cricket Association, Red Stripe and Geddes Grant Regional Cricket Series.
Football: Barbados Football Association Friendly International.
Horseracing: Elegant Resorts of Barbados Race Day / The Cave Shepherd 5000.

MARCH
Squash: Barbados Squash Rackets Association.
Horseracing: Cockspur Cup, Barbados Guineas.

APRIL
Squash: Barbados Squash Rackets Association, Barbados Squash Club Open Championships at Marine Courts, Christ Church. Barbados Fire & General Insurance Junior National Championships.
Soccer: Barbados Football Association Shell Cup Finals.

MAY
Squash: Barbados Squash Rackets Association, Barbados Fire & General Insurance Junior and National Championships.
Horseracing: Royal Barbados Police Force Trophy.

JUNE
Cricket: Barbados Cricket Association Competition.
Hockey: Barbados Invitational Champion Hockey Challenge.
Squash: Barbados Squash Rackets Association Classic.
Horseracing: Barbados Fire & General Trophy.
Volleyball: Barbados Volleyball Association Competitions.
Cricket: Barbados Cricket Association Competition.
Hockey: Barbados Invitational Champion Hockey Challenge.

JULY
Cricket: Shield Competition (alternate Sundays), Sir Garfield Sobers International Schools Tournament.
Squash: CLICO Open Championship, Rockley, Christ Church.
Soccer: Champion of Champions Game and Presentation.
Yachting: Annual Banks Regatta.

AUGUST
Hockey: Banks International Hockey Festival.
Horseracing: United Insurance Derby.
Volleyball: East Versus West Summer Slam.

SEPTEMBER
Volleyball: All St. Michael Volleyball Tournament.
Swimming: Barbados International Masters Swimming Championship.

OCTOBER
Cricket: Fred Rumsey Pro-Am Festival.
Swimming: Barbados International Masters Swimming Championship.

NOVEMBER
Soccer: Barbados Football Association's World Cup Tournament.
Judo: Barbados/South Caribbean Independence Games.
Surfing: Barbados Surfing Association 1994 Caribbean Cup.

DECEMBER
Soccer: Barbados Football Association Cup Finals.
Golf: United Insurance Open Tournament.

TENNIS: The island has an abundance of courts. A parish-by-parish list follows: Paragon Tennis Club (on Brittons Hill) and Cunard Paradise Beach, both in St. Michael; Casuarina Beach Club, Rockley Resort Hotel, and Southwinds Hotel and Beach Club in Christ Church; Crane Beach Hotel and Ginger Bay Hotel and Beach Club in St. Philip; Sandy Lane Hotel and Sunset Crest Club in St. James; and Cobblers Cove and Heywoods in St. Peter. Typical charges are B$12-16 per hr. In addition to those found at hotels, public hard and grass courts are maintained at Folkestone Park in Holetown and at the Garrison.

SQUASH: Courts can be found at the Barbados Squash Club, Rockley Resort Hotel, and Casuarina Beach Club in Christ Church; Heywoods in St. Peter; and a number of other locations.

HORSEBACK RIDING: English-style riding along scenic trails is available. **Highland Adventure Tours** (☎ 438-8069, fax 438-8070) offers trail rides. **Beau Geste Farm** (☎ 429-0139) in St. George has rides that include jumping; one hr. is B$53; a two-hour ride (including a half-hour tour of Francia Plantation) is B$100. **Brighton Riding Stable** (☎ 425-9381) in Black Rock, St. Michael offers rides for B$50 with transportation and B$45 without. **Caribbean International Riding Centre** (☎ 420-1246) is located in Auburn, St. Joseph. It charges B$30 ph for lessons and has gully rides (B$55), a trip to Hackleton's Cliff (B$110), and a ride to Villa Nova, which includes lunch and tour (B$175).

AEROBICS AND NAUTILUS: For those who are worried about missing their workout while on vacation, there's no reason to fret; a number of facilities offer classes. Contact Body Electric Exercise Studio (☎ 428-1890, Maxwell Rd.); Profile Health and Beauty Club (☎ 432-1393, Holetown); Sunfit Gym & Health Club (☎ 436-1024, Barbados Hilton Hotel); Speightstown Mall's Paramount (☎ 422-0721); and the Universal Health Club (☎ 438-8950, Windsor Hotel, Hastings).

BRIDGE: The Barbados Bridge League in Belleville welcomes vistors to its games of duplicate bridge held from Mon. to Thurs. and on Sat., ☎ 427-4839.

HIKING: The island, although not a hiker's paradise, has a number of paths, many of which run along the gorgeous Atlantic coast. A good pair of shoes is essential as the crusty coral coastline can be sharp. Bring a small water bottle because there are no facilites. One of the great conveniences for the walker or hiker is the now-antiquated standpipe where you can get a refreshing blast of clear, clean coral-filtered water.

From Jan. through Mar. the Barbados National Trust (☎ 426-2421) and the Duke of Edinburgh Award Scheme host early Sun. morning (6 AM) rural five-mile walks. Usually, you assemble in front of an old sugar plantation. It's an excellent way to meet Bajans and fellow travelers; around 300 participate. Walkers are divided into three groups: fast, medium, and slow.

Cricket

If one passion can be ascribed to Bajans, it must be love for this, the national sport. It's never hard to catch a match. If it's not going on along some back road, then you'll find an elite International Test Match (usually played between Jan. and April) or a club match in the first division competition (May to mid-Dec.). Barbados is famous for its almost religious reverence for the sport and has given the world the three "Ws" – Frank Worrell, Everton Weekes, and Clyde Walcott. The game is tightly interwoven with the island's moral fabric and is considered by some to be the national religion. The expression "it's not cricket" stands as a byword for upright moral conduct. It is one of society's unifying bonds and has been partially responsible for taking the island's stratified and isolated classes and bringing them together – a process which was a necessary precursor to independence.

HISTORY: Cricket reflected society's tiered apartheid-like structure and was originally the exclusive cultural property of the upper classes. The Wanderers, formed in 1877, along with its successor, Pickwick, were both white as a ghost in composition. But, while the former catered to the merchants, Pickwick drew its membership from the plantocracy. Another team, Spartan, maintained the "class" standards and drew from the growing pool of black and mulatto professionals. Its blackballing of black public health inspector Herman Griffith – because they felt that he was below their social station – led dissidents to found the Empire Club. Griffith, one of the game's classic players, became the first black to captain a Bajan team. This upper-class Bridgetown-centered sport soon spread island-wide. Workers, farmers, and carpenters took an interest and founded their own leagues; plantation overseers encouraged their workers to play – often providing a field and second-hand equipment – because they saw its importance as a form of social bonding. Of course, the *pukka* Barbados Cricket Association turned up its nose at these lower class leagues, but the spirited rivalry between plantations gave birth to the Barbados Cricket League – a revolutionary event which initialized the process of breaking down class and racial barriers. However, the true lower class was still excluded from participation.

CRICKET HEROES AND MASCOTS: Cricket has thrived to the point that Bajan's greatest heroes are cricketers. Frank Worley, one of the three "Ws," was knighted by Queen Elizabeth in 1964, and he peers from the face of the B$5 bill. Lethal left-hander Garfield Sobers – whom no less a personage than the Mighty Sparrow, the mightiest living calypsonian, has dubbed "the greatest cricketer on earth or on Mars" – was knighted by the Queen on the Garrison Savannah, where some of the earliest recorded matches took place. Today, to be a cricket hero results in moola as well as hoopla: a top star may receive B$50,000 per year, a fortune in Bajan economic terms. Even top players of lesser standing can find jobs teaching and coaching abroad with relative ease. Flannagan, a traveling mascot, entertained followers by attacking opponents during the

30s and 40s. Today, King Dyal – unfailingly dressed in a flashy three-piece suit – regularly appears, as he has for over three decades, to root for the opposition!

CRICKET TODAY: The sport's popularity remains high if not fanatical, despite the slight slip in performance. You'll see Bajan youth practicing everywhere, using anything that remotely resembles equipment to sharpen their skills. Cricket remains one of the few outlets for social mobility available to them. Taken together, the Association and the League, the two main cricket clubs, host 100 matches on Sat. afternoons between early June and mid-Sept. International matches are major events lasting five days (10:30 AM to 5:30 PM daily). Bajans picnic on the grounds, munching on local cuisine and shipping it down with hits of rum. You can count on Kensington Oval, the largest ground, being crammed to its 15,000 capacity on Test Match days when the local team faces off against Australia or England. Local club matches may pack in crowds as large as 4,000 to the smaller grounds. For current information, call the Barbados Cricket Association, ☎ 436-1397.

Spectator-Only Sports

In addition to cricket, Bajans are afficianadoes of other spectator sports. The new **Sir Garfield Sobers Athletic Center** in Wildey, St. Michael is certain to expand the quality and quantity of athletics in Barbados. This B$22 million athletic center features, among other things, a 4,000-seat stadium, and an Olympic-sized swimming pool. It was constructed by the Chinese government, who forked over B$16 million of the cost, and was opened on Independence Day 1992. The center caters to 12 different sports ranging from judo to boxing to basketball to bodybuilding.

HORSERACING: Garrison Savannah has been the primary location of horseracing for over eight decades and hosts the Barbados Turf Club's two annual seasons (from Jan. to May and from Aug. to Nov.) on alternate Saturdays. Entrance to the grandstand is B$10. **The Cockspur Gold Cup** usually takes place in early Mar. and includes competition from Trinidad, Martinique, and Jamaica. For information call 426-3980.

POLO: The Barbados Polo Club (☎ 432-1802) plays on Sat., Sun. and Wed. during the Aug.-to-April season on its grounds at Holders, St. James. Admission is B$5. Polo is also played at Brighton Stables in St. Michael.

SOCCER: This is one of the most popular sports. **The Barbados Cup** is the largest youth international soccer tournament. It is held annually in April.

HOCKEY: Both men and women play hockey during the local hockey season, which begins around the end of May and lasts until sometime in Nov. **The Banks Beer International Hockey Festival**, now in its second decade, is held annually in Aug. or from Aug. to Sept. Coordinator is Mike Owen (☎ 436-3911).

RUGBY: The **Barbados Rugby Club** is affiliated with the Twickenham Rugby Union and competes regularly against visiting teams and naval ships. For more information, contact Victor Roach (☎ 436-6883).

ROAD TENNIS: This sport is believed to have been invented here during the 1950s. It falls somewhere between table and lawn tennis and is played with a homemade wooden paddle and a tennis ball with its fur removed. The "net" consists of a long piece of wood with crude feet attached. It was recognized as a national sport in 1976 and has its own association, the Barbados Road Tennis Association, which organizes matches on a regular basis.

RUNNING: The **Run Barbados International Road Race Series** is held the first week in Dec. There are two courses. One follows a 26-mile (42,195 m) marathon along paved roads by the sea, and the second is a 10-km run in and around Bridgetown. It attracts competitors wordwide. Top prizes include airfare and hotel accommodation for the next year's race.

RACE WALKING: Barbados is the only nation in the world with a race-walking competition. The **Annual Carlton and A-One 5000 Safari** generally takes place on the sand track of the Garrison Savannah on Jan. 21 (Earl Barrow Day). It covers 35 laps and begins at 6 AM.

VOLLEYBALL: The Barbados Volleyball Association is heading into its second decade. It holds a number of events, including the **Trevor-Griffith Match** for the two top mens' teams and the **Peter Went Match** for the two top women's teams. The Association also participates in the Caribbean Tournament.

SOFTBALL: The more than 100 softball leagues – which play a modified version of the game using tennis balls and mahogany bats – hold contests on Sun. mornings.

Opposite: Big grins from a young St. Lucy resident

Above: St. Lawrence Gap, Christ Church

Below: Goat traffic jam

Above: Atlantis Submarine, Bridgetown

Below: Harvesting sugar

Above: Bottom Bay, St. Philip
Opposite: Crop Over celebrations
Below: Gun Hill Signal Station, St. George

Above: Harrison's Cave, St. Thomas Parish
Opposite: Bajan schoolchildren
Below: Traditional Chattel house

THIS STATUE WAS ERECTED BY
THE GOVERNMENT AND PEOPLE
OF BARBADOS TO COMMEMORATE
THE 150TH. ANNIVERSARY OF
THE ABOLITION OF SLAVERY
AND THE EMANCIPATION OF
BARBADIANS FROM THE INSTI -
TUTION OF SLAVERY.

THIS STATUE WAS UNVEILED BY

THE PRIME MINISTER
THE HON. H.B. ST. JOHN, Q.C., M.P.
ON
28 MARCH 1985

BODYBUILDING: Barbados is home to some of the world's most famous bodybuilders and many Bajans have won the Mr. World and Mr. Universe contests. **The Barbados Amateur Body Building Association** holds the Pine Hill Champion of Champions, the Independence Championships, and other events.

Conduct

Everyone tends to dress conservatively. If you want to be accepted and respected, dress accordingly. Bathing attire is unsuitable on main streets, as is revealing female clothing. Going shirtless or wearing too-short shorts is also *verboten* on streets. There are a few louts about, but Bajans are among the most polite, gracious, and hospitable people in the entire Caribbean, if not the world. Traditional Bajan culture focuses on politeness. Inquiries are usually prefaced by a "Good Morning," "Good Afternoon," or "Good Evening." These simple courtesies go a long way. Contact with the outside has brought some hustle and bustle, but the island still has the feel of a large village.

Be sure to ask people's permission before taking their picture. Generally, adults are reluctant and some feel that you are going to make fun of them, others that you are somehow financially benefitting. Children are willing subjects.

Respect private property while visiting ruins and be sure to ask permission first. All beaches on Barbados are public by law from the vegetation line down to the water. Certain hotels have attempted to restrict usage by charging an entrance fee; you can circumvent paying by entering the beach area to the side. Expect to be charged if you use private facilities like lounge chairs or changing rooms. Remember that you are sharing the beach: don't litter or make excessive noise. Expect to find hustlers hassling you on the beach. The most effective treatment is to firmly say "no thank you." Viewing the merchandise will only draw the interchange out, and you may end up buying something just to make them go away!

ENVIRONMENTAL CONDUCT: Dispose of plastics properly. Remember that six-pack rings, plastic bags, and fishing lines can cause injury or prove fatal to sea turtles, fish, and birds. Unable to regurgitate anything they swallow, turtles and other sea creatures may mistake plastic bags for jellyfish or choke on fishing lines. Birds may starve to death after becoming entangled in nets and plastic rings. Buying black coral jewelry supports reef destruction.

Opposite: "The Freed Slave," St. Barnabas Roundabout

To protect your own hide, never go snorkeling without tieing a float (such as a bright beach ball or a white plastic container) to your wrist or ankle to serve as a warning to speedboat or jetski drivers. Correspondingly, jetskiers should keep a keen eye out for snorkelers and should bear in mind that most people come to the beach to *escape* hustle and bustle. Those interested in preserving the environment should contact the **Barbados Environmental Association** (☎ 427-0619; Box 132, Bridgetown). They have occasional lectures at the Barbados Museum as well as nature walks.

UNDERSEA CONDUCT: Respect the natural environment. Take nothing and remember that corals are easily broken. Much damage has already been done to the reef through snorkelers either standing on coral or hanging onto outcroppings. Stony corals grow less than half an inch per year and it can take decades to repair the damage caused by a moment of carelessness. Keep well away just for your own protection: many corals retaliate with stings and their sharp ridges can cause slow-healing cuts. Make sure that you are properly weighted prior to your dive to ensure full control. Swim calmly and fluidly through the water and avoid dragging your console and/or octopus (secondary breathing device) behind you. Resist the temptation to touch fish. Many of them (such as the porcupine) secrete a mucous coating to protect them from bacterial infection. Touching them removes this coating and can result in death. Avoid feeding fish, which can disrupt the natural ecosystem. If you're diving, be sure you have a realistic appraisal of your own abilities and pay attention to decompression and other factors. In short, look, listen, enjoy, but leave only bubbles.

BOATING CONDUCT: Always exercise caution while anchoring a boat. Improperly anchoring can destroy wide swatches of seagrass, which take a long time to recover. If there's no buoy available, pick a sandy spot that will cause relatively little environmental impact. Tying your boat to mangroves can kill the trees so it is acceptable to do so only during a storm. Maintain the engine and keep the bilge clean. These two precautions help eliminate the unecessary discharge of oil. If you notice oil in your bilge, use oil-absorbent pads to soak it up. Be careful not to overfill the boat when fueling. Emulsions from petrochemical products stick to fishes' gills and suffocate them, and deposits in sediment impede the development of marine life. Detergents affect plankton and other organisms, which throws off the food chain. Avoid using harsh chemicals such as ammonia and bleach while cleaning your boat; they pollute the water and kill marine life. Use environmentally-safe cleaning products whenever possible; paint containing lead, copper (which can make molluscs poisonous), mercury (highly toxic to fish and algae), or TBT should not be used. When you approach seagrass beds, slow down because your propellor could strike a sea turtle. Avoid maneuvering your boat too close to coral reefs as striking the reef can damage both your boat and the reef. Avoid stirring up sand in shallow coral areas. The sand can be deposited in the coral and cause polyps to suffocate and die. If your boat has a sewage holding tank, empty it only at properly-equipped marinas. Finally, remember that a diver down flag should be displayed while diving or snorkeling.

Barbados Dos and Don'ts

Don't condescend to locals. Do treat the local people with the same respect you would like to be treated with yourself. Allow them the courtesy of answering at their own pace.

Do try local food and try to patronize local restaurants as well as gourmet bistros and those of resorts.

Don't make promises you can't or don't intend to keep. Don't make local children into beggars by acting like Santa Claus and dispensing gifts and money. In general, refrain from giving out money: it creates a cycle of dependency and creates more problems than it solves.

Don't just stay lounging around your hotel. Do get around and explore, but don't over-extend yourself and try to do too much; There's always the next visit.

Try to conserve energy by switching off lights and a/c when you leave your hotel room.

Don't dump your garbage at sea or litter in town. Do protect the environment and set a good example for others.

Don't remove or injure any coral, spear fish, remove tropical fish, or annoy turtles or touch their eggs. Do not feed fish or disturb monkeys.

ORGANIZATIONS: The **Barbados National Trust** (☎ 426-2421, 436-9033, fax 429-9055; 10th Av. Belleville, St. Michael) is the island's major historical and environmental conservation organization. They run eight properties on the island and produce the Barbados Heritage Passport as well as organizing hikes and other activities. The **Caribbean Conservation Association** (☎ 426-5373/9635/9633, fax 429-8483) is a regional non-profit NGO with

19 members; its headquarters are in Savannah Lodge in the Garrison. Members (US$15 minimum for associate membership) receive the quarterly publication, *Caribbean Conservation News*.

Services and Information

TELEPHONE: Barbados, unlike some other islands, has a fairly reliable phone system and a good supply of pay phones. In fact, the first phone service in Bridgetown started in 1883, only 11 years after its invention. To use a pay phone, wait for a dial tone *before* inserting your 25 cents; calls are limited to five minutes, after which you'll need another coin. Local calls made from your hotel room are free. Card phones are available at limited locations – including the airport, Carlisle Bay Centre, and the harbor. They use a pre-paid phone card, which makes them ideal for overseas calls. For local information, call 119. The island's area code is 809.

BROADCASTING AND MEDIA: The two major dailies are *The Advocate* and *The Nation*. *The Advocate's* motto – spread across a narrow scroll folded into divisions – lies right under its blue banner:

"For the cause that lacks assistance/against the wrongs that need resistance/for the future in the distance/and the good that I can too."

Regrettably, it's all downhill after the motto. The paper relies heavily on sensationalistic headlines with minimal coverage of the world outside Barbados. One suspects that they must be big Nancy Reagan fans because "Just Say No to Drugs" is frequently interspersed throughout the pages. The always hilarious *Weekend Investigator* is also a product of the *Advocate's* newsroom with its pink on yellow masthead and a ubiquitous "dainty, vivacious, and sexy" cover girl. It resembles an American soft porn magazine of the 1950s and is considered outrageous by the island's prim and proper. The letters column will have you rolling on the floor in stitches. Its photographers also exploit young women (domesticand foreign) by shooting them on the beaches and in the discos. Its weekend edition features the right-wing rantings of columnist Gladstone Holder, a Lyndon La Rouche defender. The *Nation* is slighty better than the *Advocate*, but only slightly. Its most controversial and outspoken columnist is Jeanette-Layne Clark. The excellent monthly *Caribbean* is more independent and radical than the dailies. *Contact* is an ecumenical newspaper that offers news and views from around the Caribbean. *Bim*, published twice a year, is the Caribbean's leading literary journal. *Caribbean Week* has Caribbean news and many travel pieces. The *West Indies Chronicle*, published by the West India Committee in London, and *British Trade Topics*, published by the British High Commission in Port of Spain, are also available. Tourist literature of value includes the annuals *Time Out in Barbados* magazine, *The Ins and Outs of Barbados*, and the bi-weeklies *The Sun Seeker* and *The Visitor* – as well as the monthly calendar-format tabloid *What's On*. Imported newspapers and magazines are unconscionably expensive. Two rags with suprisingly high circulation given their dear price are *The National Enquirer* and the amusing *Weekly World News*. Two papers are imported from Trinidad – *The Sunday Punch* ("The Love Paper") and *The Bomb* – which make the local press seem intellectual!

radio stations: The state-owned Caribbean Broadcasting Corporation (CBC) has one AM station (CBC, 900 AM) and one FM (Liberty, 98.1). The Barbados Broadcasting Service operates BBS, 90.7 FM and Faith FM at 102.1. Barbados Redifusion Service operates VOB at 790 AM, Yess Ten Four at 104.1 FM and a wired service feauring the "*Voice of Barbados*" program (790 AM).

television: The CBC introduced TV service (Channel 8) in 1964. There are roughly 200 TVs for every 1,000 Bajans. CNN shows from 6-10 AM, Mon. to Fri. and weekends from 9-1. Broadcasting hours are 5 PM to 11:45 PM Mon. to Fri., and 1 PM to 12:30 AM on Sat. and Sun. There's also a cable system.

Signal Stations

Information dissemination was a problem in the days before telephones, automobiles, and surfaced roads, particularly in a place where white slaveowners were outnumbered by their slaves. The island's chain of signal stations was first constructed with internal security interests in mind. It is thought that the Rebellion of 1816 spurred their erection, and the chain was built between 1818 and 1819. There were five stations: Highgate, Gun Hill, Dover Fort, Moncrieffe, Cotton Tower, and Grenade Hall. Signalling was performed with semaphore arms and flags. They were used to announce the arrivals of ships. When the telephone arrived in 1883, the towers swiftly lost their purpose and fell into disuse. Only Highgate (next to Banks Brewery in St. Michael) survived, but it was closed in 1961. Today, Gun Hill, Cotton Tower, and Grenade Hall have been restored and are open to the public. They provide some of the nation's best scenic lookouts.

INFORMATION: Tourist information centers are in Bridgetown, at the harbor's cruise ship terminal, and at the airport. The best map is the 1/50,000 scale government Ordnance Survey map with an index prepared by the National Trust, but the ordinary give-away one will be adequate for most travelers. A number of self-service laundromats are in the major towns and resort areas; one-hour and same-day laundry services are also available. The Rape and Crisis Center provides confidential counseling and referrals. It's open Mon. to Thurs., 6-9 PM, and Fri. to Sun., 6 PM-6 AM.

POSTAL SERVICE: District Post Offices stand in every parish (see chart). Put outgoing mail in red pillar postal boxes. Parcel post packages may be mailed from the General Post Office headquarters in Cheapside, Bridgetown. An express service guarantees delivery within 48 hours. Collectors will want to visit the Philatelic Bureau. With a deposit account, first day covers will be mailed to you.

hours: The GPO is open Mon. to Fri. from 7:30-5, and the branches are open Mon. 7:30-noon, 1-3, and Tues. to Fri. 8-noon and 1-3:15.

rates: USA Airmail $0.90 (first 10 g); postcard $0.65. Canada Airmail $0.90; postcard $0.65. Britain Airmail $1.10; postcard $0.70. Caribbean Airmail $0.70; postcard $0.45.

Post Offices

General Post Office
Cheapside, Bridgetown
436-4800
Fax: 429-8178

Welchman Hall
St. Thomas
438-6749

Grantley Adams
International Airport
428-7101

Belleplaine
St. Andrew
422-9219

Eagle Hall
St. Michael
426-1029

Horse Hill
St. Joseph
433-1319

Oistins
Christ Church
428-9534

Benthams
St. Lucy
439-8417

Welches
St. Michael
429-2436

Four Roads
St. Johns
433-1323

Worthing
Christ Church
435-7420

Folkestone
St. James
422-0325

Crittons Hill
St. Michael
426-5432

Six Roads
St. Philip
423-6204

Queen Street
St. Peter
422-2163

LIBRARIES: The **Central Public Library** (☎ 426-1744) stands next to the Law Courts on Coleridge St., Bridgetown. It's open Mon. to Sat., 9-5. Among its treasures are old books and newspapers about Barbados which may be examined. Branches are located in Christ Church, St. George, St. James, St. Peter, St. Philip, and St. Thomas parishes. Books may be borrowed for a B$20 refundable deposit.

NUPTIALS: Getting married is a big industry here and there are a number of places to do it – from aboard a yacht to the chapel of your choice. There is a three-day residency requirement (you will need to wait three days after receiving the license to get married) along with a B$100 charge for a marriage license that must be accompanied by a B$13 revenue stamp obtainable from any post office. If you are not a Catholic, you will be required to produce a) valid passports or copies of birth certificates, b) a copy of marriage and death certificate if either partner was married previously and widowed, and c) a Decree Absolute or a Final Judgment (not a Decree Nisi) if either partner has been divorced. The Decree Absolute must be translated into English if it is in a foreign language.

HAIR STYLISTS: Primadonna (☎ 435-7303) offers "hair designs," manicure, and pedicure. The **Hair Club Beauty Salon** (☎ 427-9655, 436-2165) specializes in services for "women of colour." **The Palms** (☎ 428-8712), in the Southern Palms at St. Lawrence Gap, offers hair and beauty treatments, facials, massages, and more. More can be found in the Yellow Pages. A popular beach activity is hair braiding.

EMBASSIES: The US consular section is on the first floor of Trident House in Bridgetown, ☎ 426-3574. The Canadian High Commission stands at Bishops Court Hill, St. Michael, ☎ 429-3550. The U.K.'s address is Lower Collymore Rock, St. Michael, ☎ 426-3525. The Federal Republic of Germany is at Banyan Court, Bay St., St. Michael, ☎ 427-1876.

Shopping

Stores are generally open Mon. through Sat. from 8-4, with some of them closing for an hour in the afternoon. Things are pretty much dead on Sun. and it may be difficult to find a food market open. Other than local handicrafts, there isn't much to buy that can't be found cheaper (or at nearly the same price) somewhere else.

Two of the best sources for local crafts are the Women's Self Help Cooperative (see below) and Artscraft (inside Da Costas). Another option is Pride Craft (inside Speedbird House). Unmistakably Bajan souvenirs include rum and *falernum*. Coffee liqueurs and punch de creme (rum and cream sold in the cruise ship terminal) are unique gifts.

One of the nicer things to carry back with you is some "dark crystal" sugar. The "brown sugar" sold in the US is actually bleached sugar darkened with molasses, but this is the genuine article. Dorly manufactures rum in bottles shaped like Barbados Harbour policemen for those who looking for something out of the ordinary. And, to please that stamp collecting relative, don't forget to visit the philatelic bureau inside the General Post Office at Cheapside, Bridgetown. Finally, a less conventional (and quite educational) way to buy local goods is to visit one of the many auctions; these are published in the classified section of the Sun. newspaper.

CRAFTS: These are found in Pelican Village on the Princess Anne Highway near Bridgetown as well as in many of the island's shops. Handicrafts include pottery, woven baskets, rugs, mats, coconut shell accessories, straw and *khus-khus* fans, bottle baskets, mahogany crafts, plus shell and coral jewelery. The best place to buy crafts and souvenirs is at the **Women's Self Help Cooperative**, located on Broad St. near the Careenage. It was founded in 1907 by Lady Gilbert Carter and is open Mon. to Fri. 8-4, and Sat. 8-12. Cooperative members sell a wide variety of goods, including local pottery, crochet work, loupha-fashioned dolls, home-produced peanut butter, stewed guava, guava jelly, gooseberry syrup, local cherry wine, and other delights. One major handicraft venue is **Temple Yard** in Bridgetown where the Rastas present their arts and crafts. **Chalky Mount** in St. Andrew produces traditional pottery. **Earthworks Potteries** is where ceramicist Goldies Spieler turns heaps of clay into everything from chattel houses to microwave-safe modern cookware. **Bridgetown's Articrafts**, inside Norman Centre on Broad St., features the work of artist, designer, and handweaver

Roslyn Watson who is noted for her tapestries and basketry. **Best of Barbados** is a chain of shops islandwide that showcases the varied work of Jill Walker and offers a good selection of artwork and books (including this one). **Daphne's Sea Shell Studio** (☎ 423-6180) on "Congo Rd." in St. Philip offers shell-decorated items as well as hand-painted clothing. **Wild Feathers** (☎ 423-7758) is also in St. Philip at Long Bay; it's right near Sam Lord's Castle – just follow the signs. It features carvings and paintings of native and migrant birds. **Mango Jam** (☎/fax 427-0287), at #1 Pavilion Court at Hastings, sells a line of hand-painted clothing. The work is displayed island-wide. At the airport, **Fly Fish** (☎ 428-1645) sells frozen flying fish: B$30 for 10 fish, B$46 for 20, and B$60 for 30. They also have other items.

TAPES, CASSETTES, AND VIDEOS: The most prominent record company on the island is Ice. It features the Mighty Gabby and other artists. Tapes and records are expensive. The Caribbean Broadcasting Corporation (☎ 429-2041) sells videotapes of calypso shows and other events.

DEPARTMENT STORES AND MALLS: Broad Street houses a lot of stores, including the major malls. **Broad Street: Da Costas** has a number of individual franchises and sells everything from duty-free goods to fabrics to sewing machines. **Cave Shepherd** is the island's largest department store. The air-conditioned **Norman Centre** features The Book Shop, a record store, Mother Care, and T-shirt and jewelery shops galore. **Harrison's** (also at Bridgetown Harbour) offers a cornucopia of duty-free goods; they have 13 other shops islandwide. **Mall 34** has 24 shops carrying everything from greeting cards to fashionable clothes. **Maraj and Sons** sells duty-free goods ranging from watches to jewelry items. The **Royal Shop** sells famous name watches, jewelry, and other items. Small but diverse, **Med-X Mall** has a health food store and restaurant, an ice cream parlor, dry cleaning, a stamp counter, and a pharmacy. **Elsewhere:** Located at Rockley and Hastings respectively in Christ Church, **Quayside Centre** has a number of shops and restaurants, and **Hastings Mall** has 32 shops. **Chattel House Village**, opened in 1989 at St. Lawrence Gap, consists of a group of new chattel-style houses selling local crafts and clothing, including beachwear.

BOUTIQUES: These include Swanki, Ela, Gaye Boutique, Sapodilla Island Boutique, Mademoiselle, Glitzy, and The Ritz in Holetown; Simon in Paynes Bay; Harrisons and Gailies in Sam Lord's and the Sea Shell Studio nearby; as well as various shops in Bridgetown's Da Costa and Cave Shepherd.

ANTIQUES: Prices have risen and the best goods are siphoned off abroad, but many antiques are retained in the island's greathouses. Buyers will do well to check the Sun. papers for auction listings. **Greenwich House Antiques** (☎ 432-1169) has the widest selection in the Caribbean – afficianadoes can literally spend hours browsing! It is spread out in the interior of a greathouse at Greenwich, St. James. An alternative is **Antiquaria** (☎ 426-0635), which displays its wares on three floors of an old townhouse on St. Michael's Row, opposite the cathedral, in Bridgetown. **La Galeria Antique** (☎ 432-6094) is at Paynes Bay in St. James. Others are **Claradon Antiques** (☎ 429-4713) in Belleville and **Antiques and Collectibles** (☎ 427-7368) in Hastings.

MARKETS: The local markets are always a source of entertainment as well as of unique souvenirs. They are a great place to strike up an acquaintance while you stock up on the local produce. Try the Cheapside market in Bridgetown and don't miss the Oistins fish market.

BOOKS: These are very expensive here, as are all imports. The largest bookstores are in Bridgetown, but Best of Barbados has books (including this one) at its branches island-wide. Small bookstores in Bridgetown include **Bryden's** at Victoria St. and Bolton Lane behind Cave Shepherd, **The Cloister** on Hincks St., and **Robert's Stationary** in High St. Cave Shepherd, Broad Street's most prominent business, has books, both in their first-floor crafts section and in their second-floor bookshop.

A second-hand bookshop is on Bay St. The most memorable books to buy in Barbados are the publications of the National Cultural Foundation (particularly anything scribed by G. Addington Forde) and the National Trust. Heinemann's *The A-Z of Bajan Heritage* makes a particularly attractive souvenir. You might also wish to check out local authors or the book by Lesley Sutty, *Fauna of the Caribbean: The Last Survivors* (London: Macmillan, 1993).

IMPORTED GOODS: These luxury items include a variety of clothing (cashmere sweaters, French hand-beaded and Italian handbags, and shoes); crystalware from France, Ireland, England, and Sweden; bone china from England, France, and Denmark; an international assortment of gold and silver jewelry; the highest quality Swiss and Japanese timepieces; leading brands of perfume; and a variety of Japanese cameras and state-of-the-art electronics.

DUTY-FREE SHOPPING: You must produce your travel documents to buy at duty-free prices. Some goods (spirits, tobacco, electronic and camera equipment) must be delivered for pickup at the airport or harbor before departure. Alternatively, you can just buy it there directly before leaving. Know your prices; just because an item is marked "duty free" doesn't, in fact, mean that it is.

American Customs: Returning American citizens, under existing customs regulations, can lug back with them up to US$400 worth of duty-free goods provided the stay abroad exceeds 48 hours and that no part of the allowance has been used during the past 30 days. Items sent by post may be included in this tally, thus allowing shoppers to ship (or have shipped) goods like glass and china. Over that amount, purchases are dutied at a flat 10% on the next $1,000. Above $1,400, duty applied will vary. Joint declarations are permissible for members of a family traveling together. Thus, a couple traveling with two children will be allowed up to $3,200 in duty-free goods. Undeclared gifts (one per day of up to $50 in value) may be sent to as many friends as you like. One fifth of liquor may be brought back as well as one carton of cigarettes. Plants in soil may not be brought to the US.

Canadian Customs: Canadian citizens may make an oral declaration four times per year to claim C$100 worth of exemptions, which may include 200 cigarettes, 50 cigars, two pounds of tobacco, 40 fl. oz. of alcohol, and 24 12-oz. cans/bottles of beer. In order to claim this exemption, Canadians must have been out of the country for at least 48 hours. A Canadian who's been away for at least seven days may make a written declaration once a year and claim C$300 worth of exemptions. After a trip of 48 hours or longer, Canadians receive a special duty rate of 20% on the value of goods up to C$300 in excess of the C$100 or C$300 exemption they claim. This excess cannot be applied to liquor or cigarettes. Goods claimed under the C$300 exemption may follow, but merchandise claimed under all other exemptions must be accompanied.

British Customs: Each person over the age of 17 may bring in one liter of alcohol or two of champagne, port, sherry or vermouth plus two liters of table wine; 200 cigarettes or 50 cigars or 250 grams of tobacco; 250 cc of toilet water; 50 gms (two fl. oz.) of perfume; and up to £28 of other goods.

German Customs: Residents may bring back 200 cigarettes, 50 cigars, 100 cigarillos, or 250 grams of tobacco; two liters of alcoholic beverages not exceeding 44 proof or one liter of 44 proof plus alcohol; two liters of wine; and up to DM300 of other items.

Tourism Authority Offices

Bridgetown
Harbour Road (P.O. Box 242)
Bridgetown, Barbados
(809) 427-2623/2624
Fax: 426-4048

Great Britain
263 Tottenham Court Rd.
London W1P 9AA
(011) 44171-636-9448/9
Telex: 051-262081
Fax: 011-44171-637-1496

Grantley Adams Airport
Christ Church, Barbados
(809) 428-0937/5570

Bridgetown Harbour
Bridgetown, Barbados
(809) 426-1718

New York City
800 Second Ave.
NY, NY 10017 USA
(212) 986-6516/6518
Telex: 023-666-387
Fax: (212) 573-9850
(800) 221-9831

Los Angeles
3440 Wiltshire Blvd.
Suite 1215
LA, CA 90010 USA
(213) 380-2198
Fax: (213) 384-2763
(800) 221-9831

Toronto
5160 Yonge Street, #1800
North York
Ontario M2N 6L9H3B 1P5
(416) 512 6569/6570/6571
Fax:416-512-658
(800) 268-9122

Montreal
615 Rene Levesque Blvd. W.
Suite 960
Montreal, Quebec
Fax: 514-861-7917
(514) 861-0085

Germany
Rathenau Platz 1A
6000 Frankfurt 1
West Germany Nybrogatan 87
069-280982
Telex: 041-414068+
Fax: 49-69-294-782

Sweden
Barbados Tourism Authority
c/o Hotel Investors Ltd.
S-114, 41 Stockholm
Sweden
468-662-8584
Fax: 468-662-8775

France (Agency)
Barbados Tourism Authority
c/o Caribes 102, 102 Ave. Des Champs-Elysees
75008 Paris, France
4562-6262-4226-6262
Telex: CARAIB 6420 33F
Fax: (331) 4074-0701

Bridgetown and St. Michael's Parish

Bridgetown

Bridgetown possesses a vibrancy that cities many times as large might envy. Its clamor and bustle reflects the industry and energy of the island's people. Here, you'll find historical buildings inter-mingled with modern offices; dreadlock-sprouting coconut ven-dors slashing open coconuts with machetes for waiting businessmen clad in suits and ties; and hucksters hurrying to market, produce riding smartly atop their heads.

HISTORY: Bridgetown was founded on July 5, 1628 when the soon-to-be governor Charles Wolverstone arrived with 63 other settlers. The site was selected for its harbor and definitely *not* for its proximity to a large swamp that made it an unhealthy place to live during its early years. The present name has evolved from its early appelation, "The Indian Bridge Towne" – which referred to the bridge left by the Caribs. Through the years it has been known as "The Bridge," "The Bridge Town," and "St. Michael's Town." Its fine harbors at Careenage and Carlisle Bay gave it predominance over Holetown which was settled a year earlier. Street names downtown date back to the city's founding – in honor of such prominent early settlers as High, Tudor, James, and Swan. The last was a surveyor who laid out the town and, thus, had the secondary business street named after him. Hurricanes and fire have had their toll on the earliest buildings. Bridgetown was originally a fine town of broad streets and attractive stone storehouses, but was reduced to a mass of rubble by the 1780 hurricane. Only 30 houses were left standing and 3,000 died. The town never recovered from this, the most devastating single catastrophe in the island's history. Other disasters have plagued the town as well: hurricanes hit in 1675 and 1831, and major fires ravaged in 1659, 1668, 1673, 1756, 1758, 1766, 1821, 1826, 1845, 1853, and 1860. The 1860 fire allowed the government to purchase land and build the Public Buildings and enlarge Trafalgar Square. The town has played host to such luminaries as Winston Churchill, Aldous Huxley, Paul McCartney, Queen Elizabeth II, Mick Jagger, George Washington, Sting, and Henry Morgan.

ARRIVING BY AIR: Grantley Adams International Airport is in the southeasternmost portion of Christ Church Parish. Expect long lines at Immigration. There are only two teller windows at the bank here; the tourist information may be able to change a small amount if you have cash. Curiously, if you want to use the restrooms, the two pay phones encased in pillars, or the free lines to selected hotels, you must backtrack through Immigration! Once you've finished your business inside, you should breeze through customs. Plenty of taxis are available but, if you don't have a lot of luggage, you can take one of the infrequent 12A buses out on the main road towards Bridgetown (via Oistins Town and along the coast). If you're heading towards Crane Beach or Sam Lord's Castle, you must cross the road and wait on the other side. In any case, have your B$1 exact change ready.

GETTING AROUND: The main bus terminal stands next to the Charles Duncan O'Neal Bridge on Fairchild St. Buses leave from here for Bathsheba, Sam Lord's Castle, and other locations to the S and E. Ask at the information counter for the bus gate and probable time of departure. Although this is a new terminal, the bus system hasn't improved. Expect outrageously long lines during rush hour.

There are two other terminals in town. One is the Jubliee (or Lower Green St.) at the end of Broad St., which services mainly Holetown, Speightstown, and other points N. Another and much smaller one is the Pelican terminal off Princess Anne Highway (after Temple Yard and the GPO, but before Pelican Village). From here No. 1-D goes to District D (Dunscombe) in St. Thomas; No. 2 goes to Rock Dundo via Rock Hall; No. 3 goes to Turner's Hall via Hillaby and St. Andrew's Church; and No. 4 goes to Shorey Village via Welchman Hall Gully, Harrison's Cave, and Flower Forest.

Central Bridgetown Sights

TRAFALGAR SQUARE: This is the city's heart – alive and pulsating. The square features vendors wending their way to market, policemen directing traffic, and kids cajoling each other as they pass on their way to school. Lord Nelson has gazed over the hustle and bustle – silently reliving his victory at Cape Trafalgar – since just before dawn on March 22, 1813. In the middle of his search for French Admiral Villaneuve, he steamed into Carlisle Bay, making a great impression on the Bajans. In their grief at his death, they managed to raise £2,300 for the statue in a matter of weeks. They purchased Eggington's Green, renamed it Trafalgar Square, and installed the statue as its *piece de resistance*. It was sculpted by Sir William Westmacott and is 17 years older than its London cousin. Traditionally, visiting schoolchildren have been instructed to salute it. It has also been a center of controversy and cries for its removal have been voiced periodically since 1833 (one of the most notable being the Mighty Gabby's call to "take down Nelson and put up a Bajan man"). Garbage has been dumped at his feet and protesters have used him as a backdrop, but Lord Nelson has stood unperturbed through it all, maintaining a stiff upper lip and an expression of forbearance. The only change in the statue's lifestyle over the decades has been the end of the tradition of wreath-laying on the Trafalgar anniversary, a practice halted in 1962. These days, taxi drivers wait for customers at his heels. Be sure to read the fantastically verbose inscription on the pedestal. An ironic footnote to bear in mind is that, writing home, Nelson had described Barbados as being both "barbarous" and "detestable." Before passing on, be sure to swing your binoculars upward to focus on the young Lord's finely crafted head.

FOUNTAIN GARDENS: This area functions as a watering hole – one of the town's best spots for *limin'* – and is situated to the SE of the Public Buildings in Trafalgar Square. It incorporates the Mediterranean Dolphin Fountain and the War Memorial. It was inaugurated in 1865 in commemoration of the first piped water into the city in 1861. The fountain has recently been restored to its original magnificence. The grey granite **War Memorial** obelisk was built in 1925 to commemorate those who died during WWI. It is now adorned with bronze panels featuring the island's coat of arms and the names of Bajans who died during the two great wars. Its coralstone basin is of local design.

THE PUBLIC BUILDINGS: The Houses of Parliament across the road, where the House of Assembly and the Senate convene once a week, date from 1872. The Senate and House meet in the East Wing. The Assembly's stained glass windows show personable portraits of all the Kings and Queens of merry old England, as well as the Lord Protector, Oliver Cromwell. He is placed in the rearmost window by the visitor's gallery, as if to signal his outsider status (not having royal blood). The ornately-carved Speaker's Chair was an Independence Day gift from India. The much smaller Senate chamber features enormous framed photos of Queen Elizabeth and Prince Philip; the coats of arms on the wall are those of the once all-powerful plantocracy. The extra seats in the chamber are reserved for the Governor General and the Queen. At the building's entrance stands the statue of Sir William Conrad Reeves, who served as Chief Justice from 1886-1902. Reeves, considered by the average black Bajan of the time to be an "Uncle Tom," became the first Chief Justice with African blood in the British Empire. He was staunchly supported by the island's elite and placated the Colonial Office through compromises. His moderate proposals – such as increased educational opportunities and lowering of the voting age – saved the island from falling into the grip of the Crown Colony system and, consequently, he was awarded knighthood and the position of Chief Justice. **visiting:** Seeing the House or Senate in session is an experience no visitor should miss if the opportunity avails itself. The visitor's gallery in the House overlooks the chamber below. At the beginning of a session, the enormous brass scepter, which resembles a refined, ornate version of a club, is carried in and placed in a receptacle to the front. The bewigged Speaker then enters and takes a seat in the intricately-carved chair. The Chairman of Committees sits to his right. To find out when the next, unfortunately all-too-rare, session is, call 426-5331/3717/3712.

THE CAREENAGE AND BEYOND: On the other side of Trafalgar Square in the E portion of Carlisle Bay, this marina is so named because wooden-hulled sailing vessels were careened (turned on their sides) for repair here. Larger ships berth at the Deep Water Harbour to the W of town, but smaller boats, including the city's fishing fleet, still patronize the Careenage. This marina occupies the outer reaches of what was once the Constitution River. (It was actually not a river at all, but the arm of a bay.) Today, its inner stretch has been covered with landfill. Warehouses on either side are preserved by owners DaCosta & M. N. Musson. For 300 years the Careenage reigned supreme – acting as the center of communications and mercantile activity for the island – but it has been eclipsed by the modern Bridgetown Harbour. Nowadays, it is more of note as a spiffy berth for sleek yachts and supports a beehive of nightspots. Two bridges span its length to separate the outer and inner basins: the Charles Duncan O'Neal Bridge, named after the founder of the Democratic League and the Workingman's Association (see History), and the Joseph Chamberlain Bridge (1872), named after the Colonial Secretary who helped Barbados with financial aid after the 1898 hurricane. This latter is a drawbridge that used to be raised for tall ships, but mechanical problems have rendered it stationary. At the W end of the Careenage stand the **Pierhead** and **Willoughby's Fort**. The fort was constructed on what was then Little Island in 1656 and is now occupied by the Coast Guard. The Pierhead was pastureland before it held warehouses. It used to sit across from the island and now lies adjacent to it. **Waterfront Café**, a tourist watering hole with a spectacular view, is an old warehouse. **Independence Square**, near the main bus terminal heading E from the Pierhead, is a popular center for political rallies during election times. **Independence Arch**, with its self-explanatory name, is also worth seeing. **St. Ambrose Church** was consecrated on Jan. 1, 1858 by American Reverend Joseph S. Meyers. It lies in the district's heart, a deliberate move by the Right Reverend who was disgusted by the filth and vice he found there.

BROAD STREET: This street is a major center of activity and should, perhaps, be renamed "Bustle Street." It has served as a shopping area since the 17th C. Broad Street was originally known as **Cheapside**, a name that still applies right to the end where the General Post Office and farmer's market are located. It was also known as Exchange Street or The Exchange, owing to the presence of the Merchant's Exchange. As the main shopping street in town today, it is worth a stroll for its atmosphere. Its classic architectural landmark is the **Barbados Mutual Life Assurance Building** (1895). At night, it becomes a special place for promenading – with popcorn and peanut vendors galore.

ST. MICHAEL'S CATHEDRAL: Honoring the archangel, the present day edifice stands on the site of the orginal small, primitive structure. The first building was replaced with the Church of St. Michael (consecrated in 1665) which was, in turn, destroyed in 1780 and replaced by the present structure in 1789. This was extensively renovated and changed after it was damaged by the 1831 hurricane. It became St. Michael's Cathedral in 1824. It remains essentially Georgian in appearance, but also incorporates Gothic Revival-style additions, including pointed arches in the round-topped windows and trefoil clerestory windows. Its neglected military cemetery is filled with the tombs of dignitaries and soldiers – many of them in their teens and early twenties – who fell victim to plague and yellow fever. Be sure to note the inscription commemorating Robert Hooper and the painted memorial to Thomas Duke, Treasurer in 1750. You will also see the Braithwaite memorial, the Francis Bovell memorial, and the monument recording the tragic death of Mrs. Letitia Austin. Sir Grantley Adams, the island's first premier, also lies interred here. The barely legible tablets set into the floor date from the 17th C. A good time to visit is on a Sun. afternoon when Sunday School is in session. The nation's barristers, clad in wigs and gowns, assemble here for the annual Assizes Service and you'll see the processional cross. At Sun. morning services, the angelic voices of the choirboys – dressed in high ruffed surplices and red gowns – ring out clear and true. They sang at Westminster Abbey during the summer of 1971.

VICINITY OF ST. MICHAEL'S: Behind the cathedral on the other side of St. Michael's Row stands Cathedral Square and the Masonic Temple. The latter once housed Harrison College, originally founded as Harrison's Free School by Thomas Harrison in 1733 to provide free education for indigent boys. It is the nation's oldest and most prestigious secondary school. Towering above both is the 11-story **Central Bank Building**, the highest structure on the island. It contains a small theater and art gallery. The building is flanked on its N side by the huckster mecca of **Roebuck Street**. The monument and plaque in front of it were erected in 1989 to commemorate the meeting place of the first Parliament 300 years before. **James Street**, nearby, was once the property of the Quakers – until they were swindled out of it. While in the area you might want to check out the **Iron Gardens** (☎ 426-1336) – statues constructed from old car parts – at Perry Gap on Roebuck St.

QUEEN'S PARK HOUSE: This former military home was built in 1786 and currently houses **Queen's Park Theatre**. It replaced the original structure which was destroyed in the hurricane of 1780. The commanding general of the British West Indies lived here until 1906. It is surrounded by Queen's Park, which first opened to the public in 1909. The park appears derelict, but it was given lots of TLC by the Parks and Beaches Commission in 1970. The playground, to the right of the theater/gallery, borders an enormous thousand-year-old African **baobab tree**. As the island's largest, it measures 61.5 feet (18.5 m) in girth. At night the park takes on a quieter and more mysterious ambiance. The monkeys and birds sleep in their cages, dark shadows behind the grills. You might see a gospel group rehearsing in the pavilion, using a Casio synthesizer for accompaniment.

VICINITY OF QUEEN'S PARK: Nearby, note the facade on the adjacent Ministry of Agriculture. To the N is "The Square" of Harrison College (see Vicinity of St. Michael's). On Constitution Rd. you will find another historic building that once housed Queen's College.

SYNAGOGUE: On a side street extending from James St. to Magazine Lane, stands a building that once contained the Jewish synagogue – a successor to the original that was totally destroyed by the 1831 hurricane. The island's Jewish community consisted of Sephardic Jews who probably emigrated from Brazil in the 1650s. They were isolated and ostracized, listed separately on the census and heavily taxed. By the 1850s, most of the community had migrated and only 71 remained, half of that number non-practicing. By 1926 there was only one, and the synagogue was dismantled. Some of its treasures may be seen in the Barbados Museum, but two of its five cemeteries have disappeared and its four chandeliers were sold to an American. The building – restored by the current Jewish population – now retains only its cemetery to serve as a reminder of an era past. It's open weekdays from 9-4.

PRINCE WILLIAM HENRY STREET: Prince William Henry (later to become King William IV) arrived in 1786, commanding the frigate *Pegasus*. He and his entourage laid waste to the town's principal brothel belonging to a Ms. Rachel Pringle Polgreen on Bay St. The street was named to commemorate his visit. Both sides of Hincks St. near to its base – from the car park to W.S. Munroe – are filled with Bajan color and character.

PUBLIC LIBRARY: The historic public library stands on Coleridge St. It was a gift of Andrew Carnegie and was opened in 1906. The diminutive and non-functioning **Montifiore Fountain**, the centerpoint of the triangle facing the library, is easy to pass by. It was a gift of John Montifiore way back in 1864 and was relocated here from Beckwith Place in 1940. Each of its four marble statues represent different human ideals: Justice, Fortitude, Temperance, and Prudence. A complex on this street includes the Police Station, Law Courts, and the Magistrates' Courts.

TUDOR STREET AND ENVIRONS: Parallel to Coleridge St. is Tudor Street where the Quaker meeting house once stood. One end of this street leads into Broad Street and the other end terminates in **Baxter Road:** "The Street That Never Sleeps." From dusk to dawn, evening after evening, Bajans party hard – up and down, in and out of the street's numerous rum shops and restaurants. The odors of frying fish and chicken permeate the air, and jukeboxes blare until dawn. **Suttle Street,** a respectable neighborhood now transformed into a trader's mecca, is renowned for its atmosphere. It runs into St. Mary's Row, the street's extension. **St. Mary's Church** was built in 1827 to accommodate the overflow from St. Michael's. **Lower Green Station,** another bus terminal, stands across the street here.

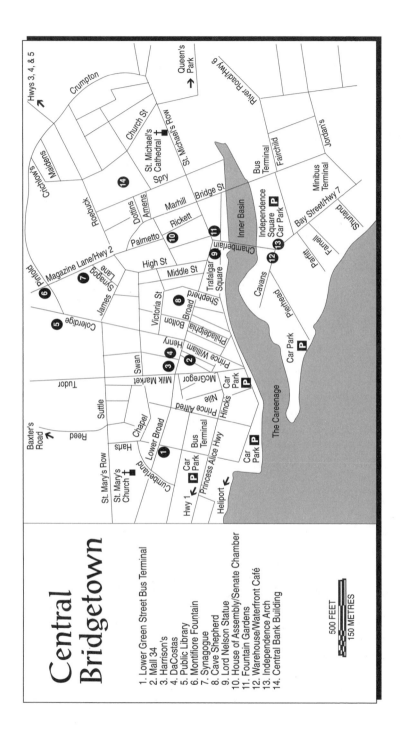

Central Bridgetown

1. Lower Green Street Bus Terminal
2. Mall 34
3. Harrison's
4. DaCostas
5. Public Library
6. Montifiore Fountain
7. Synagogue
8. Cave Shepherd
9. Lord Nelson Statue
10. House of Assembly/Senate Chamber
11. Fountain Gardens
12. Warehouse/Waterfront Café
13. Independence Arch
14. Central Bank Building

500 FEET

150 METRES

Hwys 3, 4, & 5
Crumpton
Queen's Park
Church St.
Maidens
Critchlow's
St. Michael's Cathedral
St. Michael's Row
River Road/Hwy 6
Spry
14
Roebuck
Marhill
Bridge St.
Dottins
Amens
Jordan's
Fairchild
Bus Terminal
Palmetto
Rickett
10
Inner Basin
Independence Square Car Park
Minibus Terminal
Pinfold
Magazine Lane/Hwy 2
High St
11
Chamberlain
13
Bay Street/Hwy 7
Shurland
7
Smegg Lane
Middle St
9
Trafalgar Square
12
Farrell
Parfitt
6
James
Coleridge
Victoria St
8
Shepherd Broad
Cavans
Pickheed
5
Philadelphia Bolton
Car Park
Swan
3 4
Prince William
Henry
2
Tudor
Milk Market
McGregor
Car Park
The Careenage
Suttle
Nile
Prince Alfred
Hincks
Baxter's Road
Reed
Chapel
Harts
Cumberland
Lower Broad
Car Park
Bus Terminal
Princess Alice Hwy
Car Park
St. Mary's Church
St. Mary's Row
Hwy 1
1
Heliport

☞ Traveler's Tip
A three-hour historical tour (B$50) leaves from Cave Shepherd on Broad St. from Mon. through Sat. at 10 AM. It visits many of the sights listed here. The "Hop a Tour" leaves Cave Shepherd at 10:30 and 2:30. Contact Barbados Activities Hub (☎ 431-2094; 424-8140 after hours, fax 436-1643).

TEMPLE YARD: Bajan culture reflects a synthesis between Africa and Britain. In the case of Temple Yard, the African elements predominate, merging art and craft in a colorful melange of shape and form. Here, in a series of conjoined rudimentary wooden stalls, the island's top Rasta artists show their stuff. Ceramicist Ayem, a graduate of the Jamaica School of Art, produces sculptures, reliefs, hangings, plaques and paintings. Sculptor Ras Congo has his own small house here. Innumerable crafts – wrought from bamboo, leather, coconut, seashells and other materials – are represented. Rasta culture is evident: from representations of lions to the red, green, and gold maps of Africa to the images of Marcus Garvey and Bob Marley. Music blasts from small restaurants selling *I-tal* (vegetarian) and Bajan dishes (like rice and stew). Also present is open use of marijuana and a hard sell atmosphere. This location came into being after the government moved sidewalk vendors out of areas where their parked stalls were causing congestion. A minibus terminal is here; Cheapside market stands a bit farther on as does the new General Post Office, a kissing cousin in design to the Central Bank Building. Along Princess Alice Highway, which parallels the coast, lies **Trevor Way**, named after a young man who was killed nearby. This small but flourishing park has been beautified by the Rotary Club and is maintained by the National Conservation Commission. It offers a stand of cabbage palm and mahoe as well as a great view of Carlisle Bay.

PELICAN VILLAGE: This complex – built on land reclaimed from the sea – contains cheap handicrafts as well as serious art. It is located across from Pelican Bay and near Temple Yard. The Barbados National Council has its art gallery here. Karl Broodhagen, a craftsman who began his career as a tailor, has his sculpture gallery here. He's well known for his cast bronze heads, including the one of Sir Grantley Adams which stands on a pedestal at the Government Headquarters on Bay St. "The Freed Slave," his most famous sculpture, stands at the center of St. Barnabas Roundabout at the border of St. Michael and St. George parishes. Courtney Devonish, a native of the pottery village Chalky Mount, operates a workshop here too. He has traditional pottery as well as other pieces that reflect his Italian training. **Pelican Restaurant** is the place to stop and collect some energy before exploring farther. The Industrial Development Corporation operates a shop nearby.

MOSQUE: You won't find it in any tourist brochure. This amazing anachronis is sandwiched between two chattel houses on New Kensington Rd. off Fontabelle opposite a house labeled "Bombay Villa." It is a large two-storey mosque with green tinted windows and is constructed of green and white painted concrete.

MEDFORD'S MAHOGANY CRAFT VILLAGE: This woodcarving center is run by self-taught artist Reggie Medford, who builds a wide variety of pieces from massive mahogany roots. It is open Mon. through Fri. 8-5, Sat. 8:30-1 and is located on Baxter's Road, Lower Barbarees Hill, St. Michael.

BRIDGETOWN HARBOUR: Construction was begun in 1957 and inauguration took place in 1961. More than 90 acres of land were added to the area by filling the sea with 730,000 cubic yards of quarried gravel, thus eliminating Pelican Island which lay 1,800 feet (600 m) away. On this former dependency stand the offices of the Port Manager and Harbour Master. The huge sugar warehouse, which can hold up to 80,000 tons (half of the annual crop), was built at the same time. The port can clear up to 2,000 tons of cargo per day. It has a specially built cruise ship terminal with a number of shops. (See below under Parish Practicalities.) There's also a 50-acre duty-free Industrial Park. **Kensington Oval**, nearby, features extremely competitive cricket matches.

UWI CAVE HILL CAMPUS: The nation's only university (N of town off Highway 1) has some handsome architecture. Check out the view from the library window. The grave of Sir Frank Worrell, the legendary West Indian cricketer, lies within the complex. Heading N from Cave Hill, near Batt's Rock, a high-walled house was once a "lazaretto" or home for lepers. It was subsequently converted to house the island's first radio station whose antenna still dominates the landscape to its rear.

BELLEVILLE DISTRICT: This earliest of suburban developments – many of whose homes have been restored – was developed by entrepreneurs Sam Manning and George Whitfield in 1882. They intended it to be a modern middle-class development, laying out 11 parallel avenues on 60 acres which were intersected by two parallel boulevards. A row of mahoganies was planted along Pine Rd. and 900 palm trees were placed elsewhere. Tennis courts, a masonic lodge, a cricket field, and a church were also built. Some of these lots were sold with a house.

Belleville is home to Erdiston, the Teachers' Training College. **Roland Tree House**, at 10th Avenue in Belleville, houses the Barbados National Trust's headquarters (☎ 426-2421/9033). It is not a house built in a tree, but rather one named after Mr. Roland Tree – the Trust's founder. This classic Victorian home was constructed in 1893. It is furnished with period furniture and is a fine exhibit of old local architecture. Every Thurs. ladies clad in Victorian garb show visitors around.

MOUNT GAY VISTORS CENTRE: Mt. Gay Distilleries (☎ 425-8757) is set on Spring Garden Hwy. and offers a 30-40-min. tour of its distillery along with tastings. It's open Mon. to Fri. from 9-5; admission is B$8 adults; children under 12 are free. There's also a Best of Barbados outlet here.

ALONG HIGHWAY 4: Government House, official residence of the Governor General, crowns a hill overlooking Belleville. It was constructed in 1736 and was originally called Pilgrim House, after its owner, Quaker John Pilgrim. It has suffered major damage from hurricanes, but the home and its gardens still may be viewed on special open days. The upper-class residential area of **Pine Gardens** is in the vicinity. **Bishop's Court Hill**, at its end along Highway 4, is named after the home of the island's Anglican Bishop. A commercial district past Collymore Rock contains Bank's Breweries with Wildey Industrial Park to its rear. Farther along the highway is the Barbados Institute of Management and Production.

ALONG ST. BARNABAS HIGHWAY: This highway is lined with modern technological facilities. It connects Grantley Adams International Airport with Speightstown, flanking such ultramodern edifices as the Caribbean Devolpment Bank and the Caribbean Broadcasting Corporation. It also runs past Pinelands, an ugly housing development that dates from the 1960s. Karl Broodhagen's sculpture **"The Freed Slave,"** stands at the St. Barnabas Roundabout in St. Michael. This massive statue – erected in 1986 – depicts Bussa, the leader of the 1816 slave revolt, standing in a defiant posture, his hands still wearing broken chains. Turning to the W, the Two Mile Hill road leads to Ilaro Court.

ILARO COURT: This greathouse is one of the nation's architectural wonders and is less than two miles from Bridgetown. It is framed by trees on a bluff and its stark white walls surround doors and windows that incorporate various architectural techniques.

Vivid green hoods frame the decorative wrought ironwork of its windows. Ilaro was designed and planned by American Lady Gilbert-Carter, whose husband served as Governor from 1904-11. Its interior features paintings, a grand piano, and East Asian tables. The walls of the lounge are adorned with beautiful tapestries and prints of old sailing merchant vessels. Opposite, the upholstered green and white chintz furniture gleams in contrast to the pale brown glow of the pine floor and the subdued pale grey walls. A covered arcade overlooks the rolling countryside.

The house surrounds a rectangular courtyard that looks onto a swimming pool and flowering plant garden. Long polished doors in the dining room lead out to the open verandah. Two glass chandeliers reflect light that plays on chippendale chairs, two circular dark mahogany tables, and a collection of old china. The five bedrooms are adorned with Regency dressing tables and slender four-poster beds; lily ponds and fountains embellish the grounds. Unfortunately, it may be visited only on special occasions.

TYROL COT HERITAGE VILLAGE: This restored mansion, originally constructed in 1854 and opened in 1995, centers around events in Barbados and the Caribbean from the 1930s to the 60s. It is the birthplace of former Prime Minister Tom Adams and the former residence of his father Sir Grantley Adams, the first premier of Barbados and the first (and only) Prime Minister of the short-lived Federation of the West Indies. The two-storey house is made of coralstone and has a deep basement. The surrounding four acres have a restaurant, a chattel house village selling arts and crafts, and a rum shop. For times, admission, and exact directions contact the National Trust (☎ 426-2421, 436-9033).

Heading towards Christ Church's Gold Coast

The best sites are out and around the island. Many locations of historic interest surround the city. In addition to the ones mentioned so far, others are enroute to Christ Church's tourist strip.

CARLISLE BAY CENTRE: Cruise ship passengers purchase a package ticket to this "day on the beach" resort. It features a restaurant (with daily lunchtime specials), shops, water sports, plus tuk band and steel band performances. Facilities are also available for use by outsiders, ☎ 426-6101.

ESPLANADE: This area on Bay St. provides a great view of Bridgetown harbour, complete with romantic red sails in the sunset. The now-demolished houses that once stood here dealt in smuggled goods before their purchase by the government at the end of the 19th C. A bust of Sir Grantley Adams stands in the gardens.

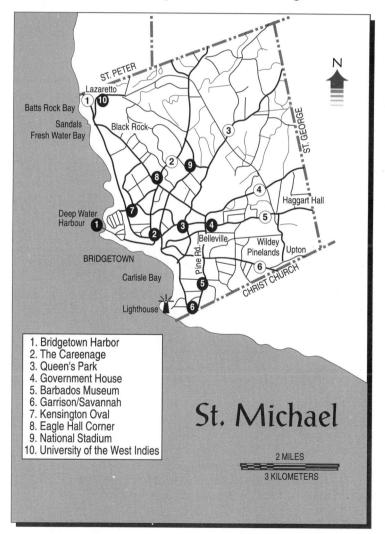

1. Bridgetown Harbor
2. The Careenage
3. Queen's Park
4. Government House
5. Barbados Museum
6. Garrison/Savannah
7. Kensington Oval
8. Eagle Hall Corner
9. National Stadium
10. University of the West Indies

St. Michael

2 MILES
3 KILOMETERS

GOVERNMENT HEADQUARTERS: The modern Government Headquarters, with its semi-circular driveway, stands on Beckles Rd. and is surrounded by begonias, poinsettias, and hibiscus. The bronze bust in front of the driveway commemorates Sir Grantley Adams, the "father" of modern Barbados.

ST. PAUL'S CHURCH: This church was rebuilt in 1831 and was once used as a garrison church. The names of many British soldiers are inscribed in stone between the aisles. The regimental crests, plaques, and flags on the wall are those left by members of the Irish regiment, the Connaught Rangers, whose religious needs spurred construction of the original structure.

CROFTON'S HOUSE: Located at the corner of Bay Street and Chelsea Road. This is one of those big deal "sights" in the Caribbean – like Alexander Hamilton's house in Christiansted on St. Croix – that has no basis in fact. Washington arrived in Barbados on November 3, 1751, on his first and only visit abroad. He stayed here with his half-brother, Lawrence, in the hope that the climate would cure Lawrence's illness. Any of the houses in the area might very well have been *the* house and, since it's fun to look at them anyway, you might as well!

Standing directly opposite is the privately-run Yacht Club, which is housed in a former military building. Farther down the road, right behind the Seaview Hotel, is a gem of a natural tract featuring palm trees, casuarinas, and hummingbirds – all bordering the beach. **Charles Fort** at Needham's Point – the largest of those constructed along the S and W coasts during the 17th and 18th C. – is named after King Charles II of England, the "Merry Monarch" who reigned from 1660-1685. A number of cannon are here.

THE GARRISON: This is the collective name for St. Ann's Fort and the Savannah as well as being its parade ground. A British garrison was permanently assigned here from 1694-1906, after which it was replaced by a volunteer force. Use your imagination to visualize batteries of troops – garbed in red and white starched uniforms – drilling in formation here. The Savannah contains a playing field (used for soccer and rugby) and a racetrack. Every Easter Monday a kite-flying festival is held here. The arms on the cupola tower of the former British Regiment guard house belonged to William IV. It was formerly the Savannah Club, but has now been transformed into the **Military Museum**.

The fort, located behind an ugly Victorian structure, dates from 1702; its signal tower was constructed around 1819 as part of the increased security in reaction to the 1816 slave rebellion. In addition to its defensive functions, the fort also served to relay messages to other parts of the island. Signal stations in other districts could hear about a slave uprising, the arrival of a ship, an impending attack, or an upcoming Council meeting. Today, it is manned by the Barbados Defence Force. You can still see the thick walls enclosing the store room, the armory, and the powder magazines. A cemetery chock full of the bones of soldiers lies behind the fort overlooking the sea.

The **Barbados Gallery of Art** was opened in 1995 on the Turf Club premises at Bush Hill here. In the area nearby, known as Needham's Point, just before the Garrison, are the Hilton Hotel (the recently restored military cemetery stands E of the Hilton) and a Mobil Oil Refinery. There's also a fine beach here. Octagonal **Needham's Point Lighthouse** was built in 1865 and is the second oldest but smallest of the island's lighthouse quartet. It is now inactive. The former abodes of colonial-era government officials stand around the Savannah; blocks of handsome arcaded red-painted brick buildings follow. They date from the post-1831 hurricane era and were originally used to house troops.

The red brick structure to the S of the Savannah along Highway 7 used to be the hospital for St. Anne's Fort; it has now been subdivided into flats. Nearby, St. Mathias Gap leads from the highway to **St. Mathias Church**. This church was consecrated in 1850 and superseded St. Paul's as the Garrison Chapel.

BARBADOS MUSEUM: This lovingly conceived and executed complex (☎ 427-0201, 436-1956) serves as a superb introduction to Barbados – one that no visitor should miss! It is housed in the old military detention barracks (constructed between 1817-1853); most of the galleries were once prison cells. As you tour, try to visualize the captives lying about rotting in rags. The building was made with rusticated limestone and yellow brick and has an arched carriageway running through the entrance; the marble fountain here was once at the local synagogue's entrance for Jews to wash their hands before attending a service. The clock, Menorah, and one of the benches also come from there. You enter at the shop where, among other things, there are wonderful antique postcards for sale.

The first dioramas in the **Harewood Gallery** are of flora and fauna and can help you appreciate what you see – both above and below water. One illustrates the life on the island's coral reefs. The displays continue as you round the corner into the **Jubilee Gallery**, which illustrates the nation's history, largely through Amerindian and colonial artifacts. Among the highlights are a cowrie shell inscribed with the Lord's Prayer, antique medical equipment, old guidebooks and other memorabilia relating to the early tourism industry, and a July 22, 1789 copy of the *Barbados Mercury*. Be sure to see Stewart Howard's caricature of the German officers a century ago. The final gallery in this wing contains a map collection.

The **Warmington Gallery** (outside and to the left) displays mock-ups of a typical bedroom and living room of a 19th-C. planter. If you're hungry or thirsty, the café next door has menus uniquely printed on paper bags! The **Challenor Gallery** displays military memorabilia. Switch on the lights and enter the Cunard Gallery next door. It contains a fine collection of antique prints and paintings, the best of which are Will Holland's hilarious sendups of the West Indian plantocracy's lifestyle. The final two galleries are exceedingly diverse. One displays a very fine collection of African musical instruments, sculpture, ceramics, and woodcarving. The other is to the rear and has hundreds of pieces of late 18th-C. china, glass, snuff boxes, rare furniture, and silver. One of the more interesting displays is a case featuring British ceramics that imitate Ming Dynasty pottery. The room's finest piece, however, is the Scotch snuff mull made from a ram's horn; it includes implements and a moustache comb. Note the carved ivory diptych and the Staffordshire ceramic figures. The freshly refurbished children's galleries bring history alive with historical dioramas and doll houses. Open Mon. to Sat. 9-5; admission is B$10 (children B$5). The museum's courtyard serves as the location for the performance "1627 and all that," and those who attend may tour the museum in the evening.

Harry Bayley Observatory

This – the E Caribbean's only observatory – opened in Jan. 1963. It is named after the co-founder of the Barbados Astronomical Society who also built the island's first medical laboratory and modern hospital. The conical structure was designed by the late Barbara Hill, an architect who wrote *Historic Churches of Barbados*. It is topped by a Celestron 14-inch Schmidt-Cassegrain telescope. Admission (only Fri. eves.) is B$8 adults, B$4 children, and B$5 each for groups. Your donations help pay the rent. Refreshments and other items are available.

A night's visit here begins with a half-hour video presentation followed by a trip up to the roof where the telescope and dome are rotated by hand and focused on whatever is in the sky; it's pretty much the luck of the draw and weather plays a big part. You should be able to see Saturn – crisp, clear, and unbelievable – or something equally impressive such as

Vega or a group of binary stars. The tower also affords a night view of Bridgetown. The delightful company of some of the 30 members present would be reason enough to make the effort. Those who have visited so far include Isaac Asimov, Claudette Colbert, Neil Armstrong, and comet authority Fred Whipple. You may find yourself a life-long amateur astronomer: their enthusiasm is *that* contagious. At the worst, you may shake off a bit of jadedness and ponder the wonders of the universe. For more information, call Bill Sutherland at 426-1317 or John Forde at 422-2394.

To get to the observatory, take Hwy. 6 from Bridgetown, pass the Texaco station on the left, then take the second right turn into the road which has a sign. Turn right and you'll see the observatory ahead.

St. Michael Practicalities

ACCOMMODATIONS: There are three major hotels in the parish. **Sandals Barbados** opened in 1995 just N of Bridgetown along the coast. It is one of the major all-inclusives. To the S of town are **Hilton International**, at Needham's Point in Aquatic Gap, as well as the **Grand Barbados** and the **Island Inn**, which are nearby.

BUDGET ACCOMMODATIONS: The outlying suburb of Belleville is a center for reasonably-priced accommodations. The **Crystal Crest** (☎ 436-6129), Pine Rd., has rooms for US$22, including breakfast and dinner. Others, from around US$20 pn (European Plan), include **The Great Escape** (☎ 436-3554), 1st Ave, and **Broome's Vacation Home** (☎ 426-4955/2937, 429-3937/4192) in Pine Gardens. **Fortitude** (☎ 426-4210) is on lower Wellington St. **Stox Inn** (☎ 427-4370), at Industry Hall on Bay St. just minutes on foot from downtown, is one of the lowest-priced guesthouses on the island, but it's also extremely spartan. You also might try **De Splash Inn Guest House**, Passage Rd., (☎ 427-8287), and **Superville Guest House** (☎ 427-5668), 3rd Ave. in Pickwick Gap on Wilbury Rd.

DINING OUT: The **Ideal Restaurant** is on Cave Shepherd's top floor. Entertainment is provided courtesy of the CNN media circus coupled with the occasional soap opera. **Amy's Place** (☎ 429-7854) is at 33 Broad St. and serves West Indian, Chinese, and other cuisines; take out is available. It also offers buffet lunches from 11-3.

The **Boatyard** is set on Bay St. at the edge of Bridgetown and is definitely geared towards the nautical crowd. Fisherman's Wharf and the Waterfront Café, both overlooking the Careenage, are the best-known seafood restaurants. **The Waterfront Café** (☎ 427-0093) is set in a restored coral-limestone warehouse and offers a platter filled with such appetizers as fish melts (flying fish roe fried in batter) and fish cakes. Try their lime squash. Live music can be found here nightly and the Tues. night buffet (B$35) is accompanied by a steelband. Entrées range from B$14-$35. **Fisherman's Wharf** (☎ 436-7778) has an excellent selection of seafood, sandwiches, and platters. Entrées start at B$24. The **Barbados Museum's restaurant** is one of the more reasonable and comfortable places to eat lunch.

out of town: The **Brown Sugar** (☎ 426-7684) is in the Garrison area at Aquatic Gap. You can dine under a pavilion filled with hanging ferns, or out on a garden terrace. Its Planter's Buffet is B$25 and entrées run from B$30. The **Schooner** (☎ 436-8719) and **Golden Shell** restaurants are in the Grand Barbados Hotel in Carlisle Bay. The Schooner was built in 1803. It is set at the end of a pier and is surrounded by the Caribbean on all sides; the specialty is seafood. **Barracks**, at the Island Inn in Aquatic Gap, emphasizes local food and is set in a former rum store dating from 1803. **The Hilton** and **The Pebble**, the latter of which caters to vegetarians, are at Needhams Point. The Hilton offers buffet dining on its terrace for lunch (B$30 including tax and service) and dinner (around B$42-$48); à la carte dishes are also available.

HEALTH FOOD: The **Pure Food Café** is on Broad St. **Super Salads** is in Carlisle Bay Centre on Bay St. **Merle's Health Shop and Restaurant** is at 114 Norman Centre, also on Bay St.

BUDGET DINING: Every Fri. **Queen's Park Restaurant** serves a buffet lunch for B$15; meals average B$9 on other days. One of the more moderately-priced and better choices is the **cafeteria** inside Cave Shepherd. It offers local cuisine like fried flying fish, cakes, and coffee; there's also a bar and take-out counter. Try the new **Balcony Restaurant** overlooking the street. Da Costa's has the **Munch Wagon** and **Ho Kwong** (Chinese buffet). On Marhill St. near Trafalgar Square, **Encore** features a variety of reasonably-priced food; items include sweet potato pie, macaroni pie, and salads. **Chefette**, across on Broad St., serves pizza, chicken, *roti*, burgers, salads, and ice cream. **Capricorn**, on nearby Palmetto St., has similar prices. The **City Centre Bar**, across the street, offers counter service. On Chapel St., **Bucaneer Barrel** features local fast food, and **Colonel Sanders** has the same stuff as stateside. **E.O.B.'s**

Cafeteria is adjacent to the Fairchild St. bus terminal and shares its canned music. Aesthetics are not a top priority – your food is served on styrofoam – but they do have reasonable food with good size portions. A sample special is steakfish, salad, rice, macaroni pie, and a small mauby for B$10.95; it's one of the few budget eating spots in town open on Sun. For snacks in this area, try the vendors out the door to the left and around the corner. In Pelican Village you can dine at the **Bongo Light Ital Restaurant**. On **Baxters Road** ladies tending coalpots sell fried fish for B$8 per large piece; some of the more famous restaurants are the Havana Restaurant, Johno's, Enid's, the Pink Star Bar and Restaurant, and Collins Bar and Restaurant. Other places to eat are on the way to Christ Church. Local restaurants include **The Boatyard**, which is equipped with a pool table and has a nautical feel. It is mainly for tourists and overlooks the water. It features seafood, a salad bar, and ice cream. Just down the road is the **Gasbros Club** where you can dine on *pudding and souse* every Fri. The **Port and Starboard** (☎ 425-6450) is out at Brighton Beach, within walking distance of the cruise terminal. After you dine, check out their water sports or lounge in their beach chairs.

FOOD SHOPPING: Budg-Buy Food is on St. Michael's Row. **Julie's Supermarket** is on Bridge St; a larger version opened in 1995 at Busser Roundabout along the Errol Barrow Highway near the Tom Adams Highway. Sample prices: Pine Hill Dairy Passion Fruit Drink, 89 cents/250 ml; Breakme Oatmeal Cookies B$3.99/8 oz; onions B$4.95/kg; potatoes B$1.99/kg; Rough Rider Condoms B$1.69/three-pack; Eveready alkaline batteries 2/B$5.99; Mt. Gay Rum B$11.89/liter; Skippy Peanut Butter B$8.49/18 oz; Bajan Cajun Hot Pepper Sauce, B$1.99/6 oz; milk B$3.05/liter; Anchor New Zealand Cheese, B$2.75/200 g; Australian cheese B$10.30/kg; kiwi fruit B$3.29/for 2; small apple 99 cents. **Buy Rite Discount Market** has stores on Broad St., Fairchild St., High St., and Swan St. **Federal Supermarket** is on Nelson St. **Rick's Supermarket** is on Fairchild St. **Cheapside Market**, a mere shadow of former times, is at the end of Broad St. just before the utramodern GPO. It still has hucksters vending their wares. There's another outdoor market on Swan St. **Harry's Vegetable Basket** is on Middle St. near Victoria. **Chick Growers Ltd**, Roebuck St., sells eggs for B$5.88/doz. and chicken for B$2.88/lb. Also on Roebuck is **Alleyne Arthur's Discount Store**, which has some good deals. One very fine place to buy food is the **Farmer's Discount Center**, which has a selection of poultry, fruit, and vegetables as well as locally-produced molasses and banana essence. It's on Beckles Rd. off Bay Rd. near the museum, and is open Mon. to Fri. 8-6; Sat. 8-1. Those needing to economize on their rum should visit the **The Grog Shop** on High St. It features cheap rum straight out of the keg; bring your own bottle. Finally, a number of gas stations have mini-marts that are open 24 hours.

bakeries: Festers Plus is on Marhill St. and High St. **Clarke Bakery** is at 32 Tudor St. **Full Stop** is on Broad St. **High Crust** is at 20 City Centre Mall and at 34 Roebuck St. **Paris** is in the Hinds Bldg. in Cheapside. **Chamel's** is on Bay St. and Hincks St.

BOOKSTORES: Cave Shepherd has a very fine bookstore – just take the escalator up. They also sell the *Sunday New York Times* (around B$22). **Robert's Stationary Store**, 9 High St., has a fine collection of local books. Air-conditioned **Bryden's Bookshop**, on Victoria St., also has an excellent selection. **The Book Shop** is inside the Wildey Shopping Plaza. **Days Books** is in the Diamond Tower Mall on Marhill St. **Island News Stand** is on the first floor of DaCosta's on Broad. St. **The Book Place**, featuring reasonably-priced used books and some very eclectic new ones, is on Probyn St. and on Bay St.

MUSIC SHOPS: CDs are expensive in Barbados, averaging about B$35 each. **Cave Shepherd** has a small record kiosk. **Dance World** is on Rickett St. **Electronic City** is inside Speedbird House on Fairchild St. **No. 1 Record Shop** is at Independence Square. **Manning's** is on Broad St. The **CD Exchange** is at Pandora's Place on Bay St.

Shopping in Bridgetown

Cave Shepherd – department store, Broad St.
Da Costas – department store, Broad St.
Mall 34 – 24 shops Broad St.
Maraj and Sons – duty-free goods, Broad St.
Med-X Mall – Broad St.
Norman Centre – air-conditioned mall, Broad St.
Harrison's – Bridgetown Harbour, Broad St., and other locations.
Royal Shop – Broad St.
Women's Self Help Cooperative – handmade items, Broad St.

CRUISE SHIP TERMINAL: This cutesy facility has a wide range of shops, but access is restricted to tourists arriving by ship. You'll find Caribbean Sounds (a well-stocked record store), a Best of Barbados outlet, a PO, a tourist information office, and carts selling books, alcohol, and souvenirs. The building cost B$5 million and resembles a village of chattel houses. There are plans to double the ship capacity from six to 12.

SERVICES: A **stamp counter** and Mid Town pharmacy are located inside Med-X Mall. The **USIS** has a small library open noon-3, Tues. to Fri., on Parry St. The local representative for **American Express** is Barbados International Travel Service (BITS), also on Parry St. One good travel agency is **YES Travel** (☎ 425-9338, fax 425-8998; P.O. Box 406, Bridgetown). The General Post Office is open from is open Mon. to Fri., 7:30-5. On Harbour Rd., the **Tourism Authority** (☎ 427-2623/2624, fax 426-4048) has a good selection of brochures in its lobby. A second branch is in the cruise ship terminal.

Useful Bridgetown Phone Numbers

Air Canada	428-5077
American Airlines	428-4170
Barbados Activities Hub	431-2094
after hours	424-8140
fax	436-1643
British Airways	436-6413
BWIA	426-2111
fax	427-4295
Liat	428-0968
or	428-0987
Mustique Airways	435-7009
Tourism Authority	427-2623
fax	426-4048

The Northern Parishes and The Scotland District

The Scotland District was named after its UK lookalike and contains the entire parish of St. Andrew and portions of St. Peter, St. Joseph, and St. John. Take your time while exploring and savour this, the only area to offer much in the way of forest glades, streams, hills, ravines, and gorges. The Scotland District was formed after the sea ate away at the island's coral cap, exposing the soft underbelly of sandstones and clays known locally as Joe's River Mud. During the rainy season, the streams transform into raging torrents that carry everything along with them. Landslides, collapsed bridges and loss of vegetation are common occurences. In 1901 nearly 100 homes and estate buildings were destroyed when 400 acres of land slid down towards the sea. Again, in 1938, 50 acres of hillside land shifted position, forcing abandonment of 100 houses in Rock Hall Village. The soil's instability can be traced to such activities as overgrazing, cultivation of steep slopes, and deforestation. These problems have a multiplying effect; each serves to intensify the effects of the other. Heavy flooding, in turn, adds to the problem when sand and silt clogs the streams. Aloes and cotton are grown in the district, which extends for 22 sq. miles and covers about 1/7th of the island. The other northerly parishes in this section are the three parishes due N of Bridgetown: St. James, St. Peter, and St. Lucy. St. James has the glamorous tourism; St. Peter contains the island's most picturesque town; and St. Lucy, the nation's northernmost parish, has some of the best scenery and most attractive traditional chattel houses.

Saint James Parish and The Platinum Coast

The so-called "Platinum Coast," plush and well heeled, is a villa-speckled oasis stretching along the coast of St. James Parish. It was once a simple paradise, but gone are the days when schoolboys would bicycle to Freshwater Bay and, unobserved, strip naked and

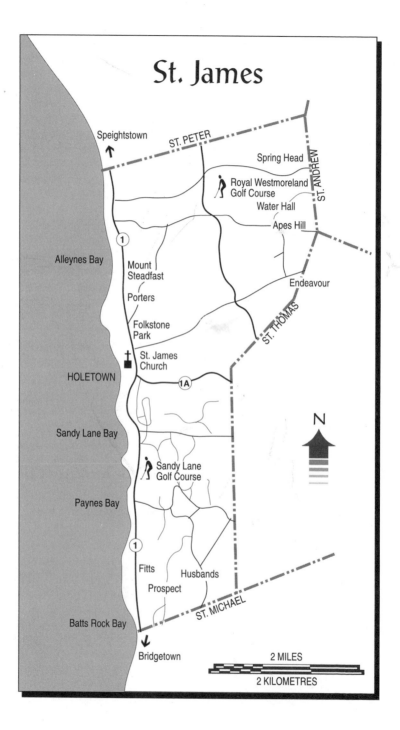

plunge into the delightful water. Things began changing in the late 20s when Burton Ward, owner of the Walmer Lodge plantation, decided to build a club house at Freshwater Bay. Out of this modest establishment – combining dance floor and rented bungalows – came Paradise Beach, once the W Coast's leading beach resort. Bajans originally shunned the coast because they feared tidal waves, the lack of the refreshing tradewinds that grace the E coast, and the distance from Bridgetown. Any visitor can see that any time lost then has been more than adequately made up for! Some of the more outstanding architecture includes two mansions of coralstone: Henrietta, E of the Sandy Lane Hotel, and Ronald Tree's on Heron Beach, completed in 1947. Today, one can still wander mile after mile of beach-lined coast, taking in the sights.

HOLDERS HOUSE: This magnificently restored greathouse is just S of Sandy Lane in St. James Parish. It was constructed some 300 years ago on a ridge, at the center of what was once a 500-acre sugar and tobacco plantation. Its two-foot-thick plastered coralstone walls have multiple louvered exterior doors for good air circulation.

Holetown

This is hardly a town at all – Sunset Crest Shopping Centre is what saves it from mere village status. But it is the parish's hub, around which all of the resort hotels seem to branch off. It still has bits of nature scattered about, despite its development. Astride a small bridge near the Discovery Bay Hotel you can observe white egrets arriving to rest in trees at dusk. And the sunsets are still marvelous along the beaches.

HISTORY: The town was once known as Jamestown in honor of James I. Its current name comes from the "hole" into which settlers could anchor their ships.

SIGHTS: The remnants of **James Fort** lie behind the back of the police station where only two coralstone walls and a cannon remain. The Holetown Police Station was originally part of the gunner's quarters for the fort. The **Holetown Monument** is just a few yards N of the police station. It is constructed of softstone blocks with a wooden cross on top, and commemorates the 300th anniversary of the landing of the *Olive Blossom* in July 1605 – an incorrect date that should actually read 1625. **St. James Parish Church** is on the left-hand side of the road a few hundred yards farther N. It was built in 1785 after its predecessor was razed by the 1780 hurricane. St. James has one of the few reminders of early church architecture as represented by the porch tower with two crudely carved pillars and a keystone over the door. Fine stone sculptures grace the walls. Among these is one commemorating Sir John Alleyne's two wives and son John; it shows a view of Eton, the famous British public school. The old bell, cast in 1696 – prior to the renowned Liberty Bell which was cast in London in 1750 – is displayed inside. The "King William" referred to in the inscription is William III. Check out the 18th-C. tombstones and the memorial tablets, especially the racy one dedicated to Sir John Gay-Alleyne's wife that hangs on the side above the steps to the balcony. In part, the 1774 plaque reads that she:

"... fweetened the Joys, alleviated the Cares, & enlightened the Pleasures of the nuptial State... "

FOLKESTONE PARK: This area is also known as Barbados Marine Reserve and features tennis courts, a playground, and an artificial reef, purposefully formed by sinking the ship *Stavronikita*, which had been destroyed by fire in 1976. It has shaded benches as well as a small but fairly expensive restaurant and is a popular picnicing spot for locals. Its small **marine museum** (☎ 422-2871/2314) offers an eight-foot aquarium and hourly slide shows from 10:30. It is open Mon. to Fri. 10-5, Sat. and Sun., 10-6; B$1 admission, 50 cents for children. Snorkeling equipment is available for rent. Note that water sports are prohibited in the areas delineated by buoys. Follow the underwater trail along seven-mile-long Dottin's Reef a quarter- mile offshore. Folkestone House, nearby, is also a former fort.

BELLAIRS RESEARCH INSTITUTE: Scientists at this division of Canada's McGill University, located next to the Folkestone, have studied tropical biology relating to sea urchins, flying fish, and plankton; wind and solar power; tropical climatology; sea turtle conservation; and the possiblilities of using brackish or purified seawater in agriculture.

HERON BAY: Ronald Tree had this house built in 1947 amid 20 acres of verdant splendor. Its grounds include a mullet-stocked pond, a citrus orchard, and coconut palm grove. Overnight visitors have included the likes of Adlai Stevenson, Winston Churchill, Aristotle Onassis, and the Queen and Prince Phillip. It's right down the road from Colony Club and across from the entrance road to Porters. If you pass it on the beach, follow the beach down to the end and turn right, past blooming jasmine and frangipani trees, before encountering banyan trees near the main road. An incredible array of striking houses are around this stretch.

PORTERS HOUSE: This is one of the island's most majestic guesthouses and now serves as a private residence. It is located near Holetown and opposite Colony Club and Heron Beach. Although parts of it do date from the 17th C., most was built in the 18th and 19th C. It is approached by a paved road lined with mahogany trees. To get to the sugar oven next door, retrace your steps, follow the main road and pass by mooing cows to enter the creepy, deteriorating remains.

FROM HOLETOWN HEADING NORTH: Taking Highway 1, pass along the coast through the villages of Mount Steadfast, Weston, and Carlton. **St. Alban's Church** stands between the highway and the sea at Lower Carlton, St. James. It was once Clarendon Fort and offers a great view from the seawall.

VAUCLUSE FACTORY: This sugarcane processing plant is named after a department in southern France's Rhone Valley. It is situated off Highway 2A. There is an excellent view from Dukes nearby. **Jack-in-the-Box Gully**, also in the immediate vicinity, has a variety of trees, but not its namesake.

PORTVALE SUGAR FACTORY: In Blowers within the E part of the parish is this huge collection of sugar manufacturing and harvesting equipment housed in the **Sir Frank Hutson Sugar Machinery Museum (☎ 432-0100)**. This restored "boiling house" was opened in 1987 when the distinguished engineer was 91. Frank personally assembled the machinery found here. Visitors may see a model windmill and taste "sling" and molasses, both of which are by-products of the manufacturing process. During the cane season (Feb. to May), you may also tour the factory. It's open Mon. to Sat., 9-5; closed on major public holidays. Admission: B$5 adults, B$2.50 children.

St. James Practicalities

ACCOMMODATIONS: The exclusive **Sandy Lane Hotel (☎ 432-1311, fax 432-2954)** is set on a 380-acre sugar estate. It opened in 1961 and was renovated in both 1991 and 1994. The hotel was envisioned by its founder Ronald Tree as "an elegant country house party in English tradition" and is a member of Forte Exclusive Hotels, Elegant Resorts of Barbados, and Leading Hotels of the World. Tree designed much of the furniture himself and Robertson "Happy" Ward, an American, was the architect.

The hotel was built with no expense spared. Portuguese masons worked on the bathrooms. For many years its golf course was the only 18-hole course on the island. Tree brought his wealthy friends with him and the neighboring 380-acre Sandy Lane Estates contains more than 100 luxurious dwellings valued between US$350,000 and $3 million each! During its nearly 30 years, Sandy Lane has welcomed many of the high-and-mighty. Among those who have sojourned here are Tom Jones, Mick Jagger, Princess Margaret, Elton John, Jacqueline Kennedy Onassis, Kevin Costner, Fidel Castro, Claudette Colbert and David Niven. Since the mid-1960s it has been run by the Forte Hotels.

The recent renovations have given the hotel attractive furniture and a beautiful chandelier in the lobby, which were designed by Heather Aguilar-Swan. On the premises there is a 3,000-sq.-foot freeform freshwater swimming pool. Complimentary water sports include snorkeling, windsurfing, waterskiing, and Hobie cat and sunfish sailing. Golf and tennis lessons are available; there are five tennis courts (two are illuminated at night), and the golf course (scheduled to expand from 18 to 36 holes) is one of the finest on the island. Use of both tennis courts and golf course is complimentary. A special Tree House Club will babysit your children while educating them. Other special young adult activities are offered as well.

The hotel has 30 suites and 91 double rooms. Suites and exclusive rooms have a TV; in other rooms you will be charged extra. All have a/c, clock radios, telephones, room safes, mini-bars, hairdryers, and private patios or balconies. Newly renovated suites have huge bathrooms with climb-in marble baths, mirrors, glass-door showers, and a separate chamber with toilet and bidet. There are a total of three phones and the stationary comes with your name embossed. The hotel also has a number of shops; transfers to and from the airport are in Rolls or private cab. Honeymoon, "Classic Gold," diving, golf, diving, and other packages are available. Rates run from B$900 for a garden-view room off-season to B$4,400 for the penthouse during the high season. Airport transfers, welcome champagne bottle and fruit basket, breakfast and dinner, plus numerous other amenities are included in the price. A total of 15% is added for tax and service. For more information call 800-225-5843.

Another of the foremost resort hotels in the area is the **Coral Reef Club**, run by members of the English expatriate O'Hara family. The hotel dates from the early 1950s when the tourist industry was just beginning. Its compact cottage villas, spread over a large area, are an economic anachronism; today's high land prices would render them unfeasible. The twin themes here are the color white and the flower hibiscus. Everything – from the staff's uniforms to the buildings – is a pristine white. Flowers are everywhere, and hibiscus is the best represented – one of the housekeepers is a genius at arrangements. The 12-acre grounds, with their labeled trees, form a small botanical garden and the villas have names like "coconut" along with a framed picture and typed description of the tree. Generally speaking, the atmosphere here is one of gentle, mellow etiquette – even the birds appear to chirp politely. Wrought iron and yellow doors beckon you into the reception and dining area. Keep in mind that the villas towards the rear have a completely different ambiance than those facing the sea at the front, which comprise just 16 out of the 75. The deluxe suites feature a kitchenette, twin bedded room, private bath, two air conditioners, large living room, and balcony. There's also a pool and two tennis courts on the grounds. Rates run from B$250 pn during the summer for a superior single to B$1,600 pn for four people in a two-bedroom suite. The nearby **Sandpiper Inn**, also owned by the O'Hara family, has similar services and accommodations. Both hotels were remodeled in 1994. In the US, call (800) 223-1108; in Canada call (416) 322-7824, and in Britain call (0171) 730-7144.

Other large resorts and hotels in the parish include Buccaneer Bay, Colony Club, Glitter Bay, Tamarind Cove Hotels, Discovery Bay, and the Royal Pavilion. All are listed under the "Hotel Finder" at the back of this book.

DINING OUT: The **Sandy Lane Restaurant** (☎ 432-1311), overlooking the ocean, is one of the nation's most elegant dining spots and it compares favorably with the best European bistros. Its menus combine French, Bajan, and international cuisines. Dress here is generally "elegantly casual." It is administered by Executive Chef, Hans Schweitzer. The restaurant offers a daily afternoon tea, a traditional Sun. lunch, and a Fri. evening buffet. Dinner offers unique starters such as kingfish sashimi with lemon and yellow peppers, *avenelles* of dorado simmered in a chardonnay sauce, or lasagne of local vegetables with cream of leek sauce. Delicious soups are offered such as chilled tomato soup with avocado guacamole or pink prawn bisque with fine champagne. Main courses include cavalli fish marinated with fresh coconut and citrus baked in banana leaves or St. Vincent coral lobster served with brunoise of mango, papaya, and spring onions. One entrée is reserved for nutritional cuisine. You even have your choice of three different rolls! A waitperson will come by with a sterling silver brush to crumb your table after the main course. Dessert delights include praline and chocolate pyramid and a platter of cheeses served with crisp celery and grapes. Dinner comes to B$178 pp without drinks. Breakfasts are served buffet-fashion and you'll always find smoked salmon and made-to- order omelettes. Sandy Lane's more casual **Seashell Restaurant** and **Beach Restaurant** (buffet lunches) are open only during high season.

Holetown dining: La Maison (☎ 432-1156) is one of the nation's foremost gourmet restaurants. It has entrées from around B$45. La Maison is set in an attractive old coralstone Bajan house right on the sea and quite near Holetown. You can sit at one of the canopied tables on the terrace and choose from salmon mousse wrapped in sliced salmon with caper-cream sauce, red snapper marinated in herbs and honey with raspberry sauce, and lobster tail and jumbo shrimp, to name just a few. **The Mews** (☎ 432-1122) on 2nd St. is run by legendary Austrian chef, Josef Schwaiger. The building is an attractive white stucco house transformed into a stylish yet intimate bistro. Dishes include kingfish with anchovy, red snapper in pine-nut crust, carpaccio of tuna, and seafood canelloni. Dining is under the stars on a patio filled with plants and a fountain or on balconies. Entrées start at B$34. **Nico's** (☎ 432-6386), a wine bar and restaurant, is on the second floor of a townhouse on 2nd St., right across from The Mews. It serves grilled fish, soups, and salads as well as a wide range of wines (B$30 a bottle and up) and champagnes (B$100 a bottle and up). Also on 2nd St. is **Min's Chinese Restaurant** (☎ 432-5481); entrées from B$14-B$25. **The Chattel** (☎ 432-5278), 2nd St., offers Bajan cuisine for around B$12 lunch, B$20 dinner; a steel band plays on Mon. and Sat. Another bistro set in a chattel house is **Ragamuffins** (☎ 432-1295), 1st St., which serves Caribbean food; it has a blackboard menu. The **Garden Grill** and **Gourmet Shop** (☎ 432-7711) offers your choice of three-course dinners for B$55; they also sell chocolates, cheese, and other delicacies in their shop. **Raffles Restaurant** (☎ 432-6557), 1st St., wins the prize for the most unusual decor. It features zebra-striped couches, painted leopards, and representations of other jungle critters. Food ranges from baked island fish to pumpkin soup and entrées run from B$40-B$65. The **Surfside** (☎ 432-2105) offers seaside dining; it's behind the PO. **The Sandpiper Inn** (☎ 422-2251) is the gourmet restaurant belonging to the hotel of the same name. Specialties include blackened salmon and a potato pancake topped with sour cream and caviar. Prices start at B$35 and run up to B$70. **The Garden Restaurant** (☎ 432-1301) serves international and creole gourmet specialties. It is set in the Discovery Bay Beach Hotel Entrées run from B$30-B$60; live entertainment is common during the season.

Derricks dining: The Carambola (☎ 432-0832), one of the island's classiest gourmet bistros, is here – around 1.5 miles S of Holetown. It overlooks the emerald Caribbean and is unique in that it combines Thai and Western dishes. Entrées – from Caribbean shrimp to dolphin fish – start at about B$40 and run up to B$90 for lobster. Appetizers include hot and sour prawn soup and *paupiette* of salmon. Take your pick from apple and cinnamon *bonbonbenière*, chocolate profiteroles, and praline *petit pot* for desert. A selection of coffee liquers (B$10-B$15) are also offered. **The Coconut Creek Club** (☎ 432-0803), set next to beach coves, serves up a variety of special dishes. Dinner is four courses for B$60.

Payne's Bay dining: Payne's Bay, a bit farther S of Holetown, has a number of great restaurants. The **Bamboo Beach Bar** (☎ 432-0910) serves a variety of seafood specialties as well as steak and chicken. It is set right on the beach and the atmosphere is casual. It has good food, snacks are served in the afternoon, and there's often entertainment at night. **Kaskades Restaurant and Bar** (☎ 432-7981) has an "English Roast Dinner" on Mon. in a garden atmosphere. It has live entertainment on some nights. Entrées run from B$35-B$65. **Smugglers Cove** (☎ 432-1741) is a gourmet restaurant with a small menu that features items such as shrimp, escargot, lobster and fresh fish steak. Dinner entrées start at B$18. It's open for lunch and dinner. **Coach House** (☎ 432-1163) is an English pub-style bistro that offers a B$20 buffet lunch weekdays with local food. Entrées run from B$30-B$60; the lunch buffet is B$20. **Neptunes** (☎ 432- 6999/1332) is a very attractive and innovative gourmet seafood restaurant set inside the Tamarind Cove Hotel. Dishes such as conch and callaloo soup, blackened snapper, and smoked marlin are on the menu. It's air conditioned and open from 6 PM nightly. Entrées run from B$30-B$60. Inside the same hotel is the **Flamingo** (☎ 432-1332), which serves gourmet dinners, and **Barbaracoa**, which serves bar-style lunches. The **Buccaneer Bay Grill** specializes in European cuisine. **The Connisseur** (☎ 432-5737), opposite the hotel here, supplies wine and other beverages as well as gourmet foods. **Fathoms** (☎ 432-2568) is a beachside seafood restaurant; it's open for lunch and dinner. Dining is on a terrace overlooking the water. Entrées range between B$30 and $60. **Frank's Beach Bar** (in the Tropicana Hotel) has reasonably- priced food as well as changing facilities. **Treasure Beach Hotel** (☎ 432-1346) houses another well-known restaurant. Entrées run from B$32-B$60.

Prospect dining: A number of restaurants can be found in Prospect. **La Cage Aux Folles** (☎ 424-2424, open only for dinner), features local, Chinese, and international dishes. Set in a restored Edwardian mansion, it's one of the island's most renowned gourmet restaurants. Start with an appetizer such as smoked salmon *à* *la Russe*, or their soup, *ajo blanco*. Follow that by an entrée like *bouillabaissse á la Rouille*, and a *petit pot au chocolat* for dessert. **Angry Annie's Restaurant and Bar** (☎ 424-0425) offers in pasta and ribs; vegetarian dishes are also on the menu. Entrées are priced from B$20-B$45. The **Rose and Crown** (☎ 425-1074) is a small, attractive seafood restaurant. It's open for dinner; entrées are B$22-B$53. **Fiesta** (☎ 425-1107) is also here, as is **Koko's** (☎ 424-4557) – a small gourmet restaurant perched on the edge of the sea. Entrées run from B$22-B$42, and there are vegetarian dishes on the menu.

Dining north of town: The **Coral Reef Club** (☎ 422-2372) serves gourmet entrées ranging in price from B$65 on up to B$130. It features a barbecue with floor show and steel band on Thurs. nights and a buffet on Sun.

Porters dining: The **Palm Terrace** and **Café Tabora's** are gourmet bistros at the Royal Pavilion (☎ 422-4444). The **Piperade** is at the Glitter Bay Hotel (☎ 422-4111) next door. It offers Californian and American cooking. **Le Chateau Creole** (☎ 422-4116), with Caribbean and cajun fare, serves food in a garden atmosphere. A well-known choice is the Colony Club (☎ 422-2335), which has the **Orchids Restaurant** (live entertainment; buffet on Mon.) and the **Ocean Terrace Restaurant** (open for lunch, including Sun. buffet). Other choices in the vicinity include **Settlers Beach Hotel** (☎ 422-3052) and its gourmet restaurant (B$60-B$120 for entrées). **Folkestone Restaurant and Bar**, set on the beach in Folkestone Park, offers *cou cou* and flying fish for lunch on Wed.

BUDGET DINING: Catamara in Holetown offers Bajan fare like fried flying fish along with peas and rice. The **Beach Club** has nightly specials. The only truly budget place to eat in town is the take-out counter inside the **99 Convenience Store**. **Holmes Bar**, a rum shop in St. James, serves food until the wee hours. It is set atop Holder's Hill – off Highway 1, opposite Tamarind Cove – and has real rural atmosphere, right down to the spicy fried chicken. **Chefette's** is likely the only fast-food emporium that has its own beach; it serves *rotis*. The **Pizza House** (☎ 432-0227) is in Holetown.

BEACH PACKAGES: The **West Beach Restaurant** (☎ 230-2730, 432-0679) gears itself towards cruise ship passengers, offering skiing, sailing, beach chairs, wave runners, banana and tube rides, and a Bajan buffet lunch for B$130; hours are 10:30-2:30, Mon. - Sat. **MARKET FOOD: Super Centre** is at Sunset Crest. **St. Elmos Variety** is in town. **Wick's Discount Wine and Spirits** sells French bread at B$3.50 per stick, as well as the obvious. A small **farmer's market** at Sunset Crest – across the road from Inn on the Beach and directly across from the 99 Convenience Store – sells fruits and vegetables. There are a number of other small markets around the parish. **bakeries: Paris** is in Sunset Crest.

ENTERTAINMENT: The **Beach Club** (☎ 432-1309) presents karaoke on Mon., fire eating and limbo on Wed. (with a dinner buffet), and Axis plays on Thurs. Most of the hotels and some restaurants provide near-nightly entertainment during the tourist season.

SERVICES: Profile Health and Beauty Club (☎ 432-1393), 1st St., offers everything from yoga classes to kung fu to aromatherapy to artificial nails. Holetown has pharmacies and other stores.

St. Thomas

St. Thomas is one of only two island parishes unexposed to the sea, St. George being the other. Three highways (Highway 1A from St. James, which runs into 2A, Highway 2, and Highway 2A) intersect the parish. Its features include the island's only cave, a nature preserve, and some examples of classic architecture.

Along Highway 2A

WARRENS: This magnificent greathouse was once the center of a working plantation, but it has been encroached upon by residential and commercial structures and no longer serves as a plantation house. It was built in 1686 and has since been preserved by its owners, the C.O. Williams Construction Company. To the E lies one of the island's most venerable baobab trees. This one was planted in 1735 and is smaller than the one in Queen's Park.

SHARON: Sharon is the oldest Moravian church on the island. It stands on the side of a hill on the main road between Bathsheba and Bridgetown. This religious edifice, constructed in 1799, is one of the few 18th-C. structures on the island which remains unaltered; it was restored to all its glory in 1989. The church's architecture reflects the middle-European roots of the Moravian faith.

BAGATELLE: Bagatelle Great House, off Highway 2A, is owned by Richard and Val Richings. It was built in 1645 and was originally the property of Lord Willoughby; it was then named Parham Park

House. In 1877, its name was changed to Bagatelle by its new owners, who took it over in partial repayment for a gambling debt. The story goes that after the property was lost, the former owner shrugged and said it was just a "bagatelle," French for a trifle. It was converted into **Bagatelle Restaurant** (☎ 421- 6767) in 1970 and Lord Willoughby's bust graces the souvenir menus supplied with the meals served here. Dining is elegantly casual and only a fixed-price dinner menu (around B$100) is served; reservations are required. The menu is Caribbean/French and the atmosphere is exquisitely elegant. Be sure to check out the art gallery upstairs if you dine here. Several miles farther on is the **St. Thomas Parish Church**, which was destroyed by hurricanes in 1675, 1780, and 1831, and was damaged by the storm of 1731.

WELCHMAN HALL GULLY: This windy, cool, and damp ravine (☎ 438-6671) opened to the public in 1961 and has now been developed as a national park. It was named after former land-holder General Williams, a Welshman, and one of the earliest colonists. Around 1860, one of his descendants cleared some acreage and planted fruit and spice trees here, before wilderness again overtook it. It was purchased by the National Trust in 1962.

You enter via an orange grove and a flower garden of bougainvillea, frangipani, and begonias. The gully is the closest you'll get to feeling what pre-British Barbados must have been like. Meet the chattering monkeys which abound on the grounds (best seen in early morning and late afternoon). The area is a paradise for birdwatchers, so definitely bring your binos. Benches are placed at intervals so you can relax and hang out; just sit very still and watch for birds and other creatures. The legendary Elephant Stalactite is a four-foot-long and wide stalactite which has merged with a stalgmite to form a large pillar. It's near the original entrance to Harrison's Cave. Vegetation includes strangler figs, tree ferns, nutmeg and clove trees. The nutmegs came from Grenada and the cloves were imported from Zanzibar. There's also a 25-foot traveller's tree, which originates in Madagascar; the thirsty visitor could gouge the trunk with a knife and drink the water collected in the interstices. At the secondary entrance you'll find a steep path leading to a lookout point with a great view. Welchman Hall is open daily (except public holidays) from 9-5 and admission is B$10 adults, B$5 children. **getting here:** From Bridgetown, take the ABC Hwy. to the Warrens Roundabout, then take Hwy. 2A and follow the signs (including those to Harrison's Cave). **in the area:** To use your time wisely, combine a visit to the gully with a trip to Harrison's Cave. A large variety of fruit trees grow in the village of Carrington nearby.

HARRISON'S CAVE: This cave is one of the largest in the Caribbean. It's located on Highway 2 near Welchman Hall. The cave had been common knowledge among locals for hundreds of years, but was not explored until 1970 by Ole Sorenson, a Danish speleologist. Heavy flooding in that year had opened up the entrance to what was to be known as crystal caverns; exploring the cave, he discovered a number of big chambers. One of the more remarkable features is the large number of virgin white, pear-shaped stalactites here. It takes 220 years for one inch of stalactite to grow, and the cave is over a half-million years old! In 1981, the government opened it to the public; it is now one of the most popular and unusual attractions.

The tour covers one mile and another two miles remain undeveloped. Tours are given every hour from 9-4 and, if you're in a group, reservations (☎ 438-6640) are advisable. Admission is B$15 adult, B$7.50 children. After buying your ticket, head for a case-lined room which displays pre-Columbian artifacts. The video show here provides a background that prepares you for what you will see. Exiting the room, you grab one of the brightly colored helmets (don't forget the protective cloth), place it on your head, and board the open-air electric bus for your 45-minute trip down into the cavernous depths. You pass by waterfalls, streams, cascades, and pools, then return after seeing the Great Falls. Your point of entry is the Great Hall, which is set 120 feet below the surface; it is divided into upper and lower levels. Continuing, you pass various formations such as "The Village." You are allowed to get out, walk around and take photos at various other points such as "Twin Falls" and "The Altar." The "Cascade Pool" features a 40-ft-high waterfall. You dismount at the cavern's lowest point and cross the side of a waterfall that plunges into a blue-green pool. You also pass the cave's natural entrance. The ladder and boat you see here are used in an emergency. **practicalities:** There's a small cafeteria and a gift shop. For more exotic dining, try the Rastafarian bamboo stand at Sturges (by the intersection of the roads to the cave and to St. Nicholas Abbey). They have drinking coconuts as well as fruit and *I-tal*(vegetarian) dishes.

FISHER POND: The two-storied Fisher Pond house, which antedates the 1831 hurricane, is set near the junction to Bathsheba. Two millwalls (ruins of windmills once used in sugar production) stand here. **Russia** or **Rusher Gully** is nearby and is marked by vertical coral cliffs running along both sides.

St. Joseph and Bathsheba

St. Joseph may be the island's smallest parish, but it is not without its delights. It offers Bathsheba, one of the island's most famous fishing villages, along with a portion of Hackleton's Cliff, a remarkable set of gardens, and a quite splendid coastline. The arriving African air here is said to be incredibly fresh and brisk, as it hasn't been near land for thousands of miles. Saharan dust has even been known to blow in on occasion. Highway 3A and the East Coast Road, which enter the parish from St. Joseph, are two of the major transportation arteries. Coming from St. George, Highway 3 descends down steep Horse Hill to Joe's River Plantation and on.

BATHSHEBA: This fishing village is 14 miles from Bridgetown, but a world apart. Its rocky terrain – one of the most photographed spots on the island – surrounds a spectacular beach. This shady beach plays host to an annual surfing competition and is named the "Soup Bowl" because of its foamy surf. The **Bonito** is a restaurant worth trying here and hotels include the **Atlantis** and the **Edgewater**. All three offer legendary Sun. brunches. The East Coast Road goes from Bathsheba along the old railway route to Belleplaine, heading up into St. Andrew.

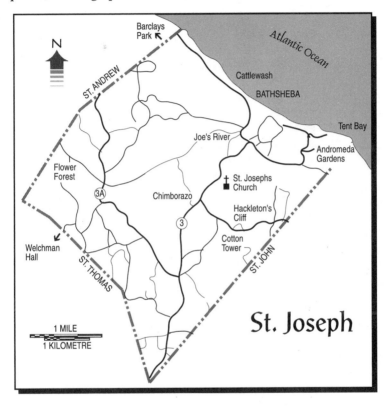

FLOWER FOREST: This tourist attraction (☎ 433-8152, fax 433-8365) consists of an expertly-landscaped forest that retains much of its original wild ambiance. It is set in the heart of the Scotland District in Richmond, St. Joseph. Just pick up a leaflet and follow it along; the 50 acres are divided into eight sections, each marked on ceramic stones interspaced on the attractive, well-manicured grounds. Allow an hour or more for your visit because this is a great place to relax; bring your sketchpad, easel, or camera. Paths rise and fall, bringing into view mango, golden apple, breadfruit, cocoa, avocado and bamboo. You'll find flowers like torch ginger, lady in a boat, Eucharist lily, sweet lime from the Philippines, Mexican breadfruit, and others. Monkeys are seen at dawn or dusk here. **practicalities:** The gardens may be reached via Highway 3A, which runs past the villages of Sugar Hill, Chimborazo, Spa Hill, Fruitful Hill, and Cane Garden. You head through attractive secondary forest on your way to the entrance. In addition to a restaurant, there's also a Best of Barbados shop here. It's open daily 9 to 5, B$10 admission; children B$5.

COTTON TOWER: Near the top of Horse Hill (also known as The Devil's Bowling Alley or Bowling Alley Hill), a byway leads to this former signal station. The three-storey structure was named after Miss Dorothy Cotton, daughter of Lord Combermere, Gov. of Barbados, and served as a message relay post. In the plantation era, messages originating from the Governor's residence in Queen's Park were relayed to St. Anne's Fort and on to Gun Hill, Moncrieffe (on the border between St. John and St. Philip), and then to Cotton Tower. Hoisting the appropriate flags, Cotton Tower's soldiers would relay the message to Grenade Hall (on the site of Farley Hill and now incorporated with the Wildlife Reserve). Construction started in 1819. One window points in the direction of Gun Hill and another towards Grenade Hall. From the top, the view takes in Parks Road Saddle back to the N and Buckden Gully to the S. Rising from atop the hill in the distance is St. Joseph's Anglican Church. Hike through the woods from Cotton Tower, passing through a break in the cliff wall, to Dacres Hill.

ANDROMEDA GARDENS: This is the island's most famous garden and was begun by the late Iris Bannochie in 1954. A visit here might be the perfect prelude or climax to a leisurely lunch at the Atlantis Hotel, the Edgewater, or the Bonito Restaurant. The flowers in these gardens cling tightly to the rocks and take their name from the mythical Greek maiden who was tied to a rock as a sacrifice for a sea monster. The massive boulders here – as wide as 27 feet (9 m) – were toppled by torrential flooding. Trees include the fustic, bearded fig, whitewood, pop-a-gun, and maypole. The lily pond, bridged by a causeway, has night- and day-blooming lillies on opposite sides. This separation allows both types to flourish because, if they were planted together, the day bloomers would soon crowd the nighties out. Ingeniously-designed bridges and paths criss-cross the gardens. Some are made of local sandstone, others of brick; some have grass, others are concrete slabs decorated with leaf imprints. Flowers include begonias, hibiscus, red ginger lillies, and bougainvilleas. In one special section, orchids jut straight up. A swimming pool was built in 1956 and the excavated soil was used to construct a terraced garden. There are large palm and orchid gardens, which – as with the entire grounds – can be explored. Singing birds complete the picture in this serene setting one which combines a British sense of orderly restraint, an E. Asian design, and a tinge of Caribbean mysticism. It's open 9-5, except certain public holidays. Admission is B$10 for adults, B$5 for children.

VICINITY OF ANDROMEDA: Tent Bay, near the Atlantis and the Edgewater hotels, is the sole location along the parish's coast where fishing boats operate. You may see fish being unloaded from 1-3 PM daily during the season. **Foster Hall Woods**, also in the vicinity, is second only to Turner's Hall Woods as an ecological preserve.

OTHER SIGHTS: Atop Spa Hill, the ruins of **Spa House** command one of the island's most magnificent panoramas – over the wild and rugged territory to the E. The name Spa spawned the name spawgee for the redlegs who lived here. At the time **Chimborazo Hill** was christened, it was believed to be the island's highest point and was therefore named after Ecuador's Mt. Chimborazo, then believed to be the world's highest peak. A small chapel atop **Gagg's Hill** is built of coralstone and features four tombstones set into the floor.

St. Joseph Practicalities

ACCOMMODATIONS: Kingsley Club (☎ 433-9422) in Cattlewash at the S base of the magnificent beach running along the E coast, is the perfect get away. With the exception of a few houses for rent, it is the sole accommodation in this area. The white and blue color scheme gives it a classic W. Indian feel to it. The guesthouse is of postwar construction and the restaurant is more than a century old. Its rooms are equipped with one or two double beds, overhead fan, and a private bath with shower. The corridor has a large selection of books and magazines. Off-season rates run from around B$48 with breakfast and B$72 with breakfast and dinner. The Atlantis and the Edgewater hotels in Bathsheba are the other two closest accommodations.

FOOD AND DINING: Kingsley Club is the exclusive venue for the Cattlewash area. Its restaurant is immaculately done up with blue-cushioned white wicker chairs and matching tablecloths and napkins. Heading N along the East Coast Road in St. Andrew are the **East Coast Café** and snackbar on the beach across from Barclay's Park; Belleplaine also has a few snackbars.

The **Atlantis Hotel** (☎ 433-9445) is best known for its buffet lunches, which are a celebration of local cuisine. It can be crowded – especially on weekends – so be sure to reserve. A typical spread is pan-fried flying fish or chicken served with rice and peas, along with vegetables and desserts. Expect to spend around B$30-B$35, including a drink and tip. The **Edgewater Inn** (☎ 433-9900) serves three meals daily plus a Sun. buffet (B$25). The small **Bonito Restaurant** (☎ 433-9034), on the main stretch in Bathsheba, features local seafood, including crab. Their Sun. buffet is quite popular with locals. The second-floor location gives a great view of the bay. A small snack bar is just down the road and rum shops are nearby.

St. Andrew

St. Andrew is one of the least-populated parishes (pop. 6,500). It retains an atmosphere and charm all its own. The parish contains part of the scenic Scotland District as well as a stretch of the East Coast Road, it also features the island's best-preserved windmill, a nature reserve, pottery village, as well as other attractions. Other than the East Coast Road, the parish's major artery is Highway 2.

CHERRY TREE HILL: Resplendent rows of wind-bent and gnarled mahogany (not cherry!) trees line the avenue leading up to it. There's a great view from the top gazing S to Chalky Mount and Hackleton's Cliff; there are also monkeys in the vicinity. A path at the base of the hill leads to the right and curves around E to a sheltered gully forested with casuarinas. A path of a few hundred yards leads to the flattened top of Mt. Stepney, known as **"The Mount."** Another path from its top heads along the escarpment's edge. One side is lined with sour grass and maypoles (century plants); the other is a dropoff. A jumble of huge boulders (some of them house-sized) covering a one-mile area rests at the foot of Mt. Stepney – the result of a 1901 landslide. A winding path leads through them to Boscobelle Church. **Paul's Point** offers a magnificent view over Gay's Cove to Pico Teneriffe. From Cherry Tree Hill, the road continues on to St. Peter.

MORGAN LEWIS MILL: Morgan Lewis Mill is the best-preserved sugar mill in the Caribbean; it's the only one on the island with its arms and well house intact. It is typical of the Dutch-style mills that once dotted the island and is the only one remaining from the days when cane was ground. There were around 500 grinding mills; they lasted until the early 1900s when they were replaced by the more efficient steam-run mills. The three-roller Morgan Lewis is of the type introduced around 1798. It was manufactured in Derby, England in 1908. Squeezing 50-65% of the sugar from the cane, these mills were a big improvement over the former cattle-powered ones that extracted only about 50% of the juice. It is run by the Barbados National Trust, which has installed a permanent display of sugar manufacturing accessories, including ladles and yokes, at the site. Climb to the top for a great view. Morgan Lewis (☎ 422-9222) is open Mon. to Fri. from 9-5, except public holidays. Admission is B$5 adults, B$2.50 children.

Windmills of Barbados

As any visitor to the Caribbean Islands can attest, the ruins of windmills and sugar factories are a prominent feature on the landscape. On many islands, they have been included in restored estates or incorporated in the construction of tourist hotels. In Barbados, one millwall even supports a radio dish antenna belonging to the Caribbean Meteorological Institute. Some are covered with the "shower of gold," an attractive climbing vine introduced from S. America.

The island's windmills were built between the beginning of the 1650s and the end of the 1700s. The Dutch are credited with their introduction. Bajan mills are taller than those found in the Leeward Islands. Historian Schomburgk wrote that the island had 506 windmills in 1848; ruins of around 100 or so still stand today. Arnold's Mill is set on a hill above Highway 2A in St. Peter. It is reputedly the oldest and dates from the 1700s. Most others date from the 1800s. The first mills were built with coral rubble, but later versions also had block stone.

MORGAN LEWIS BEACH: The area S from Chandler Bay to Green Pond offers some of the most remote places on the island. The view from Morgan Lewis Beach is of totally unexploited wilderness. Check out the view from **Paul's Point**.

ST. ANDREW'S ANGLICAN CHURCH: This church was condemned in 1842 and rebuilt from 1846-55. It is a survivor of the disastrous 1780 and 1831 hurricanes. Near the church is the Walker's sand dune, which has been threatened with ecological damage by extensive mining. High-quality clear glass cannot be produced from the island's sand, but green and amber glass can.

Shorey Village, nearby, is famous as the birthplace of legendary cricketer Conrad Hunte.

BARCLAY'S PARK: Good picnicking but dangerous swimming can be found at this 50-acre park which climbs up a hillside. It was a 1966 Independence gift from Barclay's Bank International and lies off the East Coast Road near the border with St. Joseph. There's a snackbar here. It's a good place to visit on holidays and Sundays when you can see how Bajans relax.

CHALKY MOUNT: This is actually a rugged range of hills that rise 571 feet over the road. A few potters still linger on here, a reminder of the time when this community was *the* major supplier of household ceramic items. It's a great place to see the sunset. Chalky Mount can be reached from Highway 2; take the road to the right heading off to Coggins Hill which leads up to it. A moderately

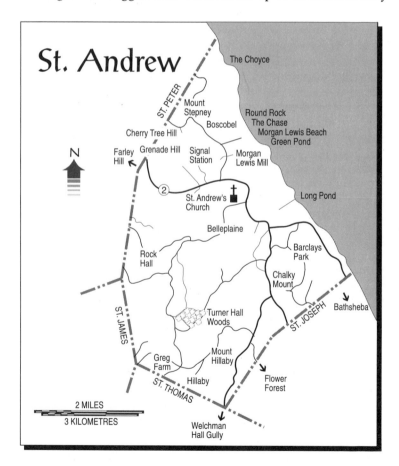

difficult path goes to the summit. Its brownish- red soil reflects the high clay content. Kickwheel-powered pottery produced here includes *conerees*, pots for pickling and cooking stews and *monkeys*, water jugs designed to cool water.

HAGGATTS AGRICULTURAL STATION: Visitors to the home of the soil conservation plan for the Scotland District can see the methods being implemented to improve the area. Because the clay foundation under the soil is impenetrable, the water slips away, taking the topsoil with it. The station is developing various anti-erosion techniques. One method is to plant grass on hillsides to hold the water; another is the use of *gaboins*, stone-filled wire baskets that slow down the flooding after rains. The center also distributes fruit trees, including mango, Barbados cherry, and citrus.

TURNER HALL WOODS: These woods, rising 600-800 feet (180-240 m) above sea level, cover 46 acres (18.6 ha) on a spur running NE from Mt. Hillaby. They form one of the island's few remaining glades, similar to other semi-evergreen forests found in Antigua, Trinidad, Martinique, and other islands. Like them, it receives 60-70 inches (150-175 cm) of rain per year. Coming here will give you a feel for how the island was before the arrival of the Europeans. **getting there:** Follow a tree-lined track from the village of St. Simon on the road to the S of Belleplaine. Where the trail crosses a bridge and ascends towards the Turner's Hall-Bridgetown road, a side trail leads to the best-preserved section of the forest.

  flora and fauna: At least 32 species of trees are present, including such Bajan stalwarts as sand box, macaw palm, silk cotton, locust, fustic, red cedar, and cabbage palm. These are supplemented by 30 species of shrubs. One tree found only here is the jack-in-the-box. Its name comes from its hollow, topless small fruit which has a small seed standing inside; it can be identified by its large, heart-shaped leaves. The woods are home to a few monkeys along with a four-foot-wide and deep hole known as the Boiling Spring; the natural gas exuded from it may flicker if ignited. **birding:** Birds seen here include the scaly-naped pigeon, the Lesser Antillean bullfinch, the Carib grackle, the gray kingbird, the black-whiskered vireo, and the Caribbean Zenaida dove.

  hiking: A five-mile (8-km), four-hour hike from Turner's Hall Woods heads E, down via St. Simon and Haggatts Factory, to Belleplaine and Windy Hill. The more difficult three-hour hike from Mose Bottom to Haggatts Factory follows a riverbed; it involves traversing rocky terrain thick with brush. A third four-mile (6.4-km), two-hour hike runs from Turner's Hall Plantation N and then W to Rock Hall village and on to Spring Head.

nearby sights: The only uninhabited valley in Barbados lies S of the woods. It's bordered by Haggarts to the E, Mose Bottom to the W, and White Hill to the S. It was populated until 30 years ago when landslides and transportation hassles forced residents to relocate. Today, it is planted with mangos and coconuts and is also used as pasture for cattle.

UP MT. HILLABY: The road through **Mount All** and **White Hill** is perched on the back of a ridge and affords spectacular views. At the top of White Hill, turn left to reach the summit of Mt. Hillaby (1,116 feet), where you can see the island from windward to leeward. To the S lie rolling fields of cane and other crops; to the N are the villages of **White Hill** and **Gregg Farm** with St. Peter's eastern ridge in the background. (Pudding and souse is for sale on Sun. at Gregg Farm village.) The best view is to the E – ravines, hills, and gullies. Mt. Hillaby is actually a dirt- covered, chalk hill and is rather undramatic in itself. The metal-capped cement stum, which reads "Inter American Geodetic Survey. Do not Disturb. Hillaby. 1953." shows you're in the right place.

BLEAK HOUSE: A plantation commanding a great view of the entire Scotland District is at the parish's W end, close to its border with St. Peter. It may be reached by following Highway 2; make the first left turn after Farley Hill Park. Its 160 acres were constructed in 1886 by order of eccentric Charles Peddlar. They are now being used for farming and animal husbandry.

St. Andrew Practicalities

BUDGET DINING AND MARKET FOOD: Belleplaine has **Belleplaine Supermarket and Snackette** and the **Likorish Bar & Grocery**. Try the **East Coast Café** and the **snack bar** at Barclay's Park.

St. Peter and Speightstown

St. Peter is the only prefecture to cross the island W to E, although the eastern portion is mighty skinny. The twin contrasts of ultra-posh St. James to the S and ultra-rural St. Lucy to the N are easily accessible. The parish's charms include one of the island's architectural gems – a ruined greathouse transformed into a national park – the island's second major town, and a wildlife reserve. An added feature are the 20-odd millwalls here, the most of any parish. **getting here:** The most popular route runs via Highway 1 from St. James, but the approach from St. Peter is particularly scenic – either via Cherry Tree Hill or Farley Hill. If you enter this way, the first attraction you come to will be St. Nicholas Abbey. Coming from St. James, on the other hand, you will doubtless be passing through Speightstown, the mainstay of the island's N.

Speightstown

This is currently the second most important town, Bridgetown being No.1, in terms of economic and cultural importance. It is all archetypal balconied houses and narrow streets, with the exception of a shopping mall, and has remained virtually unchanged for over a hundred years. It is not so much the individual buildings in this town that create its unusual ambiance, but the total effect created by the whole. The National Trust is planning restoration work here that could transform this rather shabby town into one of the most elegant in the Caribbean. One step toward this is a "Paint the Town Competition:" residents will renovate and paint their properties and receive discounts from local paint companies. Results should be apparent by the time of your visit.

The town's bypass channels traffic out of the center, thus retaining the serenity. Walk around here on a Sat. morning when the hucksters are out selling vegetables in full force. Crop Over floats are on display near the Fisherman's Café, and you might see the Salvation Army band marching on holidays and special occasions.

HISTORY: The town's name (pronounced "Spikestown") comes from the land's previous owner, William Speight, who was a member of the first assembly. The town rapidly gained importance and became well known for its trade with Bristol; it was dubbed with the sobriquets "Little Bristol" and "New Bristol." Its importance derived from two sources: poor communications between the northern parishes and Bridgetown, and from the distant financial connections of a few enterpreneurial expatriate merchants. As the merchants passed up, up, and away into the great marketplace in the sky and as intra-island communications improved, the town's prominence faded. During the days of the *Speightstown Schooner*, passage could be made to Bridgetown three times per week. The duration of the voyage was always uncertain, but it generally took

1-1.5 hours. Denmark Fort played an important role in the town's defense when Cromwellite Sir George Ayescue attacked. The town's reputation for racism and upper-class snobbery – a tradition which is, thankfully, receding – was one of its less enviable features. The island saying, "Speightstown hens don't lay home," came out of the empirical observation that the town's women frequently married outsiders. Another insightful description refers to a "Speightstown Compliment," which is a backhanded one.

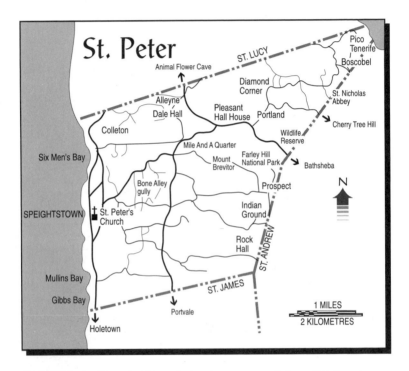

SIGHTS: St. Peter's Church, having escaped the 1780 hurricane, was destroyed by the whopper of 1831. It is at the corner of Church and Queen Streets. A Georgian-style structure stood from 1837 until 1980 when a fire destroyed all but its walls and steeple. The subsequent restoration (from 1980-83) cost B$750,000. The side of **Church St.** opposite St. Peter's Church retains some of the shops – with overhanging galleries supported by slender poles – characteristic of streets in the old days. The remnants of the **Denmark** and **Orange forts** stand in the town's center. Be sure to see the building next to the Golden Crust Bakery with religious slogans painted on brown boards covering its walls and windows. A good place to hang out is the **Esplanade** along Sand St. – delineated by a row of cannon pointing seaward. Relax on its lime green benches set below mahoe and tamarind trees filled with singing birds. Everyone is staring off into the distance – like characters in a play pausing before their lines.

IN AND AROUND TOWN: Speightstown Mall, opened in 1980, offers a wide variety of shops, banks, and fast food. **Arlington** is one of the best-preserved colonial Bajan houses; it housed the first Public Health Centre and now hosts the Lions Club (north). It was also home to the Skinner family for generations; they operated a shop on the gound floor. The building is very long and narrow, with two-foot-thick walls.

On the outskirts of Speightstown near Cobbler's Cove stand some magnificent estates. One is Claudette Colbert's mansion; if you're fortunate you might tread on the same beach spot where Ronald Raegan once basted his buns! The second is **Leamington**, the former residence of the US ambassador. Farther down the road, beautiful **Mullin's beach** is generally deserted. A popular restaurant and bar of the same name are here.

SPEIGHTSTOWN BUS TERMINAL: Speightstown's modern and comfortable bus terminal (☎ 422-2410) stands in the N part of town, near the bypass. Its mandarin-orange-striped interior offers benches, piped in music, and a monitor giving estimated departure times. All buses leaving from here originate in Bridgetown, except for the Oistins and Speightstown buses. Ask at the information counter concerning departure times. It is a virtual certainty that your bus will be late; it is also dead certain that the one time you take a quick walk and return late, your bus will have left on time! The *Boscobel bus* runs to Ashton Hall, Mile and a Quarter, Diamond Corner, the Castle, the Baltic, and on to Boscobel. The *Indian Ground bus* runs to Portland, Welchtown, Prospect, Indian Ground, and French Village. The *Josey Hill bus* runs to Checker Hall, Bourbon, Mt. Gay, and Josey Hill. The *Connell Town bus* runs to Heywood, Six Men's, Checker Hall, Harrisons, Crab Hill, Cluffs, Bright Hall, Flatfield, Connell Town, and River Bay. The *Pie Corner bus* runs to Six Men's, Pickerings, Half Acre, Spring Hall, Spring Garden, Rockfield, Pie Corner, Graveyard, and The Baltic. The *St. Lucy's Church bus* runs to Litchfield, St. Joseph's Hospital, Mile and a Quarter, Alleynedale, St. Lucy's Church, Trents, Friendship, Crab Hill, and Samond (near Archer's Bay). The *Archer's Bay bus* runs a similar route. The *Speightstown bus* covers the same route as the Indian Ground bus, but continues on to Welchtown, Greenland, Waker's, Beleplaine, and Cattlewash before climbing the hill past Andromeda Gardens to Bathsheba. The *Oistins bus* bypasses Bridgetown, but still goes by the coast from the Garrison on. If you want to get to Farley Hill, take an *Indian Ground* or *Bathsheba bus*; for St. Nicholas Abbey, then jump on a *Boscobel bus* and, for the magnificent stretch of coast around Little Bay, take the *Pie Corner bus* to the end of the line.

HEADING NORTH: Heywood Beach lies opposite the all-inclusive **Almond Beach Village** tourist development (one of the island's largest resorts), to the N of Speightstown. No one has ever satisfactorily explained why the small bay farther on, once a whaling center, is known as "Six Men's." One story has it that six Indians were found there by arriving settlers. Today, it features tattered fishing boats resting on wood blocks and oil drums amid the wrecks of cars. Turn left at the nearby junction where houses are named "Snugness" and "Snug Haven." Past **Sherman's Bay**, another fishing area, is a narrow but long sand beach. You will often see boats being caulked prior to painting during the fall months in preparation for the winter season. In the distance is a loading ramp extension belonging to the economically-ailing Arawak Cement Plant. Next up the road is the **Half Moon Bathing Facility**, which has a rather small beach. To reach **Maycock Bay**, continue along the main road until the turn-off past the cement plant. This narrow bay, only 100-200 feet (60-90 m) wide, stretches for about a mile and is the most spectacular location before Harrison Point. Two steep trails lead down to the beach and the ruins of Maycock's Fort. At nearby **Harrison Point** stands the compound of the Barbados Defence Force, formerly the US Naval Facility. The facility itself is off-limits, but a track leads down to **Harrison Point Lighthouse**, from which another path at its base leads to the rugged, eroded coast. The lighthouse dates from the 1920s. **Hangman's Bay** lies to the S nearby.

ALL SAINTS CHURCH: This is the oldest church on the island and was constructed in 1649. It stands 1.5 km from the district of Mile and a Quarter. It succumbed to the 1831 storm, having already braved the hurricanes of 1675 and 1780. A foundation stone was laid in 1839 and the rebuilt church was consecrated in 1843 – only to be demolished some 40 years later after structural problems were uncovered. The present version dates from 1884. Its 17th-C. graveyard holds the remains of William Arnold, allegedly the first Englishman to set foot on Barbados. Back on Highway 2A is monkey-inhabited **Baker Woods** and, at its end, **Sion Hill Gully**, populated with rubber trees, runs under the road. From **Pleasant Hall** off Highway 2A, a narrow and twisting road leads through the **Second High Cliff. Arawak Cave** is immediately at the beginning of this to the right. The cave has a small carved sculpture in the shape of an Indian head.

BONE ALLEY GULLY: This gully, also known as Whim Gully, lies near Speightstown off Highway 1. Despite the forbidding name, it is actually a wide-open natural area – a great place to go for a walk. Sailor Gully and Rock Hall are two other impressive locations. They are N of Speightstown and can be accessed by Highway 2A. **The Rock** – a set of 80-ft-high (25 m) vertical white cliffs festooned with thick vines – overlooks 80-ft-deep, 300- yard-long Sailor's Gully. **Orange Hill** offers a panoramic view of the area.

MOUNT BREVITOR AND VICINITY: Indian artifacts have been found in caves between Mount Brevitor and Portland, and in a large stalactite- and stalagmite-laden cave underneath the hill. The caves were used by the Indians for burial and, possibly, religious ceremonies. Don't miss the wonderful view of the leeward coast. Other great views can be had from the road that connects Rock Hall to Mount Brevitor.

ALLEYNE DALE HALL: This was built by the Terril family around 1680-85; it was known as The Terrils until the nickname Cabbage Tree Hall stuck – after the long avenue of majestic towering cabbage palms that once flanked the entrance road. Sir John Alleyne purchased the plantation house in the 18th C. It was said that the ghost of the last Terril – who committed suicide and was interred in the cellar – still paced the hallways. Sweet lime hedges, more than a century old, surround the three-storey building. The mill-wall here, built in 1861, is the island's tallest. Washing Pond, also on the estate, has the reputation for never drying up – even under the severest drought.

PROSPECT: This relatively high (823 feet) area near St. Peter's Parish is named for its view. It's off a side road down the highway just before Farley's as you approach from Speightstown. The sea is visible on both sides and it's a great place to picnic. Walking through Prospect Woods will bring you to another fine viewpoint, with Cleland downhill and Chalky Mount off in the distance.

FARLEY HILL NATIONAL PARK: This is one of the island's top tourist attractions. The mansion commanded a view of the ocean on three sides until the demon fire so and thoughtlessly destroyed it some years back. Today, several acres of verdant parkland here contain carefully cultivated tropical vegetation. The grounds offer a variety of fruit trees; cross the bridge below the greathouse ruins near the parking lot to find a grove of casuarina, young mahogany, and whitewood. Don't miss sitting on the lime green benches which are sheltered by casuarina trees. The bluff is cooled by the ocean breeze and commands a dramatic view over the rugged Scotland District and the coast.

history: The greathouse entrance, standing 900 feet (275 m) above sea level, was once lined with towering cabbage palms. A side mahogany staircase led upstairs to the bedrooms. Distinguished visitors over the years have included Prince Alfred, The Duke of Edinborough (in 1861), Prince Albert Victor, and Prince George (later King George V). In 1956 the house was camouflaged almost unrecognizably for its incognito role as the mansion, "Belle Fontaine," in the 20th Century Fox production of the classic flick, *An Island in the Sun*. The coral gates in front of the ruin were brought in during the film's production. Queen Elizabeth II unveiled a statue here for the opening ceremonies when it was declared a national park (after its purchase by the Barrow Government in 1966). Open daily 9-6; a parking fee is charged. Highway 1 leads down from Farley Hill to the W toward the parish's more populated sector and on through to Speightstown.

BARBADOS WILDLIFE RESERVE: This project of the Barbados Primate Center should, more accurately, be described as an open-air zoo as most of the animals have been imported. It gives you an opportunity to observe the island's green monkeys (see Fauna in the Introduction) and other indigenous and not-so-native fauna close at hand. A gravel road across the highway almost due N of Farley National Park runs through the sugarcane fields and leads to the entrance. There's a small covered restaurant along a brick path that heads past aloe vera and clumps of cactus plants frequented by sportive sunbathing monkeys. You might see a gigantic solitary box turtle meandering by while munching on a plant. His head moves back and forth as though he were a mechanical windup toy. The turtles and monkeys pop into view everywhere, but it takes a bit more doing to spot the raccoons (now extinct elsewhere on the island), wallabies (from Australia), hares, otters, and deer that frequent the glade of young mahogany trees. The information center is beautifully constructed and has circular brick flooring, picnic benches of polished wood, and hanging, encased charts and diagrams. Try to peek into the closed-off breeding center in its rear where the monkeys are kept prior to export. Open the screen door just past the center to enter the aviary. Multicolored parrots squawk at the top of the tall, cylindrical cage to the rear – discursing, no doubt, on the subject of their visitors' frivolous finery. On the edge of the pond around the back you'll find four pelicans, a gift of former Florida Sen. Birch Bayh. They may be bedded down for a nap; after awakening they preen themselves fastidiously, never venturing a glance at the snoring cayman lying below. The reserve is not a place to be rushed through.

Grenade Hall is an old signal station (in operation from 1819-1887) that has been refurbished as part of an "ecotourism" project and incorporated as part of the reserve. One difference between the current and original towers has been the introduction of stairs to the observation deck. You can see Dover Fort and Cotton Tower by peering through a telescope here. The forest has a nature trail and Indian artifacts – unearthed during the restoration process – are on display. The reserve and signal station are open daily 10-5; admission to both is a pricey B$20 for adults; B$10 for children. Note: Visitors should keep in mind that this reserve exports monkeys for medical research – a practice that is controversial among Bajans and visitors alike.

ST. NICHOLAS ABBEY: This greathouse – the oldest on Barbados – is the island's architectural highlight. It is near Cherry Tree Hill and Farley National Park in St. Peter and is one of only three greathouses of Jacobean origin surviving in the Americas; the other two are Drax Hall (also on Barbados) and Bacon's Castle in Virginia. St. Nicholas (☎ 422-8725) is approached by a mahogany-lined avenue. It is open Mon. to Fri. from 10-3:30; admission is B$5; children under 12 are free.

history: It is thought that Richard Beringer, who owned the 400- acre estate in the 1650s, had the house constructed during that decade. Its formal garden, gables, and four fireplaces call to mind an English country mansion. The sash windows and interiors date from the 17th C. The house was never used by Santa Claus nor any member of the clergy as an abbey, despite its name. Incredibly, the mansion weathered the severe hurricanes of 1675, 1780, and 1831. The two front rooms were paneled in 1898, using the nearly-extinct West Indian cedar.

on view: There's a display of old photos and journals, and a film presentation twice daily that depicts Bajan life circa 1935. The former outhouse in the back – which once housed four unpartitioned seats – now encloses a generator. Farther to its rear is a monkey-populated gully.

nearby sights: The ruins of the estate's sugar factory lie to the N, just to the right side; it has been closed since 1947. Some gnarled mahogany trees surround the tractors here and green, waving tassels of cane stretch as far as the eye can see. **Boscobel** can be reached by following the narrow road behind via Diamond Corner. A large red-roofed Anglican church stands here next to the ruins of a mill adorned with a shiny bright red mailbox. Alternatively, continue over to the left and climb up and over Cherry Tree Hill.

St. Peter Practicalities

ACCOMMODATIONS: St. Peter's pre-eminent resort is unquestionably **Cobbler's Cove**. The stately main building was originally known as Camelot and owned by the Haynes family during the 1940s. When Aland Godsal, a descendant of the Colleton family, took over, he instructed the architect to "design a hotel that we would enjoy staying at." The delightful result was this establishment, a series of two-storey black and white wooden suites grouped around a manicured lawn. The suites have a front room which, after the white vented accordion doors are opened, face the patio and lawn. The resort is designed and known for its "outdoor casual living." Off the kitchen is a small kitchenette with an honor bar; a kettle is available upon request. Sliding doors connect the front with the bedroom and adjacent bath. Cobbler's Cove is said to be more country home than hotel and, while an ideal honeymoon spot, is hardly suited for flashy yuppies. The summer crowd here tends to be family oriented; the winter season draws a somewhat older, more established traditional type. The guests are comfortable with their wealth and have no need to flaunt it. The atmosphere combines the British stiff upper lip with the Bajan welcoming smile and right hand extended in greeting – i.e., the ambiance is neither too loose nor too formal. In addition to the tennis courts and swimming pool, the following water sports are available free of charge: waterskiing, windsurfing, sunfish sailing, snorkeling, and use of the glass-bottom boat. Prices range from a low of US$185 for one person during the summer to US$990 for the Camelot Suite around Christmas. For more information or reservations call 1-800-223- 6510 in the US; 1-800-424-5500 in Canada. With the exception of the all-inclusive Almond Village, all of the other major hotels are grouped around Speightstown down the road from Cobbler's Cove. These include **King's Beach, Sugarcane Club, Eastry House Hotel**, and the **Sandridge Beach Hotel**. Apartment units include **Gibbes Garden, New Haven Mansion, and Sunset Sands**. The **Tides Inn Guest House** (☎ 422-2403) is an English-run bed and breakfast, but you can also cook your own food. It's near the sea in Gibbs. See the "Hotel Finder" for details.

DINING OUT: **Cobblers Cove Restaurant** (☎ 422-2291) is renowned for its French cuisine. Dinners range from B$105-B$150. Sun. buffets during the season feature a live steel band. **Sandy's**

Restaurant (☎ 422-2361) is at the Sandridge and serves dinners from B$30. **Kings Beach**, also down the road, has a number of restaurants.

In Speightstown, local restaurants with tourist prices include **L'il Ole Bristol, Shirley's**, and **Reddydun**. The **Mango Café** (☎ 422-0704) serves good seafood; entrées range from B$22-B$42. Diners at **Caroline's** are entertained by music most evenings. **Chirzel's Garden** in Gibbs features low sodium and vegetarian dishes among its entrées. **Mullins** (☎ 422-1878) is a popular bar-restaurant set by the beach of the same name. It's open for three meals daily and there's dancing in the evenings. The **Legend Restaurant** (☎ 422-0631) serves New Bajan Cuisine. Entrées start from B$17 and can go up to B$50. It's also at Mullins.

BUDGET DINING: The best budget place in Speightstown is **Fisherman's Pub**, which has a real local feel. They offer authentic, reasonably-priced local food including stew, chicken, and, in season, fish. Their bar is one of the few that offers draft Banks Beer. **Pizza Man Doc** (Mon. to Sat., 10-10) sells Bajan-style pizza at bargain prices; a slice is just B$1.75, a small warmed bread and cheese sub sells for B$1.25. The **Local Dishes Bar and Restaurant** is on Orange St. You should also try **Adriana's Ice Cream Shop** just inside the mall. Colonel Sanders is to its rear.

MARKET FOOD: Hucksters line the main road just past the esplanade; they sell giant avocadoes, papaya, yams and the like. At the fish market farther along, you'll see the perpetual domino game going on next to the wire grill windows. **Elmer's** is the town's only supermarket and is back past the esplanade.

sample prices: Pine Hill Dairy milk, B$2.82/litre; Pine Hill Dairy orange juice, B$3/litre; Sunflower margarine, B$2.85/lb.; New Zealand cheese, B$10.50/kg; carrots, B$7.99/kg; aubergine (eggplant), B$3.96/kg; broccoli, B$11.60/kg; local alfalfa sprouts, B$3.49/6 oz; apples B$7.45/kg; pineapples, B$4.12/kg; onions B$4.40/kg; bran bread (16 oz.), B$2.20; 2 litre Pepsi, B$5.28; Cadbury's Fruit & Nut Bar (200g), B$6.85; Ivory soap (bath size), B$2.79; Cheerios (15 oz), B$8.50; Kellogg's Cornflakes (12 oz.), B$6.48; Canadian-made Skippy Peanut Butter (500g), B$6.54; Rite Paper Towels, B$3.40/roll; *Weekly World News* ("UFO Captain is Soviet Prisoner") and *Time*, B$5.

St. Lucy

This semicircular parish, which caps the top of the island, presents rough and ragged scenery at every turn. Its classic small chattel houses – the best of which can be seen in the villages of Greenridge and Connell Town near Archer's Bay – are gradually being supplanted by bland stone bungalows. The thin soil lowland with small hills and cliffs bear the brunt of the Atlantic storms.

On foot is the best way to tour this parish and its fine coastline speckled with dramatic viewpoints. The lush countryside – its black and white cattle grazing contentedly and fine fields of green and growing cane – is simply a pleasure to experience.

ST. LUCY'S CHURCH: St. Lucy's was constructed after the 1831 hurricane. The church, along with its sweet lime hedges and Palladian windows, stands near Alleyndale greathouse. To get here from River Bay take the road heading towards the center of the parish.

ARCHER'S BAY: This popular spot is one of the island's most beautiful and is home to hordes of chirping birds and butterflies that flit and hover over wildflowers. The large grassy area above the bay – populated by cud-chewing cows and lackadaisical goats – is sheltered by giant casuarinas that sway in the light sea breeze. A path leads from the cliff down to the rock-strewn bay where jade water clashes against the eroded bluffs. Two stout, gigantic stone columns guard the entrance to the beach on the right. The *Archer's Bay bus* terminates at a mini-mart where you can get last minute provisions. A track from nearby **Crab Bay** leads through sugarcane fields to **Duppies**, a premier surfing spot. Cluff's millwall can be seen in the distance.

ANIMAL FLOWER CAVE: This set of sea caves at the island's northernmost center is carpeted with "sea flowers" and adorned with rock formations. It is justly famed for its yellow sea anemones. These short, cylindrical marine animals feed with the tentacles attached to their tops; these contain nematocysts, stinging cells that paralyze prey. The tentacles move captured prey to the anemone's mouth. Fertilization occurs underwater. Down in the cave, you can see a few small purple anemones. Their numbers vary with the conditions, but they are diminishing these days. The cave itself is quite an intriguing place: it has formations that resemble a turtle, a hand, and a lizard, and the view through the cave and out to sea is splendid and worth the visit in and of itself.

The above-ground café has namecards galore, thousands of them covering the walls and ceilings, tacked up with glue and then varnished on. It also has a collection of hanging banners, including "Yorkshire," "Barbados Rum," and "Cornish Pastries." The Wards, who own it, serve drinks and sandwiches. The surrounding land is currently barren, but it once produced cane under the name of Animal Flower Plantation. A perpetual domino game goes on in the nearby shed selling corals; a huckster also vends her goods here. A colony of wooden signposts out towards the sea point the way to such destinations as Germany, the US, and Venezuela with the distance indicated in kilometers. Waves crash against the sharply convoluted coral cliffs – sending salty spray into the air with poetic violence. Check out the seaward view from the parking lot.

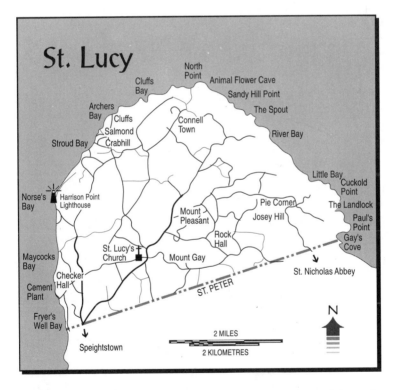

NORTH POINT: The abandoned ruin you pass heading S from the cave area is what remains of North Point Resort, a top resort in the 60s. The ruin contains the remains of what was once the island's sole Olympic-sized swimming pool. If you walk down across the coral-encrusted plain, littered with patches of cacti, you can still reach the beach. What appears to be a coral block fortification surrounds the sand, continually pummeled by hyperactive waves. Back from there, the buildings have the look and feel of a bombed war zone. Another interesting site right next door is a set of dried-up ponds which were formerly used as salt processing ponds until the 1940s. Seawater would be pumped in and, after its evaporation, the salt would be collected. From the North Point walk to the W, following a path that passes a series of pointed promontories alternating with coves.

THE SPOUT: This attraction can be viewed from the North Point, but is actually at **Ladder Bay** near River Bay. The sea spurts like a geyser through the hammer-headed coral promontory in jets as high as 100 feet.

RIVER BAY: This bleak but scenic park is a famous and favorite spot for Bajan picnics. Its name stems from a small stream flowing to the sea here. The bay is cut into chalk and limestone and features spectacular wind-blown coastal scenery. Wind rushes through casuarinas and the rambunctious Atlantic crashes into **The Point**, a jagged outcrop. Changing facilities and picnic tables are found here. From River Bay, a 1.5-mile track leads to Little Bay and Waits Bay.

LITTLE BAY TO BOSCOBEL: This is one of the most spectacular stretches of coast on the island if not in the Caribbean. To get here, either drive or take a *Pie Corner* bus to the end. At **Little Bay**, waves pummel an outlying coral outcrop and spray flies into the air. The overflow rushes into a wide trough where you can either lay back and let it roll on top of you or move towards the front and meet the surf head on. Climb up on top of the doughnut-shaped arch for a magnificent view. Along the coast to the right you pass a series of indentations along a bleak, windswept, coral-encrusted plain until you come to another major bay. After that is a track sheltered by casuarina trees that serve as a windbreak for the palm tree grove to the rear. Soon you will come to a magnificent view of **Pico Teneriffe** across the way. It rises to the S side of Cove Bay (Gay's Cove) and appears higher than its few hundred feet. On misty days, it is said to resemble a sorrowful and anxious Madonna gazing seaward in search of her wandering fishermen. This location, **Paul's Point**, is touted widely as the island's most attractive spot. Decide for yourself. **Gay's Cove Beach** below – which can be reached by a goat track – consists of rounded stones. Continue along the side, following the pink splotches of paint that mark the way until you reach Boscobel, a nondescript jumble of houses along the road. It is possible to walk from above the village to Morgan Lewis Beach, but the path is convoluted and can be difficult to find without guidance. The local rum shop is at the top of the hill on the right as you descend to the village. Note the collection of beer can rings that have been pounded into the tarmac by passing vehicles. Wait here if taking a bus; minibuses generally turn around up here.

GOAT HOUSE BAY: This beautiful scenic spot near the Rockfield corner 1,800 feet E of St. Clement's Village, lies smack in the middle of an unspoiled stretch reaching from River Bay to the twin bays of **Chandler** and **Laycock**.

The Southern Parishes

St. George

The parish is mostly flat and landlocked – as the Bajans say, "it has no sea." The fertile and fecund rolling fields of cane firmly remind one of its link with King Sugar. St. George is home to large sugar estates such as Valley Plantation and Salters, as well as to Bulkley Sugar Factory, the parish's sole remaining sugar refinery. The number of residents in the parish is growing rapidly; population in the parish's western portion grew at an average annual rate of 23% during 1970-1980.

DRAX HALL: St. George Valley is one of the best places to explore the dynamics of cane growing in Barbados and Drax Hall is one of the estates where cultivation began. This estate is another in the line of Jacobean-style plastered coralstone greathouses that once dotted the island. It is the only one still in the possession of the original owners. Sir James Drax, the builder and family patriarch, was one of the movers and shakers behind the sugarcane industry who became the island's richest planter. He improved the manufacturing process by bringing a Dutch model of a sugar mill to his estate and experimenting with it. The house, built during the mid-1800's, overlooks one of the nation's largest sugar estates. The powerful influence of this estate on the area is reflected in nearby place names such as Drax Hall Woods, Drax Hall Jump, and Drax Hall Green. A 50-ft-high millwall stands to the E off Highway 4. The white millwall and ruined boiling house of Redland cottage stand off the main highway nearby. **visiting:** Visitors are not unwelcome, but there is not a lot to see here; a fence and menacing attack dogs surround the house.

BRIGHTON GREAT HOUSE: Brighton has been under the control of the Pile family for over 100 years and is one of the island's oldest greathouses. A marble slab in the S wall reads "Wisheir" and is dated 1652. Thick columns of mastic wood support the roof with its 20-ft (6-m) beams; its walls were fabricated from a mix of corn husks and rubble.

BYDE MILL: The exact age of this home is a mystery, but it is thought to have been built by a Joshua Steele who leased the estate in 1777. It is set several miles farther E of Brighton Greathouse on Highway 4B in the parish's eastern tip near its borders with St. Philip and St. John.

ST. GEORGE'S PARISH CHURCH: This church is at the top of Rectory Hill, which runs off the crossroads at the end of Salters at Charles Rowe Bridge. It is filled with monuments, some of which are by well-known English sculptors. Its most famous tomb is that of the Honorable Richard Salter (d. 1776), sculpted by Nollekens. Philadelphia-born and London-famed Benjamin West painted *The Rise to Power*, a depiction of the Resurrection which serves as the church's altarpiece. The painting was relegated to an outhouse wall for years due to a falling out between the donor and the rector at the time. The eye of the painting's centurion was poked out by the finger of an irate thief because he claimed it was staring at him too intently. A painting on copper entitled *The Descent from the Cross* hangs in the N porch. The church also has antique silverware. From here, ascend to Gun Hill.

GUN HILL: This signal station served double duty: as a communications point and as a convalescent station for sick soldiery. A full-sized milk-white limestone lion – a representation of the British Imperial Lion – is set off Fulsier Road just below it. The lion was carved out of the rock by Henry Wilkinson of the "ninth Regiment of Foot – Adjutant General" in 1868. Its Latin inscription translates as follows: "It shall rule from the river to the sea, and from the sea, to the end of the world." Wilkin's inspiration for this is said to have been a box of matches with a lion drawn on them. Climb the stairway to have a look. The towering signal station is farther up and its panoramic view has been praised by visitors over the centuries. It is definitely a not-to-be-missed sight. It is accessible by car.. The small museum inside was opened in 1982. In 1994 the National Trust waged a battle to halt the destruction of the old military barracks here; the Sandiford government had ordered it torn down. It's open Mon. to Sat. from 9-5, except public holidays; B$8 admission for adults, B$4 for children.

FRANCIA PLANTATION: This small yet stately greathouse, opened to the public for the first time in 1989, stands on a wooded hillside at the heart of a working plantation. It is situated near Gun Hill. The home contains antique furniture along with a fine selection of old prints and maps. Be sure to see the charming fountain featuring a youth holding an umbrella. The house was constructed by Frenchman René Mourraille; he had settled in Brazil, but relocated to Barbados after marrying a Bajan. It's open Mon. to Fri., 10-4; B$6 admission. **Note:** This is a private home and the residents get very peeved when visitors arrive after closing time.

St. John

This parish, rich in sugar plantations, is hillier than neighboring St. George; its entire NE is dominated by the imposing Hackleton's Cliff. The major highways running through here are 4 and 3B. St. John contains a number of greathouses, one of the nation's most intriguing and scenic churches, a splendid coastline as well as the nation's oldest college. Martin's Bay is home to the local fishermen.

HACKLETON'S CLIFF: This 997-ft-high (305-m) cliff, topped by a line of casuarinas, rises 12 miles from Bridgetown. The cliff was carved several million years ago at a time when powerful pummelling tidal waves pulverized the Scotland District, eroding its coral cap. At its top, the breathtaking view extends from Pico Teneriffe in the N to Ragged Point in the E. Note the reforestation work going on here and at Joe's River. The latter will cover 85 acres marked with trails and is to be named "**Joe's River Tropical Rainforest**." For information, call the National Conservation Commission (☎ 425-1200).

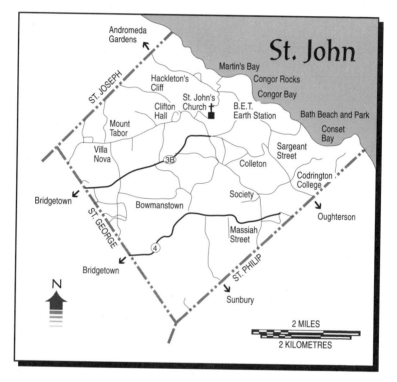

ST. JOHN'S PARISH CHURCH: This small church is off a feeder road which runs into Highway 3B approximately 14 miles from Bridgetown. It lies in the center of the island's most productive sugarcane acreage. St. John's can be approached from Malvern via Edey's Village and Clifton Hall. It is framed by frangipani and overlooks the Atlantic coast, where waves crash continuously on the reef 800 feet below. This is the quintessential English church set in the tropics. St. John's interior sports high-backed pews and a double staircase of light-colored cedar that extends up to the organ gallery. Its wooden pulpit allegedly contains six varieties of hardwood: ebony, locust, mahogany, machineel, oak, and pine. The original was built in 1676 and was destroyed by a hurricane in 1831; the present structure dates from 1836. Be sure to step outside for the magnificent view of Pico Teneriffe on the left and the lighthouse at Ragged Point, St. Philip off in the distance to the right. Note "**The Chair**" carved out of the cliffs; it marks the southward bend in the topography. By the sundial at the back you may view the dish antenna at Bath below. Outside lie the tombs of 17th- and 18th-C. planters – so large they seem fit for emperors! Elizabeth Pinder's beautifully-carved memorial was sculpted by Sir Richard Westmacott. Probably the most famous grave on the island is that of the Greek expatriate, **Ferdinando Paleologus**. Paleologus (church warden and surveyor) owned Clifton Hall, a nearby cotton plantation. When the church was razed by the 1831 hurricane, Ferdinando was discovered in a vault under the organ loft embedded in quicklime – his head facing W in accord with Eastern Orthodox traditions. The faded pink tombstone in his memory, which stands to the side of a vault to the rear, was erected in 1906. From the church, a road swings left to the N, passing the Newcastle greathouse and heading towards **Martin's Bay**, a fishing village. There is a raised coral reef close to shore; search for shells here.

hiking: The surrounding semi-wild area, known as **Glen Burnie**, has a path following the old railroad line, which leads into Bath (a bathing beach with facilities) in neighboring St. Joseph's Parish and then on to Consett Bay. Another route would be to hike the three miles (4.8 km) from Martin's Bay to Bathsheba along the old railway track.

CODRINGTON COLLEGE: Barbados' first institution of higher learning, just 15 miles from Bridgetown, was originally built in modified Italian Renaissance style. Unfortunately, only the main building's open portico and the exterior of the principal's home survive. Be sure to check out the lines of poetry inscribed at the swimming pool. This theological college for the training of West Indian clergy stands on one of Codrington's former plantations overlooking Conset Bay. It is approached by a row of stately cabbage palms – some of which are reputed to be more than a century old. The college was constructed, owned, and operated by the Society for the Propagation of the Gospel in Foreign Parts, an organization which, during the 1700s, put forward the radical and highly-controversial concept that slaves had souls and should, therefore, be converted to Christianity. The local elite weren't exactly wild about this notion, but Christopher Codrington, a wealthy landowner and Oxford graduate, bequeathed his plantation to the society in 1710. It is now part of the University of the West Indies.

The college has some very interesting architecture. Check out the chapel which features a glass mosaic of the Good Shepherd hanging over the altar; enormous carved mahogany sanctuary rails and gates; and an altar composed of ebony, lignum vitae, and cordia pedestals. Codrington's family home stands next to the college, overlooking a lily pond and small park. It is constructed of coral with a roof-long balustrade and a seven-pedimented window out front; it is now used as the Principal's lodge. Fire gutted its interior in 1887. A new feature on the premises is a short **nature trail**.

FROM CODRINGTON COLLEGE: Following the road from the college to the S, which descends a steep hill, you'll find the entrance to **Conset Bay** on the left. Fishing boats land here in the afternoons, or you may be entertained by troupes of bounding, mischievously playful green monkeys. Good walks can be found in this area. Another route is to follow Sergeant Street and take a right down Bath Hill. The **Bath Factory ruins** are nearby. The **Bath Beach facility** has a bathing area and a small forest. **Quintyne** is a freshwater spring near Bath which has seven stately cabbage palms. **St. Mark's Church**, overlooking Conset Bay and College Savannah, is worth visiting for its view alone. A road leads from there through Fortescue Plantation to the picturesque fishing village at Skeete's Bay. View Conset Bay from Coach Hill. You can also follow the abandoned railway tracks from Codrington College to the E coast at **Tent Bay**; take the Bridgetown-bound bus back from Bathsheba.

VILLA NOVA: This beautiful greathouse, located N off Highway 3B to the left from Four Cross Roads, is built on a ridge overlooking the St. John and St. Phillip tablelands. It rises 830 feet (256 m) amid six acres of woods and gardens. The house was constructed in 1843 by Edmund Haynes and has been a private residence – as opposed to a working plantation house – since 1907. It was passed from the Haynes family to the Avons to the Hunts and on to its present owners, who opened it to the public. The home features wide porches, a parapet roof, and latticed wooden arches and balustrades. It has a light and airy ambiance, but its thick walls ensure survival in a hurricane. Antiques here include a Regency secretaire and a Chippendale "pie crust" table. Many claim it is the island's best specimen of a 19th-C. greathouse. Be sure to tour the beautiful garden, where you will find a profusion of orchids, a multitude of ferns, and trees such as the bearded fig, breadfruit, frangipani,

Barbados cherry, flamboyant, and citrus. It's open Mon. to Fri. from 10-4. Admission is B$8 adults, B$4 children; ☎ 433-1524. **Note:** An 80-bed luxury resort is scheduled to open here in 1996; call for information.

CLIFTON HALL: This privately-owned Georgian-style greathouse is two miles (three km) away from Villa Nova. It is currently closed to the general public. The house has a three-sided arcaded verandah and a double staircase leading to a central porch.

MOUNT TABOR: Tabor is one of two remaining Moravian churches. It was built around 1850 and its hilltop height commands a view of the woods down to the sea in the distance.

EASTMONT: This 19th-C. house is the home of the former Prime Minister, H. Bree St. John. His ancestor, mulatto blacksmith Miller Austin, purchased the estate in 1895 – thus setting a historical precedent. It is located off the road leading S into St John from Clifton Hall.

St. John Practicalities

FOOD AND DRINK: The **Coconut Inn** (☎ 433-2697) is a unique place to stop and eat on a Sun. afternoon as you head to Villa Nova. It also functions as a basic bed and breakfast, charging around B$30 pp. Meals are available on request. It's "not a commercial enterprise," say the owners, who have a semi-hydroponic garden out back.

St. Philip

St. Philip is the island's largest parish (pop. 18,500), and is also one of the most remote. It is the home of calypsonians such as Red Plastic Bag, and the clannish inhabitants have their own manner of speech. Its topography consists of thin soil lowland with small hills and cliffs with caves, which bear the brunt of the Atlantic storms. Aloes and cotton are grown here and tobacco is farmed in the Boscobel District. Lively warblers, known locally as "grass canaries," flit through the sour grass lining the parish's eastern shore. Highways 4B and 5 are two of the main roads running through the parish. Highway 6, from Christ Church to the S, runs through the oil fields to get here. The parish's best known sight is Sam Lord's Castle, which lies off of Highway 5 on a cliff above Long Bay. The center is Six Roads, the only place on the island where six roads intersect. You'll find a health center, doctors and a pharmacy, library, video shops, and government housing here.

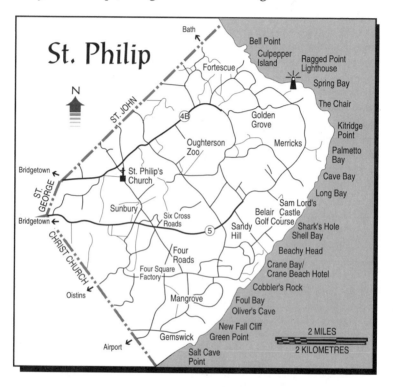

SUNBURY HOUSE: This early-18th-C. plantation house was refurbished in 1981. It is a small historical museum of Bajan life with collections of antique furniture, antique buggies, and agricultural vehicles. An exhibition center is in the old yam center. The bronze bell hanging in the belfry is dated 1766. It was originally known as Chapman's, but John Henry Barrow changed the name in 1816 in order to match his British estates. The house and grounds covered 413 acres when it was purchased in 1838 by Thomas and John Daniel. Thomas Daniel, who was busom buddies with Sam Lord, installed chandeliers to match those of his friend's home, and Lord's personal claret set can be found in the living room. Sunbury Plantation House is open from 10-4:30 daily. Admission is B$8 adults; B$4 children. The estate also features a courtyard restaurant

(☎ 423-6270, fax 423-6270), which is open for breakfast and lunch; dinner parties (B$120 pp) and cocktail parties (B$75 pp) can be catered to by special arrangement. It is located near Highways 4B, 5, and 6. In its vicinity are St. Philip's Parish Church and the nationalized Woodbourne oil fields.

OUGHTERSON ZOO PARK: This unusual wildlife breeding and environmental education project (☎ 23-6203, fax 423-6167) covers 22 acres and contains a large variety of birds, plants, and animals. Its greathouse is filled to the brim with oriental and Bajan antiques. Admission is B$10 adults, B$5 children. It's open daily from 10-5.

Oughterson takes its name from merchant Arthur Oughterson, originally of Brighton. The home differs from other sugar plantation greathouses of its era in that it has only one storey – intended to protect it in the event of hurricanes which hit the Atlantic side very hard. Walls are thick and the typically-Georgian sash windows each sport an elaborate wooden hood on their exterior to keep out harsh sunlight and protect against strong winds. Stays (small swivelling metal clips) are attached to the windows on either side and are used to mount wooden hurricane shutters; hinged outer screens are on the main doors and serve a similar purpose. The home's tiles came from ships which brought them from Bristol to Speightstown.

The house is packed with unusual antiques, many of which have animal themes. As with the real animals, their presence here reflects the former owner W. T. Miller, a marine biologist who started collecting them as a hobby. He decided to turn his avocation into an income, recognizing the demand for tourist attractions as well as the necessity of continued environmental education among locals and tourists. Note the Chinese screen, the cabinet with its little menagerie of East Asian animals, and the framed Japanese woodblock prints adorning the walls. There's also a stuffed crocodile and a giant moth in a glass case. Be sure to visit the room in the rear which is 300-odd years old – the oldest part of the house. (The rest of the house dates from about 1840.) Look for the adorable white mice, innocent of their fate, in little aquariums; you'll see them – all pink noses and soft fur – pussyfooting over the sleeping pythons who are dreaming of their next meal. In the same room, the heavy metal scuba diver's helmet harkens back to the days of yore when diving was a true adventure limited only to a few.

The former outbuildings and paddocks in the rear have been converted to house animals. Before you head out to frolic in and among our animal cousins, be sure to note and heed the sign reading "Please do not annoy, torment, pester, play, molest, worry, badger, harry, harrass, heckle, persecute, irk, vex, disquiet, tease, nettle, or ruffle the animals." Out here, you'll find caged monkeys, including squealing squirrels and capuchin monkeys. Noisy birds include the endangered St. Vincent parrots, which have been bred on the premises. They're a sight to see with their shades of green, yellow, light blue, and orange when they spread their wings. Other parrots include blue-and-gold macaws from Guyana, Amazonian parrots, and moustache parrots from Australia. Box turtles plod along, while peacocks stroll on the lawn and crocodiles sleep in their pond. There's also a little agouti, armadillos, and zebras, which are kept in a corral. An enclosure holds a family of Brazilian tapirs and you can even find bunny rabbits and hamsters. There's a small orchid house. A short nature trail to the rear takes you past a pond with ducks and labeled trees: cabbage palms, cherry trees, and others. The fish pond out front is used for breeding tilapia. There's a small café here, which is not always open. Oughterson has future plans to breed wildlife, namely rare Caribbean species, in particular the various endangered Caribbean parrots.

near Oughterson: Three Houses Park at the intersection of the roads to East Point, Bayfield and Bridgetown, Somervale, and Church Village – is a good picnic spot if you brought your own lunch.

FOUL BAY: Chancery Lane Beach here provides treacherous swimming amid coconut palms felled as a result of the 1955 hurricane. The bay is a popular recreation spot. It received its unromantic name because it was a "foul" or unsuitable anchorage for ships. The nearby **cliffs** from Oliver's Cave S to Gemswick are the island's highest – rising over 100 feet (35 m).

CRANE BEACH: Crane Beach is one of island's most popular. It lies about 13 miles (21 km) from Bridgetown and 2.5 miles (4 km) SW of Sam Lord's Castle. The surrounding towering cliffs make it a beautiful place to spend moonlit nights. Nature lovers have been enjoying this splendid spot since the 1700s. You cannot enter the beach from the Crane Bridge Hotel (see following Practicalities section for review) unless you pay an admission fee; you must walk around past it and then turn down. Exercise caution while swimming here. It's possible to cross this beach and reach Shanty Beach, Beach Head, and Shell Beach, but you will have to climb up and then down again several times.

Sam Lord's Castle

This "castle" is now a Marriot Hotel, but the main structure itself is still open for inspection. It was originally built as a 19th-C. country house and stands on a rocky bluff, overlooking a coral beach graced with coconut palms and sea grapes. Its interior combines elegant plaster ceilings and finely crafted woodwork with an attractive staircase. The adjoining dining and drawing room is also a fine display of craftmanship. Some of the furniture adorning the hotel was owned by Sam Lord, including the brass lion's-claw-footed dining room table. The "dungeons" downstairs have been transformed into carpeted air-conditioned offices.

HISTORY: Legend has it that Samuel Hall Lord hung lanterns in the coconut trees facing Cobbler's Reef off the S coast in the 1800s. When approaching sea captains – lured by lights they assumed to be those of the Carlisle Bay anchorage – neared shore, they capsized and were overtaken by Sam and other scoundrels. There is no doubt that the man himself was a complete knave, although this story is likely apocryphal. Truth or fiction, Sam somehow got the money to build the house – known also as Long Bay Castle – around 1820. It's called a "castle" because of its battlement-style notched roof; it combines Georgian symmetry and balance with Gothic details, as do the crenellated roof and mouldings above the windows. The stucco interior was crafted by English and Italian workmen brought over to do the job. Its ceilings are wonders to behold; the one in the saloon is a replica of one in Windsor Castle. But getting back to the story... Sam died on Nov. 5, 1845 in England leaving debts behind of £18,000 – an astronomical sum at the time.

VICINITY OF SAM LORD'S CASTLE: There's some great hiking in this area on the way to Ragged Point and then beyond to Culpepper's Island. Go back out to the ticket window and head around the corner following the narrow, unpaved road running along the side of the resort. A staircase at the end leads down to a vendor-free beach facing an exposed coral formation just off the coast. If you keep walking, there's an abandoned house set on the cliff and, still farther, the **ruins of Harrismith plantation house** overlook a palm-tree-studded beach. Next is a villa perched above yet another beautiful beach at Bottom Bay. Take the road to the right and continue walking with the wall on your right and the small Stonehenge-like ruined concrete and wire structure to your left. After passing another cove and beach, you will enter a windswept coral bluff, marked at its perimeter by a row of bent casuarina trees. Follow this along – peering periodically over the bluff at the knockout views of pounding surf – until the lighthouse comes into view. It sits atop **Ragged Point**, aptly named after its jagged limestone cliffs beseiged by surf. This bleak area only gains some color when the bright agave or Spanish needles are in bloom. It was built of coralstone extracted from a nearby quarry in 1875. Passing by some cows, turn up where an abandoned bus stands next to a house. Follow along – passing more goats and cows along the way – until you reach an asphalt road with a rum shop up on the right just past the stand pipe to your left. From here you can take a bus back to Bridgetown; continue the easy walk to Sam Lord's; or carry on to Culpepper Island. In any case, the lighthouse is a must. If you should meet the trickster near here who claims to sell "tickets" to the lighthouse, brush him off!

CULPEPPER ISLAND: This is the nation's sole remaining island dependency and it lies 35 yards offshore past the grounds of Whitehaven mansion. The 75-by-105-foot (25-by-35-m) coral island rises to 20 feet (7 m) above sea level. The only way to get on the island is to swim.

St. Philip Practicalities

ACCOMMODATIONS: Crane Beach Hotel has the oldest history of any hotel on the island. Its name, as well as that of the beach, derives from the type of freight elevator installed behind its pier that was eventually buried by sand drifts. This hotel's deck overlooks one of the island's most spectacular beaches and juts out over the edge of the cliff, resembling the prow of a cruise ship. The main building's design, shaped in large part by architect Oliver Messel in the early 1970s, can best be described as Mediterranean cool white. The pool, overlooking the beach, features two Roman columns and the bronze statues reflect a similar theme. The 14-room hotel was originally known as the Marine Villa; the main part of it is some 180 years old. Suites are beautifully appointed. A sample one-bedroom suite features hardwood floors of pickled pine, antique mahogany furniture, tropical-patterned canopies hanging over the king size bed, and walls of white coral brick. Wooden doors open onto the balconies or terrace equipped with a chaise lounge; views vary, but the raging ocean is ever-present. A large living room has three tables and a couch; there's a gigantic closet with a full length mirror off the bedroom, and the bath features a huge mirror and a sunken tub. The kitchenette has a sink, kettle, and a pre-stocked refrigerator/honor bar. There are two pools and four tennis courts. There's also a private locked stairway to the beach. Rates run from a low of US$100 for a standard room to a high of US$600 for a two-bedroom penthouse. For more information and reservations call 1-800-387-3998.

Sam Lord's Castle remains the parish's top resort – at least until the completion of the Crane Hotel expansion. The grounds begin with the ticket window where visitors (but not guests) must pay for admission. Bellhops ferry passengers' luggage to their rooms around the manicured grounds. Fountains and a variety of pools are in the rear of the plantation house. You will be given a map when checking in. The resort features three pools, a beach, tennis courts, two restaurants, an activities center with a small library, barber shop, beauty salon, games room, video theater, gym, and beach towel check out. The beach is at the end of the property down a set of stairs. There's nary a dull moment here and, as you prepare for bed, you'll find out why. The custom is to turn down your sheets and lay a copy of the extensive list of events (tomorrow on one side, the following day on the reverse) on your sheet, along with a small flower. It tells you when the sun rises and sets, what band will be playing in the evening, what tours are scheduled, and various other tidbits. Every morning a copy of *The Nation* and *The International Herald Tribune* are delivered to your door, providing literary fodder for your morning meal. In your bedside table you'll find copies of the Mormon Bible and Marriot's own autobiography – featuring photos of him with luminaries such as Nixon and Reagan. Room prices range from US$115s/d in the summer to US$500 for a one-bedroom suite in the busiest portion of the winter season. For more information, call 800-223-6388 in the US; (171) 591-1100 in London; or (08) 20 73 85 in Stockholm.

alternatives: Other hotels include **Ginger Bay** and **Robin's Nest**. A 500-room hotel is scheduled to replace the racetrack in 1996-1997; contact the tourist board for information. Budget travelers might try the **Ragged Point Motel** at Merricks (☎ 423-8021).

DINING OUT: Sunbury Plantation House serves breakfast and lunch in its courtyard restaurant; it also offers traditional English tea. A special feature here is the three-course meal served at an antique mahogany table with silver service; reservations are required (☎ 423-6270). Another famous local restaurant is the Crane Beach Hotel's **Panoramic Restaurant** (☎ 423-6220), which overlooks the magnificent beach. It serves a large Sun. brunch. Sam Lord's Castle has the **Wanderer** and the **Seagrille** (open evenings only). They also serve tea in the drawing room above the activities center from 3-4:30 daily.

Christ Church and the Gold Coast

Christ Church dominates the prettiest portion of the island's S coast and has paved the way for Barbados' tourist industry. The narrow coastal route runs through a gamut of hotels, inns, restaurants, fast-food emporiums, and shopping malls – with the occasional splash of blue sea and golden sand coming into view. Its phenomenal population growth has made the parish a center of business activity. The northern half is dominated by sugar estates such as Staple, Newton, Bentleys, and Grove. Sea Island Cotton grows at Spencers and Fairy Valley near the airport. The major roads are Highway 7, which parallels the sea from Hastings to Oistins before veering inland to run past the airport, and Highway 6, which cuts through its pastoral core. Highway 7 runs past the following areas from W to E: Hastings, Rockley, Worthing, St. Lawrence Gap, Dover, Maxwell, and Oistins.

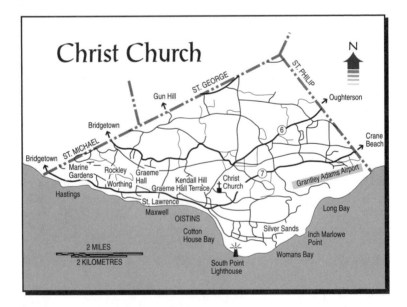

HASTINGS: The red-painted barracks bordering St. Anne's Fort in neighboring St. Michael's Parish have been converted to apartments. Its name comes from the village of Hastings, the island's first seaside resort built in the 1820s on coastal land belonging to the Hermitage Plantation. Most of its original 11 buildings were constructed near the Ocean View Hotel. One of them, Hastings

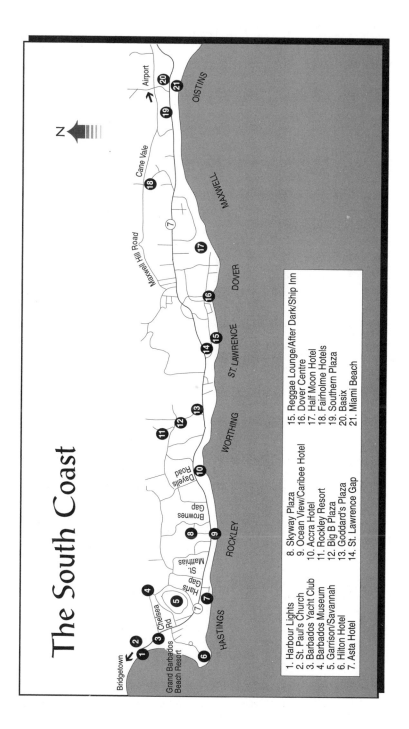

The South Coast

1. Harbour Lights
2. St. Paul's Church
3. Barbados Yacht Club
4. Barbados Museum
5. Garrison/Savannah
6. Hilton Hotel
7. Asta Hotel
8. Skyway Plaza
9. Ocean View/Caribee Hotel
10. Accra Hotel
11. Rockley Resort
12. Big B Plaza
13. Goddard's Plaza
14. St. Lawrence Gap
15. Reggae Lounge/After Dark/Ship Inn
16. Dover Centre
17. Half Moon Hotel
18. Fairholme Hotels
19. Southern Plaza
20. Basix
21. Miami Beach

Bridgetown
Grand Barbados Beach Resort
Chelsea Rd
HASTINGS
Harts Gap
St. Matthias
Brownes Gap
Daysells Road
ROCKLEY
WORTHING
ST. LAWRENCE
DOVER
MAXWELL
Maxwell Hill Road
Cane Vale
OISTINS
Airport

N

Bath or Villa Francia, was restored in 1987. During the 1880s and 90s, Hastings Rocks peaked in popularity and trams ran from Bridgetown to the Marine Gardens and the rocks. The now residential **Marine Gardens** and **Navy Gardens** lie off Highway 7 to the S. They were once a naval hospital and homes for the Admiral and his assistants respectively. The beaches from here to Oistins are beautiful, but development has killed the coral reefs, thus eroding the sand and speeding the decline of beaches such as Accra, Worthing, and Dover. At Dayrell's Road, N of Hastings and E of the Garrison Savannah, is the field belonging to the Wanderers, the nation's oldest cricket association. Pleasant beach bars in this area include the **Wave Breaker**. **Keswick Windsor House** and **Hastings Plaza** are the main shopping areas.

ROCKLEY: The next stretch of tourist-oriented coastline, Rockley, is chiefly noted for its medium-sized beach, which is always packed with tourists. Here you might see dreads braiding tourists' hair while other vacationers smear on applications of aloe. At the end of the beach to the right a small path leads to an unfrequented cove. Nearby **Accra Beach** is named after the hotel; the visitor will soon discover why its nickname is "Sin Beach."

WORTHING: This area is best known for its small beach and profusion of inexpensive guesthouses. Among the more notable are **Rydal Waters, Summer Place on the Sea, Shells**, and **Crystal Waters**. The **Oasis** is more expensive. All are listed in the Hotel Finder. A good place to hang out is the **Carib Beach Bar,** which specializes in fruit daiquiries and has live entertainment on weekends. **Rockley Golf and Country Club** (☎ 435-7873, fax 435-8268) is also here.

ST. LAWRENCE GAP: This is the parish's main restaurant and entertainment district. Other eating establishments are found on the main road and on Maxwell Coast Road, off Highway 7. There's a small beach near the entrance where fishing boats dock. This area is fun to walk around and have a gander at night, even if you're not a club fan. **Coffee and Cream Gallery**, near Divis Southwind, is the island's only café/art gallery. For details on dining and entertainment see "Entertainment" in the "Introduction" and the "Christ Church Practicalities" section which follows.

Out and About in St. Lawrence Gap

This area is where much of the island's nightlife is headquartered. Here are some of your choices:

After Dark. The island's classiest club. Good live music.

The Reggae Lounge (☎ 435-6462). Next door to After Dark. Cover can be applied against your bar tab.

Ship Inn (☎ 435-6961) features bands nightly. Cover redeemable in drinks. Small dance floor.

Other hotels have live music and performances. Check with the Casuarina or Divi Southwinds. Bands to watch out for include Splashband (reggae), Crossfire and Square One (calypso), and Spice (reggae fusion).

YARICO'S POND: A local folk song tells the legend of this pond at Kendal (off the Ashford-Kendal road). Yarico, an Indian woman, became infatuated with Inckle, a British sailor whom she had rescued while he was exploring a neighboring island. She took care of him until a search party from Barbados discovered them and then she returned to Barbados with him. Inckle, an ungrateful lout, found a new woman and sold Yarico into slavery. She either drowned herself here or bore her son by the side of this pond, depending upon which version of this story you hear. Unfortnately, this is not the correct pond: that one has disappeared.

GRAEME HALL SWAMP: Graeme Hall is one of the island's few remaining swamps. It covers 78 acres (31 ha) and is situated off Highway 7. Take the trail along the swamp's N side. It features some white as well as a few remaining red mangroves and is the sole remaning habitat for sedge – a grass that grows more than a yard high. The snowy red seal coot breeds here in the winter. Yellow warblers and cattle egrets are also numerous; the latter leave at daybreak and return to nest each evening. Other birds to be seen here include the green-backed heron, the osprey, finches, the common gallinule (red seal coot), the belted kingfisher ("rainbird"), the Caribbean coot, the yellow (golden) warbler, the double-crested cormorant, as well as a variety of grassquits, sandpipers, and terns. Unfortunately, because many migratory birds arrive during the winter, it also attracts local hunters.

OISTINS: This is the nation's premier fishing village and is set just six miles from Bridgetown. It was originally named Austin's Bay after an outrageous drunken lout. It was here that the 1652 articles for the capitulation of the island – pledging obedience to Cromwell and his commonwealth Parliament – were signed by the Royal Commissioners of Barbados after troops defending the island were defeated. This formerly primitive fishing entrepot has developed dramatically in recent years. It is now a regional center. Two hectares of land were reclaimed from the sea and much of that is devoted to the fishing industry. **Miami Beach**, the town beach, was an accidental creation. The Coast Guard spent B$3 million building a barrier to be used for mooring ships. No sooner had they finished than the sand, trapped by the new obstruction, came rolling in! Oistins now has two shopping centers: **Oistins Shopping Plaza** and **Southern Plaza**. It is an ideal place to base yourself if you're staying for a while and need a spot to relax. **buying fish:** Oistins market is one of the best places in the island to buy fish. Expect to pay B$5/lb. for fish; flying fish vendors sell 10 fish for $9. Fresh seasoning (B$5-B$10 per bottle) is also available. Just marinate the fish in it, then roll the fish in flour with breadcrumbs and deep fry.

The Mystery Of Chase Vault

The Chase Vault is in the parish church's cemetery seven miles from Bridgetown. The stories surrounding it are one of the island's enduring mysteries. Whenever the Eliot family tomb was pried opened during the 19th C. to inter a fresh corpse, coffins were found askew, some had re-arranged themselves and were battered and splintered as though the occupant had been engaged in some joust. Other coffins were lying on end or had been seemingly involved in postmortem mate swapping with another box! This happened on four occasions, but only lead coffins were affected. Vincent Combermere, Governor of Barbados, made impressions with his seal on the mortar when the vault was shut on July 7, 1819 and was present on April 20, 1820 when the vault was unsealed. This time the door opened to mayhem and disorder. The coffin of an infant had been tossed into a corner and the heavy coffin of Samuel Brewster, murdered the previous year in a slave rebellion, had shifted position. This was the last straw; the vault was subsequently emptied. Similar happenings have also occurred in Wiltshire and St. Michael's Cathedral – also with lead coffins. It is now thought that gas exuded from decomposing corpses is responsible, although no one knows for sure. Eight burly men would have been needed to move the coffins, and sand was placed on the floor but no footprints appeared. The Chase Vault remains empty.

NEWTON PLANTATION: NE of Oistins is Newton Plantation. It can be reached by following Lodge Road E for 1.5 miles (2.5 km) to a four-way crossing. Take a left on the road heading N and then turn right. This working sugarcane plantation has served as the setting for the ceremonial delivery of the last canes marking the beginning of the Crop Over Festival.

ENTERPRISE COAST ROAD: Runs along the way to the South Point past coastal forests. Thorn scrubs and sweet briars populate this road along with machineel. Sand dunes are stabililized by seaside yam, splurge, and bean plants; other dunes lie in the vicinity of Long Bay, Christ Church. The **Silver Sands Resort** is among the hotels in this area. At **Paragon**, the three-mile (5-km) coastline is bound by cliffs. A series of little rocky coves stretch out for a mile (1.5 km) from the N corner of **Long Bay**. A great view can be had from Penny Hole Rock and Salt Cove Point. The **South Point Lighthouse** is the island's oldest, dating from 1851. It was originally designed for display at London's Great Expedition; the prefab iron structure was dismantled and installed here in 1852. **birding:** Watch for magnificent frigatebirds, brown boobies, brown pelicans, gulls, terns and swifts.

LONG BEACH: This 1.5-mile (2.5-km) beach stretches from Paragon (near the airport) to Inch Marlowe Point. It is located along the site of the former Inch Marlowe Swamp – drained to make way for tourist development. Big things were planned for the property, but they failed to materialize.

Christ Church Practicalities

ACCOMMODATIONS: Major hotels in the parish are the Caribee, Coconut Court, Golden Beach, Ocean View, Regency Cove, and the Windsor Arms at Hastings; the Accra, Blue Horizon, and Rockley Resort at Rockley; the Sandy Beach and Worthing Court at Worthing; Andrea on the Sea, Dover Beach, Half Moon, Southern Palms, Divi Southwinds, Casuarina, and Spinnakers in St. Lawrence Gap; and the Golden Sands, Rainbow Reef, San Remo, Sand Acres, Benston Windsurfing Club, and Welcome Inn in Maxwell. For details check the "Hotel Finder."

APART-HOTELS: The luxury-priced **Bresmay** (☎ 428-6131/7340/7722; fax 428-7722) offers 69 fully-equipped and very attractive air-conditioned apartments. The studio apartments, situated poolside, can hold one to three persons and have twin beds and kitchenette; one-bedroom units hold two to four and have a living room. The oceanfront deluxe studios hold one or two and have twin or double beds and a TV; oceanfront deluxe one-bedroom units also have a living room and can hold two to four. Rooms are on both sides of the road. The pink building is newer and faces the ocean. There is a small snack bar. The **Monteray** and **Mirabelle** apartments are under the same management. The Monteray offers 18 spacious studio and one-bedroom units with pool and gardens, and the Mirabelle has seven apartments.

BUDGET ACCOMMODATIONS: The **Roman Beach Apartments** (☎428-7635) in Oistins are, perhaps, the best deal in the parish. Mrs. Francis Roman and family have been winning their guests' patronage for decades. The simple rooms were remodeled in 1995 and have a fan, sink, stove, cooking utensils, and a shower. Miami Beach is just across the road, and the library, a supermarket, bakery, restaurants, and the fish market are all within a few minutes walk. To get here from Bridgetown, make a right by the police station and then turn left. They charge B$50-B$70 summer and B$95-B$110 winter; tax and service are added. The inexpensive **Gaskin's Vacation Hotel** (☎ 428-4748) has both rooms and apartments, along with a TV lounge. It is in the Enterprise area and also near Miami Beach. The **Flamboyant Restaurant** (☎ 427-5588) in Hastings is owned by Mr. Bryan Cheeseman. He charges around B$50 s/d, and B$70 s/d for studios, one-bedrooms with kitchen, and B$90 for a two-bedroom place. Accommodation is spartan but functional; prices include tax. The **Fairholme** (☎ 428-9425) in Maxwell has 31 rooms and studio apartments with kitchenettes priced from B$50 s, B$60-B$110 d year-round. It's attractive and has a restaurant. You can also try the **Beaumont** (no listed tel.) nearby. George De Mattos runs **Summer Place on the Sea** (☎ 435-7424) in Worthing. The **Antoine Guest House** (☎ 420-4463/3261) is on Maxwell Main Rd. in Christ Church. **Dover Woods Guest House** (☎ 420-6599) is in Dover Woods. Other small guesthouses include **Pegwell Inn** (☎ 428-6150) in Welches, **Rio Guest House** (☎ 428-1546), in St. Lawrence Gap, **Rydal Waters** (☎ 435-7433) in Worthing, **Shells Inn Guest House** (☎ 435-7253) on 1st Av. in Worthing, and **Woodbine Guest House** (☎ 427-7627).

DINING OUT: There is a greater concentration of restaurants along this parish's coast than in any other area; something can be found to suit virtually anyone's taste and pocketbook.

   Rockley dining: The **Sugar Reef Bar and Restaurant** (☎ 435-8074) offers a Sun. buffet (noon-2:30) as well as lobster and other seafood specialties. The **Abbeville Hotel and Bert's Bar** (☎ 435-

7924) is opposite the beach. It offers poolside dining and is suited to TV sports fans. Entrées are around B$22. The **Crown Restaurant**, inside the Riviera Beach Hotel, serves Chinese food. **Cloud 9 Restaurant** (☎ 435-7880) at Club Rockley sells a B$100 "passport," which entitles you to free drinks and live entertainment as well as entry to the disco on weekends. The **Quayside Mall** has three places offering counter service: **Callalloo** features Caribbean dishes; **Bistro Italia** has Italian food (including pizza); and **Toppers** serves ice cream. After-dinner entertainment here can be found in **Rockies** where you can get zombied out over video games. A **Chefette** is adjacent. The **Pizza Joint** (☎ 435-7136) is another option for pizza lovers.

Hastings dining: The Flamboyant, set in an old white house, is right off the side of the road in back of a flamboyant tree. It serves up a wide selection of international and Bajan dishes in a romantic, candlelit setting. The **Ocean View Restaurant** (☎ 427-7821) is inside a historical building. It specializes in Old World cuisine; dinners run from B$25-B$65. The Bajan buffet (with floor show) from Thurs. to Sat. evenings is B$75. The **Ile de France** (☎ 435-6869) sits in Windsor House and is open only for dinner. Its famous for its French cuisine. Entrées run from B$35 to B$60; a good wine list is available. The well-known gourmet Italian restaurant **Da Luciano** (☎ 427-5528) is inside a historical building here. Other options in Hastings are the **Pirate's Inn** (☎ 426-6273) and the **Sandy Bank Beach Bar & Restaurant** (☎ 435-6689), which offers a comprehensive bar along with hearty food. Austrian chef, Josef Schwaiger owns the island's first wine bar, **39 Steps** (☎ 427-0715). It is set in a pink chattel house in Chattel Plaza and is a yuppie hangout. The **Mervue House Restaurant** (☎ 435-2888) serves entrées priced from B$28 to B$60. It's inside a historic house in Marine Gardens. There's also the unusually (given the typical fast-food emporium's average decor) decorative and tasteful **Shakey's**, which features sit-down service, vegetarian subs and mini pizzas.

Worthing dining: Those wishing to sample Trinidadian-style (i.e., East Indian) *rotis* should head for the **Roti Hut**. One moderately-priced local restaurant nearby is the **Carib Beach Bar** right next door. The **Asta Restaurant** (☎ 427-2541) offers a BBQ on Tues. evenings and live music nightly. It serves three meals daily; lunch ranges from B$18-B$30 and dinner entrées from B$20-B$32. **Guan Dong**, 3rd Ave. in Worthing, is a popular Chinese restaurant. The bar and restaurant belonging to **Shells Guest House** is also here. Dishes range from dolphin chablis (B$26) to red snapper Florentine (B$26) to *rotini alla casa* (B$18). The latter is pasta cooked in cream of curry sauce with shrimp, crab meat and vegetables.

St. Lawrence Gap dining: There are a number of restaurants. Gourmet **Josef's** (☎ 435-6541) serves entrées ranging from B$36-B$70. The same management runs **Southern Accents Restaurant** (☎ 435-7246) in the Little Bay Hotel, which offers food from SE Asia and the Caribbean; entrées run from B$24 to B$36. **The Pisces** (☎ 435-6564) is a gourmet restaurant specializing in seafood; the herbs and fruit come from their gardens. It has an extensive wine list and serves a continental breakfast, lunch and dinner. Entrées are priced from B$28 to B$60. **China Gardens** is in Maxwell. **Secrets Restaurant** (☎ 435-9000) on St. Lawrence Rd. offers seafood, pasta, vegetarian, and other dishes. Romantic candlelit dinners are served on the oceanfront deck. Right near the Gap's entrance is **David's** (☎ 435-6550), owned and operated by the Bajan and American couple who run the Coffee and Cream Gallery. It serves formal Bajan cuisine (entrées range from B$25 to B$50) and is open daily for dinner. The **Witch Doctor** (☎ 435-6581) offers dishes such as flying fish *aux fruits de mer*, lobster thermidor, and chicken *piri piri*. The **St. Lawrence Fishing Boat** (☎ 435-7112) has a variety of seafood and meat dishes, including creole shrimp, grilled lobster, seafood crêpe, and a seafood cold plate. It's open for three meals daily. **Tapps on the Bay** is a bar and grill offering snacks and live entertainment nightly. The **Captain's Carvery** and the **Ship Inn Pub** serve food from lunch sliding right into the evening, when they become a major nightspot. Buffets (B$20) are served from noon to 3, Sun. to Fri. Dinners are around B$40. **B4 Blues** (☎ 435-6560) serves international and Caribbean dishes; they also have a live blues band around once a week. The Chinese-style **Jade Garden** (☎ 428-2759) offers a wide variety of seafood. **Susie Yong** in the Bresmay is another popular restaurant. **Divi Southwinds** (☎ 428-7181) has a floor show on Tues. nights and a beach BBQ and steel band on Sat. It offers entrées from B$22 to B$65. **The Steak House** (☎ 428-7152) is set in a traditional house and serves hunks of dead cow flown in from the US; it also has a salad bar.

St. Lawrence Gap informal dining: The **St. Lawrence Pizza Hut** is in the St. Lawrence Steakhouse Complex and offers BBQ and fish. **Boomers** serves reasonably-priced dishes. A **Pizza Man Doc** (which also serves *rotis* and flying fish) and **Mike's Deli** are along the main road. The **Watering Hole** on the main road has cheap *rotis* and other dishes. Another place nearby offers both fish and cheese cutters. **Mr. Tee's Super Donuts** is on the main stretch in the gap. The Chattel House Shopping Village has the **Ice Cream Shoppe** and **Friendlies Delicatessen & Bar**. It is right off the Gap's main road. Vendors across from the Ship's Inn sell burgers and fish sandwiches. The **Limers Bar & Restaurant** is a relaxed place with karaoke.

Dover dining: The **Mile Tree** is next to the Dover Convention Centre, just down the road and across the street from the Ship Inn. It specializes in seafood. Dishes range from appetizers like Caribbean reef octopus to fish chowder to your choice of six selected fish cooked to order – any style from grilled to blackened to jerked. Sauces offered include *meunière*, papaya, pineapple, coconut, and rum. Meat dishes and a "vegetarian delight" plate (B$18) are also available. The nearby **Meridian Inn** restaurant serves very reasonably-priced (B$6.50-B$10.50) vegetable, meat, and shrimp curries. They are served Guyanan-style (with *dhal puri*) or Trinidadian-style (with *roti*). They also deliver: call 428-4051. **The Casaurina** (☎ 428-3600/9500) offers a buffet (B$48) accompanied by a floor show on Sat. nights. **Le Petite Flambé** and the **Garden Restaurant** are inside the Southern Palms, and the **Dover Reef Restaurant** (☎ 428-3600) is inside the Casuarina Beach Club. **Luigi's** (☎ 428-9218) in Dover Woods is the area's best-known Italian restaurant. It serves up a variety of pasta and seafood specialties; prices are between B$22 and B$44 for entrées.

Maxwell Coast Road dining: The **Mermaid** (☎ 428-416) serves creole and international dishes; prices range from B$22 to B$50 for entrées.

Oistins dining: Cafeteria-style **Granny's** – open every afternoon (except Sun.) from around 4 until 11 – dishes out chicken gizzards fried in a special batter, macaroni pie, and curried stew, among other delights.

near Oistins: A number of hotels and restaurants are clustered near the coast. The **Peach and Quiet** (☎ 428-5682), Inch Marlow, offers set menus ranging from B$30-B$40 for a three-or four-course meal. The **Silver Sands Resort** (☎ 428-6001) in Enterprise serves a Bajan buffet and features a live band on Sun. evenings. The **Long Beach Club** (☎ 428-6890) serves three meals daily and also has BBQs and buffets. **Round Rock Apartments on the Sea** (☎ 428-7500) has a seaside bar and restaurant. A full breakfast runs around B$10 and dinner entrées are B$20 to B$30.

SHOPPING: Many boutiques are in Hastings and in Quayside Centre in Rockley. **Lindsay's** in St. Lawrence Gap sells tee-shirts featuring his own designs. **Correia's Jewellery** is in Hastings Shopping Plaza. A new and used bookshop, **Baobab Book & Curiosity Shop** is in Balmoral Gap in Hastings. **Jam-Pac Music** has stores next door to the After Dark club in St. Lawrence Gap and also on the Worthing Main Rd. opposite the Shell station and Plantation Supermarket. The **Chattel House Shopping Village** (set right off the Gap's main road) has a number of attractive boutiques.

Onward from Barbados

BY AIR: Liat flies to Anguilla, Antigua, Caracas, Dominica, Grenada, Guadeloupe, Georgetown (Guyana), Martinique, Montserrat, Nevis, Port of Spain, San Juan, St. Croix, St. Kitts, St. Lucia, St. Maarten, St. Thomas, St. Vincent, Tobago, and Tortola.

BY SHIP: The *M/V Windward* (☎ 431-0449/0937/0451, fax 431-0452) sails between St. Lucia, Barbados, St. Vincent, Trinidad, and Isla Margarita or Guiria (alternating weeks) in Venezuela. There are 60 cabins (at rates from B$20 pp pn and up), and deck class is also available; rates for deck are B$79 (B$120 RT) to St. Lucia, B$92 (B$142 RT) to St. Vincent, B$120 (B$180 RT) to Trinidad, and B$212 ($296 RT) to Venezuela. It leaves on its southbound route from Barbados on Sun., arrives in St. Vincent on Mon., Trinidad and Venezuela on Tues., passes through Trinidad again on Thurs., and stops in St. Vincent and then heads back to Barbados on Fri. From Barbados, it goes to St. Lucia on Fri. and returns Sun. For more information, contact Windward Agencies Ltd., #7 James Fort, Hincks St., Bridgetown, Barbados.

Island Wide Accommodation Finder

All prices are in US$, Inexpensive: less than $50/d pn, Moderate: $50-100, Expensive: $100-200, Luxury: $200 over

St. Michael's Parish

Broome's Vacation Home, Pine Gardens, 426-4955/2937, 429-3937/4192. Guesthouse; inexpensive.

Crystal Crest Guest House, Pine Road., Belleville, 436-6129. Guesthouse; inexpensive. **facilities:** restaurant.

De Splash Inn Guest House, Passage Rd., 427-8287. Inexpensive.

Fortitude, Wellington St., 426-4210. Guesthouse; inexpensive. Six bedrooms. **facilities:** fans. **location:** walking distance from beach.

Grand Barbados Beach Resort, Aquatic Gap, 426-0890. Luxury, 133 superior and deluxe rooms. **location:** on beach. **facilities:** air conditioning, pool, suites available, complimentary water sports and tennis. **notes:** fax 426-9823; in the US call 800-227-5475.

Hilton International, Needhams Point, 426-0200. Expensive/luxury, 185 bedrooms. **location:** on beach. **facilities:** two restaurants, air conditioning, suites available, pool, tennis, health club, shops, televisions. **notes:** fax 436-8948; in the US call (800) HILTONS.

Island Inn Hotel, Aquatic Gap, Garrison, 436-6393. Expensive all-inclusive, 25 units. **location:** on beach, less than a mile from the center of Bridgetown. **facilities:** air conditioning, pool, restaurant, conference room. **notes:** restored old building. Fax 437-8035; in the US call (800) 221-6509; and in Canada call (800) 424-5500.

Nautilus Beach Apartments, Bay St., 426-3541. Moderate, 14 units. **location:** on beach. **facilities:** studio and one-bedrooms available, maid service, air conditioning.

Paradise Villas, Black Rock, 424-4581/429-4830. Moderate/expensive, 15 units. **location:** near Paradise Beach. **facilities:** one- and two-bedrooms available, maid service, air conditioning.

Sandals Barbados, Black Rock, 428-0888, 424-0889. Luxury all-incusive, 172 units. **location:** on beach. **facilities:** air conditioning, five pools, tennis courts, five restaurants, health club, live entertainment, theater. **notes:** fax 425-1384. Opened in 1995.

Sandrift Paradise Beach Apartments, 424-2062/3367. Moderate. 12 units. **location:** near beach. **facilities:** one- and two-bedrooms available, maid service, air conditioning, balconies.

Superville Guest House, 3rd Ave., Pickwick Gap, Wilbury Rd., Belleville, 426-2831. Guesthouse; inexpensive.

The Club, Hastings, 436-7604. Moderate,16 units. **location:** on beach. **facilities:** air conditioning, pool, restaurant, disco. **notes:** fax 427-1411; in US call (718) 284-3737.

Tower Hotel, Black Rock, 424-3256. Moderate, 14 units. **location:** on beach. **facilities:** one-bedrooms available, maid service, air conditioning, pool, tennis courts, breakfast, refrigerators and kettles in rooms.

Walmer Lodge Apartments, Black Rock, 426-5935. Inexpensive/expensive, 10 units. **location:** near beach. **facilities:** studio and one- and two-bedrooms available, maid service, air conditioning.

St. James Parish

Almond Beach Club, Vauxhall, Holetown, 432-7840. Luxury all-incusive, 161 bedrooms. **location:** on beach. **facilities:** a/c, one- and two-bedrooms available, three pools, tennis, fitness center, TVs, boutique. **notes:** call (800) 425-6663 in the US. Live entertainment nightly. Extremely popular.

Angler Apartments, Derricks, 432-0817. Moderate, 13 units. **location:** on beach. **facilities:** studios and one- and two-bedrooms available, maid service, air conditioning/fans. **notes:** fax 432-0817; in the US call (305) 477-3470; in the UK call 01223 845522.

Beachcomber Apts, Paynes Bay, 432-0489. Expensive, nine units. **location:** on beach. **facilities:** studio and one- and two-bedrooms available, maid service, air conditioning, pool, tennis courts. **notes:** fax 432-2824.

Buccaneer Bay, Paynes Bay, 432-1362. Luxury, 29 bedrooms. **location:** on beach. **facilities:** air conditioning, suites available, pool, TV, lounge. **notes:** fax 432-7230.

Chrizel's Garden, Prospect, 438-0207. Guesthouse; inexpensive-moderate, seven bedrooms. **facilities:** suites available, television available, kitchenette available. **notes:** fax 438-0207.

Coconut Creek Club, Derricks, 432-0803. Luxury, 53 cottages or low-rise units. **location:** high on a bluff overloooking two beaches. **facilities:** air conditioning, pool, free water sports, television available, souvenir shop, babysitting service, exchange dining with Colony Club and Tamarind Cove. **notes:** fax 422-1726. Intimate resort. Owned by St. James Beach Hotels chain.

Colony Club, Porters, 422-2741. Luxury. 76 bedrooms. **location:** on beach. **facilities:** air conditioning, pool, free water sports, tennis nearby, croquet, shuffleboard, television on request **note:** fax 422-2335. Set amid seven acres of gardens. Intimate resort. Owned by St. James Beach Hotels Chain.

Coral Reef Club, St. James Beach, 422-2372. Luxury, 75 bedrooms. **location:** on beach. **facilities:** air conditioning, suites available, kitchenette available, pool, tennis courts, television on request. **notes:** fax 422-1776. See review in travel section.

Crystal Cove, Fitts Village, 432-2683. Luxury, 88 bedrooms. **location:** on beach. **facilities:** air conditioning, suites available, kitchenette available, pool, disco, mini-mart, tennis courts.

Discovery Bay Beach Hotel, Holetown, 432-1301. Luxury, 85 bedrooms. **location:** on beach. **facilities:** air conditioning, kitchenette available, pool, tennis courts, gourmet restaurant. **notes:** fax 432-2553. Classic plantation-style design, wedding packages available.

Glitter Bay Resort, Porters, 422-5555. Luxury, 162 bedrooms. **location:** on beach. **facilities:** air conditioning, suites available, kitchenette available, restaurant, pool, health club, tennis courts. **notes:** fax 422-3940; in the UK call (081) 367-9949 or fax (081) 367-9949; in the US and Canada call (800) 283-8666 or fax (212) 545-8467. Elegant Spanish-style architecture. Greathouse on premises constructed by Sir Edward Cunard in the 1930s. Set next to sister Royal Pavilion.

Golden Palm Beach Hotel, Sunset Crest, 432-6666. Expensive, 71 units. **location:** on beach. **facilities:** one-bedrooms available, maid service, air conditioning, pool, bar. **notes:** fax 432-1335.

Homar Rentals, Sunset Crest, 432-6750. Moderate, 104 units. **location:** walking distance to beach. **facilities:** one-bedrooms available, maid service, air conditioning, pool, tennis, restaurant. **notes:** fax 432-7729. Includes four different hotels under one management.

Inn on the Beach, Holetown, 432-0385. Luxury, 20 compact studio apartments and one penthouse suite. **location:** on beach. **facilities:** air conditioning, suites with kitchen, pool, restaurant. **notes:** fax: 432-2440; in the US call (800) 840-6636 or (212) 840-6636; and in Canada call (800) 468-0023 or (809) 432-0385.

Na-Diesie Apartments, Holetown, 432-0469. Moderate, 20 units. **location:** on beach. **facilities:** studio available, maid service, air conditioning, pool, tennis courts.

Pineapple Beach Club, Vauxhall, 432-7840. Luxury all-inclusive, 147 bedrooms. **location:** on beach. **facilities:** air conditioning, suites available, pool, restaurant, fitness center, squash and tennis. **notes:** in the US call (800) 345-0356; from Florida call (407) 994-5640.

Royal Pavilion Hotel, Porters, 422-5555. Luxury, 75 bedrooms. **location:** near St. James Beach, next to sister hotel, Glitter Bay. **facilities:** air conditioning, suites available, pool, tennis, health club, two restaurants, golf, TV lounge. **notes:** fax 422-3940; in the UK call (0181) 367-9949; in the US and Canada call (800) 283-8666.

Sandpiper Inn, St. James, 422-2251. Luxury, 46 bedrooms. **location:** on beach. **facilities:** air conditioning, suites available, pool, tennis, restaurant, free water sports. **notes:** fax 422-1776. Attractively-furnished rooms in garden setting. Renovated in 1994. See review of sister hotel Coral Reef Club on page 158 for contact numbers.

Sandy Lane Hotel, St. James, 432-1311. Luxury, 112 bedrooms. **location:** on beach. **facilities:** air conditioning, suites available, pool, tennis courts, golf course. **notes:** see review on page 157.

Settlers Beach Hotel, St. James Beach, 422-3052/1372. Luxury, 22 two-bedroom villas. **location:** on beach. **facilities:** air conditioning, suites with kitchens, pool, restaurant, exchange dining, tennis and golf nearby. **notes:** fax 422-1937. Attractive garden and grounds.

Smuggler's Cove Hotel, Paynes Bay, 432-1741. Luxury, 21 bedrooms. **location:** on beach. **facilities:** air conditioning, kitchenettes, one-bedrooms available, pool. **notes:** fax 432-1749.

Sun Rentals, Sunset Crest, 432-7930. Moderate, 54 units. **facilities:** one-bedrooms available, maid service, air conditioning, pool, tennis courts, restaurant.

Tamarind Cove, Paynes Bay, 432-1332. Luxury, 117 bedrooms. **location:** on beach. **facilities:** air conditioning, suites available, kitchenette available, pool, restaurants, complimentary water sports (except diving), nearby tennis. **notes:** fax 422-1726. Owned by St. James Beach Hotels chain.

Treasure Beach Hotel, Paynes Bay, 432-1346. Luxury, 25 luxury two-bedroom villas with kitchens. **location:** on beach. **facilities:** air conditioning, suites available (including one two-bedroom penthouse), kitchenette available, pool, restaurant, casino, six tennis courts, water sports (including scuba), nightclub, and golf nearby. **notes:** fax 432-1094. Garden setting, attractive grounds.

Tropicana Beach Hotel, Lower Carlton, 422-2277. Moderate, 26 bedrooms. **location:** on beach. **facilities:** air conditioning, suites available, kitchenettes, volleyball, windsurfing, sailing, snorkeling, restaurant.

Traveller's Palm, 266 Sunset Crest, 432-7722. Moderate, 16 units. **location:** on beach. **facilities:** one-bedrooms available, maid service, air conditioning, pool, restaurant.

Tropic Apartments, Sunset Crest, 432-5949. Inexpensive-moderate, Five units. **facilities:** one-bedrooms available, kitchens, maid service, fans, access to pool. **notes:** fax 435-6649.

St. Peter's Parish

Almond Beach Village, St. Peter, 422-4900. Luxury all-inclusive, 306 bedrooms. **location:** on beach. **facilities:** air conditioning, suites and kitchenettes available, pool, tennis courts, golf course. **notes:** fax 422-0617; call (800) 425-6663 in the US. Extremely popular so reserve well ahead.

Cobbler's Cove, Road View, 422-2291. Luxury, 38 units. **location:** on beach. **facilities:** air conditioning, suites available, pool, tennis, water sports included. **notes:** fax 422-1460. See review on page 182.

Gibbs Gardens, Gibbs, 432-6562, Inexpensive, three one-bedroom cottages. **location:** walking distance to beach. **facilities:** maid service. **notes:** fax 432-5616. Middle cottage has living room; all share covered patio.

Karekath, Speightstown, 425-1498. Moderate, five bedrooms. **facilities:** maid service, air conditioning. **notes:** fax 424-8427.

Kings Beach Hotel, Road View, 422-1690. Luxury, 57 bedrooms. **location:** on beach. **facilities:** air conditioning, television, pool, restaurant, tennis, live entertainment nightly, complimentary water sports. **notes:** fax 422-1691. Connecting rooms available for families. Spanish-style resort near Speightstown.

New Haven Mansion, Gibbs, 424-4529. Expensive, six bedrooms. **location:** on beach. **facilities:** air conditioning, pool, maid service. **facilities:** two-, three-, and four-bedrooms available, maid service, kitchenettes available, air conditioning, pool, disabled access. **notes:** fax 424-2180. Converted plantation house.

Sandridge Beach Hotel, Road View, 422-2361. Expensive, 52 bedrooms. **location:** on beach. **facilities:** air conditioning, suites and kitchenettes available, pools, tennis, restaurant. **notes:** fax 422-1965.

Sugarcane Club, Maynards, 422-5026. Moderate, 20 bedrooms. **facilities:** air conditioning, suites available, pool, free shuttle to beach, television available, restaurant. **notes:** fax 422-0522.

Sunset Sands, St. Peter, 438-1096. Luxury, four bedrooms. **facilities:** air conditioning, maid service. **notes:** fax 438-1096.

St. John's Parish

Coconut Inn, Sherbourne, 433-2697. Inexpensive, three bedrooms. **facilities:** restaurant. **notes:** basic bed and breakfast charging around B$30 pp. Meals available on request. Difficult to get to via public transportation. On Villa Nova Road.

St. Joseph's Parish

Atlantis Hotel, Bathsheba, 433-9445. Moderate, eight bedrooms. **location:** beautiful viewpoint. **facilities:** restaurant. **notes:** simple rooms in an old plantation house constructed in 1882. Some rooms have private balconies. Surfing nearby.

Edgewater Hotel, Bathsheba, 433-9900. Moderate. 20 bedrooms. **location:** beautiful viewpoint. **facilities:** restaurant, pool. **notes:** fax 433-9902; in US fax (213) 388-5478. Family-owned Euopean-style inn. Surfing nearby.

Kingsley Club, Cattlewash, 433-9422. Moderate, seven bedrooms. **location:** across from non-swimmable but beautiful beach. **facilities:** fans, restaurant. **notes:** fax 433-9226. See review on page 169.

St. Philip's Parish

Crane Beach Hotel, The Crane, 423-6220. Luxury, 25 bedrooms. **location:** overlooking beach. **facilities:** air conditioning, suites available, pool, tennis. **notes:** fax 423-6220. See review on page 200.

Ginger Bay Beach Club, The Crane, 423-5810. Luxury, 16 bedrooms. **location:** on beach. **facilities:** a/c, suites available, pool, tennis court, TV lounge, restaurant. **notes:** fax 423-6629. Beach accessed by natural cave.

Sam Lord's Castle, Long Bay, 423-7350. Luxury, 256 bedrooms. **location:** on beach. **facilities:** air conditioning, suites available, pools, tennis courts, water sports. **notes:** fax 423-5918. See review on page 201.

Ragged Point Motel, Merricks, 423-8021. Inexpensive.

Robin's Nest Hotel, Long Bay, 423-6088. Inexpensive, 16 bedrooms. **location:** near Sam Lord's Castle and the airport. **facilities:** a/c, suites and kitchenette available, pool.

Christ Church Parish

Abbeville Hotel, Rockley, 435-7294. Expensive, 21 bedrooms. **location:** near Rockley beach. **facilities:** a/c, pool. **notes:** fax 435-8402. Satellite TV in bar.

Accra Beach Hotel, Rockley, 435-8920. Expensive, 52 bedrooms, including 21 studio apartments. **location:** on beach. **facilities:** air conditioning, suites and kitchenettes available, optional TV, pool. **notes:** fax 435-6794. Three acres of tropical gardens. Most rooms have balconies. Water sports and other facilities available nearby. Studio wing recently renovated.

Adulo Apartments, Rockley, 426-6811. Moderate, 14 units (two-bedroom and studio apartments). **facilities:** maid service, air conditioning/fans, televisions available, pool, tennis courts.

Andrea-on-Sea Hotel, Dover, St. Lawrence Gap, 426-6021. Luxury, 58 air-conditioned bedrooms plus 18 suites. **location:** on beach. **facilities:** air conditioning, kitchenette available, pool, tennis, restaurant, TV lounge.

Asta Apartment Hotel, Palm Beach, Hastings, 427-2541. Expensive, 60 apartments with kitchens. **location:** on beach. **facilities:** air conditioning, pools, restaurant, televisions, phones. **notes:** fax: 426-9556.

Bagshot House Hotel, St. Lawrence Gap, 435-6956. Expensive, 16 bedrooms. **location:** on beach. **facilities:** suites available, kitchenette available, restaurant. **notes:** Small hotel with tasteful rooms.

Beaumont, Hastings, 425-4659. Guesthouse; inexpensive. Four bedrooms.

Benston Windsurfing Club, Maxwell, 428-9095. Moderate. 14 bedrooms. **location:** on beach. **facilities:** kitchenette available **notes:** fax 435-8954.

Bernita Apartments, Maxwell Hill, 428-9115. Moderate/expensive, 12 units. **facilities:** maid service, balconies, fans, studio, one-and two-bedrooms. **notes:** fax 429-4854. Walking distance to beach.

Blue Horizon Beach Apartments, Rockley, 435-8916. Moderate-luxury, 118 suites. **location:** on beach. **facilities:** air conditioning, kitchenette available, pools, TV lounge, mini-mart. **notes:** fax 435-8153.

Blythwood Beach Apartments, Worthing, 435-7712. Expensive, 14 units. **location:** on beach. **facilities:** one- and two-bedrooms available, maid service, air conditioning, kitchenettes, oceanfront balconies, pool. **notes:** fax 436-7684. Studios and one-bedrooms connect.

Bona Vista, Rose Garden Ave. (off Golf Club Rd.), Rockley, 435-6680. Guesthouse; inexpensive. Three bedrooms. **notes:** kitchen facilities.

Bresmay Apartment Hotel, St. Lawrence Gap, 428-6131. Expensive. 50 bedrooms. **location:** on beach. **facilities:** a/c, suites and kitchenettes available, pool, snack bar, TV available. **notes:** see review on page 207.

Cacrabank Beach Apartment Hotel, Worthing, 435-8057/60. Moderate, 21 units. **location:** on beach. **facilities:** studio and one-bedrooms available, maid service, air conditioning, pool, private patios.

Carib Blue Apartments, 60 Dover Terrace, 428-2290. Inexpensive/moderate, 15 units. **facilities:** studio available, maid service, air conditioning, meals to order. **notes:** fax 428-5140. On hillside overlooking cricket/football ground.

Carib Caban, Worthing, 435-7423. Moderate, 17 units. **location:** on beach. **facilities:** studio and one-bedrooms available, maid service, air conditioning, restaurant, pool, private patios.

Caribbee Beach Hotel, Hastings, 436-6232. Moderate, 55 bedrooms. **location:** on beach. **facilities:** a/c, radio, TV, phone, kitchenettes, restaurant, slot machines, conference facilities. **notes:** fax 436-0130; in the US call (800) GO-BAJAN; in Canada call (800) 261-7044.

Casuarina Beach Club, Dover, 428-3600. Luxury, 130 rooms. **location:** on beach. **facilities:** a/c, suites and kitchenettes available, pool, tennis courts, volleyball, live entertainment, restaurant, TV lounge, mini-mart. **notes:** fax 428-1970. Landscaped luxury apart-hotel. Extremely popular.

Chateau Blanc Apartments, Worthing, 435-7518. Inexpensive/moderate, nine units. **location:** on beach. **facilities:** studios and two-bedrooms available, maid service, air conditioning/fans.

Club Rockley Barbados, Golf Club Rd., Rockley Resort, 435-7880. All-inclusive, 131 units. **location:** on beach. **facilities:** kitchenette available, a/c, tennis, golf course, squash. **notes:** fax 435-8015.

Coconut Court Beach Apartments, Hastings, 427-1655/6. Luxury. **location:** on beach. **facilities:** air conditioning, studios, suites and kitchenettes available, pool, tennis courts, Hobie cats. **notes:** fax 429-8198. Family-owned. Recently-constructed block of studios.

Coral Sands Apartments, Worthing, 428-9828. Inexpensive/moderate, nine units. **location:** on beach. **facilities:** two- and three-bedrooms available, maid service.

Crystal Waters, Worthing, 435-7514. Inexpensive bed and breakfast, five bedrooms. **location:** on beach. **facilities:** television in lounge, bar and snackette.

Divi Southwinds Hotel and Beach Club, St. Lawrence Gap, 428-1457. Luxury, 166 bedrooms. **location:** on beach. **facilities:** air conditioning, suites and kitchenettes available, pool, tennis courts, live entertainment, diving, restaurant, shops. **notes:** fax 428-4674. Attractive grounds. Dive packages available.

Dorisville Apartments/Goldwater Flats, Dover, 428-8686/1751. Inexpensive/moderate, 20 units. **facilities:** one- , two- , and three-bedrooms available, maid service, air conditioning. **notes:** two separate units. Walking distance to beach. Two-bedrooms can be connected to studios.

Dover Beach Apartment Hotel, St. Lawrence Gap, 428-8076. Moderate, 39 bedrooms. **location:** on beach. **facilities:** air conditioning, pool, tennis court, restaurant, kitchenettes. **notes:** fax 428-2122.

Fairholme Hotel and Apartments, Maxwell, 428-9425. Inexpensive/moderate, 31 bedrooms. **facilities:** air conditioning or fans, suites and kitchenettes available, pool, tennis courts.

Fedey, Dover, 428-4051. Expensive, 12 units. **location:** on beach. **facilities:** studio available, maid service, air conditioning.

Flamboyant, Hastings, 427-5588. Guesthouse; inexpensive. Seven bedrooms. **location:** near beach. **facilities:** kitchenette available, air conditioning/fans, restaurant, beauty salon.

Four Aces Cottages and Apartments, St. Lawrence Gap, 428-9441. Inexpensive/moderate, 14 units. **location:** on beach. **facilities:** one- and two-bedrooms available, maid service, air conditioning.

Fred-La-Rose Bonanza Apartments, 4th Av., Dover, 428-9097. Moderate/expensive, 17 units. **location:** on beach. **facilities:** studios, one- , two- , and three-bedrooms available, maid service, air conditioning.

Gentle Breeze, Rendezvous, 435-8946.

Golden Palm Beach Apartments, Palm Beach, Hastings, 426-6784. Moderate/expensive, 25 bedrooms. **location:** on beach. **facilities:** a/c, pool, TV lounge, mini-mart, kitchenettes, restaurant. **notes:** fax 429-5818.

Golden Sands Apartment Hotel, Maxwell, 428-8051. Moderate/expensive, 27 bedrooms. **facilities:** air conditioning, pool, restaurant. **notes:** fax 428-3897. Dorm-style accommodation available.

Half Moon Beach Hotel, St. Lawrence Gap, 428-7131. Expensive, 29 bedrooms. **location:** on beach. **facilities:** air conditioning, suites available, pool. **notes:** fax 428-6089.

Hythe Villa, Welches, 428-3717. Guesthouse; inexpensive. Six units. **facilities:** air conditioning. **notes:** fax 429-7392.

Inchcape, Silver Sands, 428-7006/7902. Moderate/expensive, six units. **location:** on beach. **facilities:** studios, one- and two-bedrooms available, maid service, air conditioning, cook available.

Indramer Beach Hotel, Worthing, 435-7377. Guesthouse; inexpensive. 13 rooms.

Kingsland Palace, Kingsland Terrace, 420-9008. Inexpensive; guesthouse. Eight units.

Kingsway Apartments, Maxwell, 428-8202. Moderate/expensive, three units. **location:** on beach. **facilities:** studios, one- , and two-bedrooms available, maid service, air conditioning, pool, tennis courts. **notes:** fax 436-1853. Remodeled old Bajan house.

Leeton-On-Sea Apartments, Maxwell, 428-4500. Inexpensive, three studios. **location:** on beach. **facilities:** maid service. **notes:** very reasonable charge of around B$50 d summer, B$60 d winter. Owners live on premises.

Little Bay Hotel, St. Lawrence, 435-8574/7246. Moderate/expensive, 10 bedrooms. **location:** on beach. **facilities:** a/c and ceiling fans, one-bedroom suites available, restaurant. **notes:** fax 427-7826. One of the island's oldest hotels; famed for its celebrity clientele. Mediterranean architecture.

Long Beach Club, Chancery Lane, 428-6890. Moderate/expensive, 24 units. **location:** on beach. **facilities:** one- and two-bedrooms available, maid service, fans, ramps for disabled, pool, balconies.

Magic Isle Beach Apartments, Rockley, 435-6760. Moderate/expensive, 30 units. **location:** on beach. **facilities:** two-bedroom available, maid service, air conditioning, access for disabled, pool. **notes:** fax 435-8558.

Mango Bay Club, Holetown, 432-6044. Moderate/expensive, 64 units. **location:** on beach. **facilities:** air conditioning, pools, balconies, restaurant, entertainment nightly, tennis, watersports. **notes:** fax 432-5297.

Maresol Beach Apartments, St. Lawrence Gap, 428-9300. Moderate/expensive, nine units. **location:** on beach. **facilities:** one- and two-bedrooms available, maid service.

Melrose Beach Apartments, Worthing, 435-7984. Inexpensive, 15 units. **facilities:** one-bedrooms available, maid service, air conditioning, nearby path to beach.

Meridian Inn, Dover, 428-4051. Inexpensive/moderate, 12 units. **location:** on beach. **facilities:** one- and two-bedrooms available, maid service, restaurant and bar. **notes:** fax 420-6495.

Merrywing Apartments, Rockley, 435-8916. 50 units. **location:** on beach. **facilities:** one- and two-bedrooms available, maid service.

Miami Beach Apartments, Enterprise, 428-5387. Inexpensive/moderate, 12 units. **location:** on beach. **facilities:** one- and two-bedrooms available, maid service, mini-bar.

Mirabelle Apartments, St. Lawrence Gap. Moderate/expensive, 50 units. **location:** on beach. **facilities:** one- and two-bedrooms available, maid service.

Monteray Apartment Hotel, Dover, 428-9152/6786. Moderate/expensive, 22 units. **location:** on beach. **facilities:** studios, one- and two-bedrooms available, maid service, air conditioning, pool.

Myosotis Apartments, Dover, 428-6484/3517. Moderate, 11 units. **facilities:** studios and two-bedrooms available, maid service, a/c.

Na-Diesie Apartments, Holetown, 432-0469. Moderate, 20 units. **location:** on beach. **facilities:** studio available, maid service, a/c, mini-mart, arcade, disabled access on ground floor, restaurant. **notes:** fax 432-2715.

Oasis, Worthing, 435-7930. Moderate/expensive. 35 units. **location:** on beach. **facilities:** a/c, suites available, pool, restaurant. **notes:** fax 435-8232.

Ocean View Hotel, Hastings, 427-7821/2/3/4/5/6. Moderate/expensive. 35 units. **location:** on beach. **facilities:** air conditioning, suites available, pool, ceiling fans in some rooms, restaurant, mini-mart, cabaret show, water sports. **notes:** fax 427-7826. One of the island's oldest hotels, known for its celebrity clientele.

Palm Garden, Worthing, 435-6406. Moderate. 18 bedrooms. **location:** on beach. **facilities:** air conditioning, kitchenettes, pool. **notes:** fax 429-8220. Another of the island's oldest hotels; famed for its celebrity guests.

Peach and Quiet Hotel, Inch Marlow, 428-5682. Moderate. 24 units. **location:** on beach. **facilities:** suites available, fans and a/c available, pool, balconies, restaurant. **notes:** fax 428-4957. Snorkelling pool stocked with exotic fish.

Pegwell Inn, Welches, 428-6150. Guesthouse; inexpensive. Four bedrooms. **location:** next to shopping plaza and opposite beach. **facilities:** fans, television lounge, restaurant.

Pirates Inn Hotel, Hastings, 426-6273. Moderate. 25 studios and one-bedrooms. **location:** on beach. **facilities:** maid service, air conditioning, pool, restaurant, water sports, balcony or patio. **notes:** fax 436-0957.

Rainbow Reef Hotel, Dover, 428-5110. Moderate/expensive. 43 bedrooms. **location:** on beach. **facilities:** air conditioning, suites and one-bedrooms available, kitchenette available, pool, water sports. **notes:** fax 428-5395.

Regency Cove Hotel, Hastings, 435-8924. Moderate/expensive. 30 bedrooms. **facilities:** air conditioning, suites and kitchenettes available, pool. **notes:** fax 426-9010. Recently renovated.

Rio Guest House, St. Lawrence Gap, 428-1546. Guesthouse; inexpensive. Seven bedrooms. **location:** convenient for shopping, beach, and nightlife. **facilities:** fans, television lounge. **notes:** under Swiss-Bajan management.

Riviera Beach Hotel, Rockley, 435-8970. Moderate. 24 units. **location:** on beach. **facilities:** air conditioning, restaurants. **notes:** fax 428-4957; in the US call 508-477-0555, fax 508-477-6555.

Rockley Resort and Beach Club, Rockley, 435-7880. Expensive/luxury. 111 units. **location:** off beach; shuttle available. **facilities:** air conditioning, suites and kitchenettes available, pools, tennis courts, golf course. **notes:** fax 435-8015. Country club atmosphere.

Roman Beach Apartments, Miami Beach, Oistins, 428-7635/2510. Guesthouse; inexpensive. Nine units. **location:** across from beach. **facilities:** kitchenettes, shared phone. **note:** fax 428-7635. See review on page 208.

Rostrevor Apartments, St. Lawrence Gap, 428-9298. Moderate/expensive. 44 apartments. **location:** on beach. **facilities:** one-, two-, and three-bedrooms available, as well as studios, maid service, air conditioning, pool, gourmet restaurant, snack bar, mini-mart, TV/VCR rental available, wheelchair accessible. **notes:** fax 428-7705: in the US call 800-462-2526; in Canada call 822-2077.

Round Rock Apartments On Sea, Silver Sands, 428-7970. Moderate. Seven units. **facilities:** studios and two-bedrooms available, maid service, air conditioning, restaurant, windsurfing. **notes:** fax 428-7970.

Rydal Waters Guest House, Worthing, 435-7433. Guesthouse; inexpensive. Six bedrooms. **location:** opposite beach. **notes:** fax 428-8826. Family-run. Breakfast served upon request.

Salt Ash Apartment Hotel, St. Lawrence Gap, 428-8753. Moderate. Eight units. **location:** on beach. **facilities:** studios available, maid service, air conditioning, bar.

San Remo Hotel, Maxwell, 428-2822/2816. Moderate. 23 rooms. **location:** on beach. **facilities:** air conditioning, suites and kitchenettes available, restaurant. **notes:** fax 428-8826. Family-run.

Sand Acres Hotel, Maxwell, 428-7141/7234. Expensive. 37 suites. **location:** on beach. **facilities:** air conditioning, televisions, pool, tennis courts. **notes:** fax 428-2525.

Sandy Beach, Worthing, 435-6689. Expensive/luxury. 89 bedrooms. **location:** on beach. **facilities:** air conditioning, suites and kitchenettes available, pool, restaurant, disabled access, water sports. **notes:** fax 435-8053.

Sandy Cove Apartments, Landsdowne-On-Sea, Enterprise, 428-4358/8451. Moderate-expensive. Four units. **location:** on beach. **facilities:** two- and three- bedrooms available, maid service.

Sea Breeze Beach Hotel, Maxwell Coast Rd., 428-2825. Expensive. 60 bedrooms. **location:** on beach. **facilities:** air conditioning, kitchenettes, pool, restaurants, two-bedroom suites and studios available, disabled access, water sports, TV lounge. **notes:** fax 435-8053. Family-run.

Sea Foam Haciendas, Worthing, 435-7380. Moderate/expensive. 12 units. **facilities:** two-bedrooms available, maid service, air conditioning. **notes:** fax 435-7384; from the US call (800) 462-2526.

Seaview, Hastings, 426-1450. Expensive. 18 bedrooms. **location:** on beach. **facilities:** pool, squash and tennis courts, two restaurants, air conditioning. **notes:** fax 436-1333. Intimate romantic beachfront hotel. Canopied mahogany beds.

Shangri-La Apartment Hotel, 428-9112. Expensive. 43 units. **facilities:** studios and one-bedrooms available, maid service, air conditioning, pool.

Shells Inn, Worthing, 535-7253. Guesthouse; inexpensive. **notes:** bar and restaurant attached. B$30 s, B$50 d plus 15% tax and service for rooms.

Shonlan Airport Hotel, 8 Coverly Terrace, 428-0039. Inexpensive. 16 two-bedroom apartments. **facilities:** air conditioning, kitchenettes and televisions available. **notes:** fax 428-0160.

Sichris Hotel, Rockley, 435-7930. Expensive. 24 suites. **facilities:** a/c, kitchenette available, pool, restaurant, tennis and golf nearby.

Sierra Beach Apartment Hotel, Hastings, 429-5620. Moderate. 22 units. **location:** on beach. **facilities:** studios, one- and two-bedrooms available, maid service, air conditioning, pool, restaurant. **notes:** fax 429-5621.

Silver Rock, Silver Sands, 428-2866, 420-6083. Moderate/expensive. 33 bedrooms. **facilities:** windsurfing club, kitchenette available, restaurant. **notes:** fax 420-6983.

Silver Sands Resort, Silver Sands, 428-5936. Expensive. 106 units. **location:** on beach. **facilities:** air conditioning, suites available, restaurants, ramps for disabled, kitchenette available, pool, tennis courts, mini-mart. **notes:** fax 428-3758.

Southern Palms Beach Club, St. Lawrence Gap, 428-7171. Expensive/luxury. 93 bedrooms. **location:** on beach. **facilities:** air conditioning, suites and kitchenettes available, pool, tennis courts, restaurants. **notes:** fax 428-7175.

Southern Surf Beach Apartment Hotel, Rockley, 435-6672. Moderate. 12 units. **facilities:** studio available, kitchens, balconies, maid service, air conditioning, pool. **notes:** fax 435-6649.

St. Lawrence East and West Apartments, St. Lawrence Gap, 435-6950. Moderate. 75 units. **location:** on beach. **facilities:** studios and one-bedrooms available, maid service, a/c, pool, restaurants, balconies.

Standel Apartments, 3rd Avenue, Maxwell Coast Road, 420-5430. Moderate. Eight units. **facilities:** studios, one- and two-bedrooms available, kitchenettes, balconies, maid service, air conditioning, pool, televisions, disabled access. **notes:** fax 435-6649.

Summer Place on the Sea Guest House, Worthing, 435-7424. Guesthouse; inexpensive. Seven bedrooms. **location:** convenient, on beach. **facilities:** kitchenettes available. **notes:** fax 435-6621.

Summerset Apartments, Dover, 428-7936. Moderate. Seven units. **facilities:** one- and two-bedrooms available, maid service, air conditioning.

notes: Caribbean-style house with lawn and units stretched along in a horizontal row.

Sunhaven Beach Apartment and Hotel, Rockley, 427-3550. Expensive. 35 units. **location:** on beach. **facilities:** air conditioning, suites and kitchenettes available, pool, restaurant. **notes:** fax 435-6621.

Sunshine Beach Apartments, Hastings, 427-1234. Moderate. 10 units. **location:** on beach. **facilities:** studios and one-bedrooms available, maid service, travel agency.

The Nook Apartments, Rockley, 436-6494. Inexpensive. Four units. **location:** on beach. **facilities:** two-bedrooms available, maid service, air conditioning, pool.

Treehaven, Rockley, 435-6673. Inexpensive. Three bedrooms. **location:** next to shopping plaza and opposite beach. **facilities:** maid service, air conditioning.

Vacation Hotel, Enterprise, 428-4748. Inexpensive. 15 bedrooms. **facilities:** kitchenettes available.

Welcome Inn Apartment Hotel, Maxwell, 428-9900. Expensive. 110 studios, superiors, and standard rooms. **location:** on beach. **facilities:** air conditioning, suites and kitchenettes available, pool, entertainment, restaurants. **notes:** fax 428-8905. In the US call 800-223-6510 or 201-902-7738; in Canada call 800-424-5500. Mediterranean-style. Long-stay rates available.

Woodbine Guest House, Rockley, 427-7627. Guesthouse; inexpensive.

Woodville Beach Apartments, Worthing, 435-6693. Moderate. 28 units. **location:** on beach. **facilities:** studio available, maid service, air conditioning, pool. **notes:** fax 435-9211.

Worthing Court Apartment Hotel, PO Box 43 W, Worthing, 435-7910. Moderate/expensive. 24 bedrooms. **facilities:** air conditioning, suites available, pool, TV available, restaurant. **notes:** fax 435-7374. Rooms range from studio to one-bedroom, MAP supplement offered. In the US, call (800) 223-9815 and in Canada call (800) 468-0023.

Glossary

backra, buckra – Nickname for poor white. Its name likely originates from the 'back row' of the church to which the less-prosperous Bajans were relegated. Other names for these much maligned folk include "redlegs" and "ecky-becky."

Big Six – The group of large companies said to dominate the island's commerce.

Bim – Nickname for islanders. Apparently derives from Major Byam who defended the royalist cause (1650-52). His followers became known as 'Bims.' Although the term may be applied to all Bajans, it is sometimes used only to mean white Bajans. The island is also referred to as Bimshire.

calabash – Small tree native to the Caribbean whose fruit, a gourd, has multiple uses when dried.

callaloo – Caribbean soup made with callaloo greens.

Caribs – Original people who colonized the islands of the Caribbean, giving the region its name.

cassava – Staple crop indigenous to the Americas. Bitter and sweet are the two varieties. Bitter must be washed, grated, and baked to remove the poisonous prussic acid. A spongy cake is made from the bitter variety as is cassareep, a preservative which is the foundation of West Indian pepperpot stew.

cays – Indian-originated name which refers to islets in the Caribbean.

century plant – Also known as *karato, coratoe,* and *maypole*. Flowers only once in its lifetime before it dies.

chattel house – Basic Bajan dwelling. "Chattel" is an old legal term denoting "movable property." As most Bajans own their home but not the land it is built on, the name seemed suitable. Set on very basic foundations – such as a layer of rocks – the houses are typically built with an uninsulated wood frame construction with lap-board siding and corrugated metal peak red roofs. These box-like structures have traditionally been expanded as the family (and its wealth) grows.

cohobblopot – Cooking a large number of things together in the same pot. Today, this expression is used to denote the final Crop Over event at the National Stadium which brings together the year's top performers, bands, and dance troupes.

conch – Large edible mollusk usually pounded into salads or chowders.

corn 'n oil – Falernum with dark rum added to mix.

cou-cou – Stirred corn meal mixed with okra. When served with flying fish, it forms the national dish.

cutlass – The Caribbean equivalent of the machete. Originally used by buccaneers and pirates.

duppy – Ghost or spirit of the dead which is feared throughout the Caribbean. Derives from the African religious belief that a man has two souls. One ascends to heaven while the other stays around for awhile or permanently. May be harnessed by good or evil through obeah. Some plants and birds are also associated with duppies.

falernum – A sweet liquor consisting of white rum matured with lime and almond.

guava – Indigenous Caribbean fruit, extremely rich in vitamin C, which is eaten raw or used in making jelly.

Johnny – Descendant of Scottish or Irish indentured servants.

jug jug – A thick purée made from guinea corn, flour, peas, and a minced mix of meat, onions and herbs. Served with ham slices at Christmas.

landship – A friendly society serving as a form of lower-class insurance against sickness, unemployment, and death. Run by an 'admiral' who has members assigned to his 'ship.' Its naval imagery and attire are often prominent at funerals and at Crop Over festivities.

leeward – Side of Barbados facing the Caribbean Sea.

love vine – Orange parasitic vine found on Jamaica, St. John, Barbados, and other islands. Resembles nothing so much as the contents of a can of spaghetti.

machineel – Small toxic tree native to the Caribbean. Its fruit, which resembles an apple, and milky sap are lethal.

mauby – A bitter-sweet, frothy beverage made with dried mauby bark, cinnamon, orange peel, mace, cloves, sugar, and water.

meeting turn – Informal financial cooperative for mutual savings. Each person takes a turn receiving the kitty's contents at each session.

millwalls – Ruins of windmills used in sugar production.

Mr. Harding – Effigy of the cruel slave driver of yore. Usually constructed from sugarcane trash and dressed in an old black coat and top hat and burned at the Crop Over festivities.

obeah – Caribbean "magic" imported from Africa. Although it is virtually extinct on Barbados, an 1806 law making its practice a felony punishable by death is still on the books.

parish – Unit of local administration.

poinciana – Beautiful tropical tree that blooms with clusters of red blossoms during the summer months. Originates in Madagascar.

red legs – Nickname for poor white Bajans who are descendants of indentured servants. Refers to the sun's effect on their skin. Other similar terms include: backras, backra johnies, ecky bekkies, poor whites, spawgees, or white niggers. Predominantely found today in St. John, St. Joseph, and St. Andrew.

Scotland District – A hilly, eroded area of NE Barbados.

sea grape – West Indian tree, commonly found along beaches, which produces green, fleshy, edible grapes.

sensitive plant – Also known as mimosa, shame lady, and other names. It will snap shut at the slightest touch.

star apple – Large tree producing segmented pods, brown in color and sour in taste, which are a popular fresh fruit.

taro – Tuber also known as sasheen, tannia, malanga, elephant's ear, and yautia.

tuk band – Strolling musicians playing calypso-type music. Often joined by spontaneous dancers.

Booklist

Travel and Description

Arciniegas, G. Caribbean: *Sea of the New World*. New York: Alfred A. Knopf, 1946.

Blume, Helmut. (trans. Johannes Maczewski and Ann Norton) *The Caribbean Islands*. London: Longman, 1976.

Bonsal, Stephen. *The American Mediterranean*. New York: Moffat, Yard and Co., 1912.

Caimite. *Don't Get Hit by a Coconut*. Hicksville, NY: Exposition Press, 1979. Memoirs of an Ohio painter who escaped to the Caribbean.

Forde, G. Addington, Sean Carrington, Henry Fraser, and John Gilmore. *The A-Z of Bajan Heritage*. Bridgetown, Heinemann Caribbean: 1990. The definitive encyclopedia by the island's top experts. If you only buy one book about Barbados, this is the one to read and treasure.

Hart, Jeremy C. and William T. Stone. *A Cruising Guide to the Caribbean and the Bahamas*. New York: Dodd, Mead and Company, 1982. Description of planning and plying for yachties. Includes nautical maps.

Huber, Joyce and Jon. *Best Dives of the Caribbean*. New Jersey: Hunter Publishing, Inc., 1994. A travel guide focussing on diving and snorkeling in the Caribbean. Knowledgeable authors share their dive, accommodation, and general travel tips.

Morrison, Samuel E. *The Caribbean as Columbus Saw It*. Boston: Little and Co. 1964. Photographs and text by a leading American historian.

Naipaul, V.S. *The Middle Passage: The Caribbean Revisited*. New York: MacMillan, 1963. Another view of the West Indies by a Trinidad native.

Radcliffe, Virginia. *The Caribbean Heritage*. New York: Walker & Co., 1976.

Rapp, Laura and Diane. *Cruising the Caribbean: A Passenger's Guide to the Ports of Call*. New Jersey: Hunter Publishing, Inc., 1994. Detailed guide book to the history, points of interest, walking tours, shopping and daytrips at each port. Maps.

Rodman, Selden. *The Caribbean*. New York: Hawthorn, 1968. Traveler's description of the Caribbean by a leading art critic.

Ward, Fred. *Golden Islands of the Caribbean*. New York: Crown Publishers, 1967. A coffee table book. Beautiful historical plates.

Wood, Peter. *Caribbean Isles*. New York: Time Life Books, 1975. Includes descriptions of such places as Pico Duarte in the Dominican Republic and the Blue Mountain region of Jamaica.

Flora and Fauna

Kaplan, Eugene. *A Field Guide to the Coral Reefs of the Caribbean and Florida*. Princeton, N.J.: Peterson's Guides, 1984.

de Oviedo, Gonzalo Fernandez. *Natural History of the West Indies*. Chapel Hill: University of North Carolina Press, 1959.

Sutty, Lesley. *Fauna of the Caribbean: The Last Survivors*. London: Macmillan, 1993. Beautifully illustrated, informative, and heart-rendingly written, this book makes fascinating reading and is a must for all environmentally-concerned visitors.

History

Campbell, P.F. *The Church in Barbados in the 17th Century*. St. Michael: Barbados Museum and Historical Society, 1982.

Comitas, Lambros. *The Aftermath of Sovereignty: West Indian Perspectives*. New York: 1973.

Deer, Noel. *The History of Sugar*. London: Chapman, 1950.
Handler, Jerome S. *Plantation Slavery in Barbados*. Cambridge: Harvard University Press, 1976.

Harlow, Vincent T. *History of Barbados , 1625-1685*. Negro University Press: 1926.

Hoyos, F.A. *Barbados: A History from Amerindians to Independence*. London: Macmillan Caribbean, 1978.

Hoyos, F.A. *Grantley Adams and the Social Revolution*. London: Macmillan Caribbean.

Hovey, Graham and Gene Brown, eds. *Central America and the Caribbean*. New York: Arno Press, 1980. This volume of clippings from *The New York Times*, one of a series in its Great Contemporary Issues books, graphically displays American activities and attitudes toward the area. A goldmine of information.

Hunte, George. *The West Indian Islands*. New York: The Viking Press, 1972. Historical overview from the Western viewpoint with information added for tourists.

Kortright, Davis. *Cross and Crown in Barbados: Caribbean Political Religion in the late 19th Century*. P. Lang Publishers, 1983.

Knight, Franklin W. *The Caribbean*. Oxford: Oxford University Press, 1978. Thematic, anti-imperialist view of Caribbean history.

Levy, Calude. *Emancipation, Sugar, and Federalism*. Gainesville: Univeristy Press, 1980.

Lignon, Richard. *A True and Exact History of the Island of Barbados* (1647). London: Frank Cass & Co. Ltd., 1970.

Mannix, Daniel P. and Malcolm Cooley. *Black Cargoes*. New York: Viking Press, 1982. Details the saga of the slave trade.

Schomburgh, Sir Robert, *The History of Barbados*. 1971.

Watson, K. *The Civilized Island of Barbados, A Social History 1750-1860*. Bridgetown: Caribbean Graphics.

Beckles, Hilary. *Afro-Caribbean Women & Resistance to Slavery in Barbados*. London: Karnak House, 1988.

Beckles, Hilary. *Black Rebellion in Barbados: The Struggle Against Slavery, 1627-1838*. Bridgetown, Barbados: Antilles Publications, c 1984.

Beckles, Hilary. *Corporate Power In Barbados: Economic Injustice in a Political Democracy*. Bridgetown, Barbados: Lighthouse Communications, c 1989.

Beckles, Hilary. *A History of Barbados: From Amerindian Settlement to Nation-State.* Cambridge [England]; New York: Cambridge University Press, 1990.

Beckles, Hilary. *Natural Rebels: A Social History of Enslaved Black Women in Barbados.* New Brunswick, N.J.: Rutgers University Press, 1989.

Beckles, Hilary. *White Servitude and Black Slavery in Barbados, 1627-1715.* 1st ed. Knoxville: University of Tennessee Press, c 1989.

Holder, John W. *Codrington College: A Brief History.* Bridgetown, Barbados: 1988.

Howard, Michael. *Dependence and Development in Barbados, 1945-1985.* Bridgetown, Barbados: Carib Research & Publications, 1989.

Politics and Economics

Barry, Tom, Beth Wood, and Deb Freusch. *The Other Side of Paradise: Foreign Control in the Caribbean.* New York: Grove Press, 1984. A brilliantly and thoughtfully written analysis of Caribbean economics.

Blanshard, Paul. *Democracy and Empire in the Caribbean.* New York: The Macmillan Co., 1947.

Duncan, Neville C. *Women and Politics in Barbados, 1948-81.* Cave Hill: Institute of Social and Economic Research, University of the West Indies, Barbados, 1983.

Gooding, Bailey W. and Justine Whitfield. *The West Indies at the Crossroads.* Cambridge, MA: Schenkmann Publishing Co., Inc., 1981. A political history of the British Caribbean during the 1970s.

Matthews, Thomas G. and F.M. Andic, eds. *Politics and Economics in the Caribbean.* Rio Piedras: Institute of Caribbean Studies, University of Puerto Rico, 1971.

Mitchell, Sir Harold. *Caribbean Patterns.* New York: John Wiley and Sons., 1972. Dated but still a masterpiece. The best reference guide for gaining an understanding of the history and current political status of nearly every island group in the Caribbean.

Sociology and Anthropology

Abrahams, Roger D. *After Africa*. New Haven: Yale University Press, 1983. Fascinating accounts of slaves and slave life in the West Indies.

Callender, Jean H. *Bajan Society, Past and Present*. Cave Hill: Main Library, University of the West Indies (Barbados), 1981.

Dann, Graham. *The Bajan Male: Sexual Attitudes and Practices*. London: Macmillan Caribbean, 1987. A survey, built into book form, which tackles the male, his role in society, socialization, etc.

Dann, Graham. *Everyday Life in Barbados*. The Hague: Smits Drukkers-Uit-gevers B.V., 1976. A fascinating compilation of studies dealing with topics as diverse as picnics and the rum shop.

Forde, G. Addington. *Folk Beliefs of Barbados*. Barbados: National Cutural Foundation, 1987.

Horowitz, Michael H. *People and Cultures of the Caribbean*. Garden City, New York: National History Press for the Museum of Natural History, 1971. Compilation of social anthropological essays.

Art, Architecture and Archaeology

Alleyne, Warren. *Historic Houses of Barbados*. Bridgetown: Barbados National Trust.

Buissert, David. *Historic Architecture of the Caribbean*. London: Heinemann Educational Books, 1980.

Fraser, Henry & Hughes, Ronnie. *Historic Houses of Barbados*. Bridgetown, Barbados National Trust: Art Heritage Publications, c 1986.

Gosner, Pamela. *Caribbean Georgian*. Washington D.C.: Three Continents Press, 1982. A beautifully illustrated guide to the "Great and Small Houses of the West Indies."

Hill, Barbara (Henry Fraser. ed.). *Historic Churches of Barbados*. Bridgetown: Art Heritage Publishers, 1984.

Lewisohm, Florence. *The Living Arts & Crafts of the West Indies.* Christiansted, St. Croix: The Virgin Islands Council on the Arts, 1973. Local crafts illustrated.

Music

Bergman, Billy. *Hot Sauces: Latin and Caribbean Pop.* New York: Quill, 1984.

Marshall, Trevor. *Folk Songs of Barbados.* Barbados: Cedar Press, 1981.

Warner, Keith. *Kaiso! The Trinidad Calypso: A Study of the Calypso as Oral Literature.* Washington, DC: Three Continents Press, 1982. An intriguing, well-written study of calypso, its origins, and its effect on society.

Language

Collymore, Frank A. *Notes for a Glossary of Words and Phrases of Bajan Dialect.* Bridgetown: Barbados National Trust, 1955.

Forde, G. Addington. *De Mortar Pestle: A Collection of Bajan Proverbs.* Barbados: National Cutural Foundation, 1987. This book not only lists Bajan proverbs, but gives their near-equivalents in the Caribbean and Africa.

Literature

Braithwaithe, Edward. *Mother Poem.* Oxford and New York: Oxford University Press, 1977.

Braithwaithe, Edward. *Sun Poem.* Oxford and New York: Oxford University Press, 1982.

Callender, Timothy. *How Music Came to the Ainchan People.* St. Michale, Barbados: 1979.

Drayton, Geoffrey. *Christopher.* London: Secker and Warburg, Collins, 1961.

Foster, Cecil. *No Man in the House*. New York: Ballantine, 1992. A portrait of growing up and life under British rule set in 1964.

Fowler, Robert. *Spoils of Eden*. New York: Dodd Mead, 1985.

Hoover, Thomas. *Caribbee*, 1st ed. Garden City, N.Y.: Doubleday, 1985.

Humfrey, Michael. *No Tears for Massa's Day*. London: John Murray, 1987.

Hutchinson, Lionel. *Man from the People*. London: Collins, 1969.

Kellman, Tony. *Black Madonna Poems*. Bridgetown, 1975.

Jackman, Oliver. *Saw the House in Half*. Washington, D.C.: Howard University Press, 1974. The classic expatriate novel set in London and Lagos.

Jackson, Carl. *East Wind in Paradise*. London: New Beacon Books Ltd., 1981.

Lamming, George. *The Emigrants*. London: Allison & Busby, 1980.

Lamming, George. *Of Age and Innocence*. London: Allison & Busby, 1981.

Lamming, George. *In the Castle of My Skin*. London: Schocken, 1983. His most famous novel.

Lamming, George. *The Pleasure of Exile*. London: Allison & Busby, 1984.

Small, Jonathan. *The Pig Sticking Season. Jamaica Poems, 1985*. Bridgetown: 1966.

Index